The Campus History Series

LOUISIANA STATE UNIVERSITY

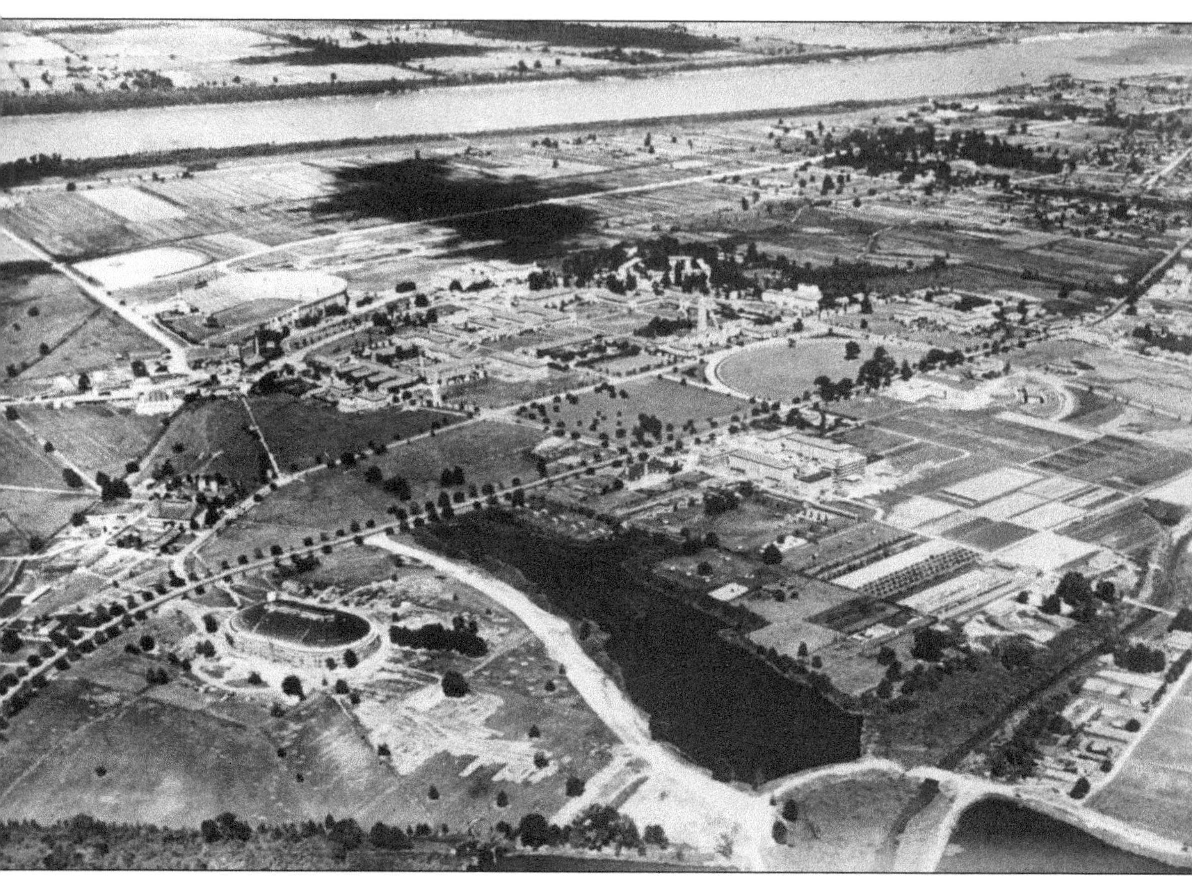

This aerial view of campus from 1937 shows the rapid expansion that took place during that decade. The John M. Parker Coliseum (lower left), Evangeline Hall (center, near the garden plots), and Grace King Hall (center) were under construction. The baseball field (top left) had been laid out, but the grandstand had yet to be constructed. (Office of the Chancellor Records, RG #A0001, Louisiana State University Archives, LSU Libraries, Baton Rouge, Louisiana.)

ON THE COVER: Taken in 1932, this Jasper Ewing photograph is of the Cadet Band on the Parade Ground. At this time, the band had about 100 pieces, but would grow to over 250 by the end of the decade. Also seen are oak and magnolia saplings that were planted around the Parade Ground and elsewhere on campus. (LSU Photograph Collection, RG #A5000, Louisiana State University Archives, LSU Libraries, Baton Rouge, Louisiana.)

The Campus History Series

LOUISIANA STATE UNIVERSITY

BARRY COWAN
WITH A FOREWORD BY DR. WILLIAM L. JENKINS

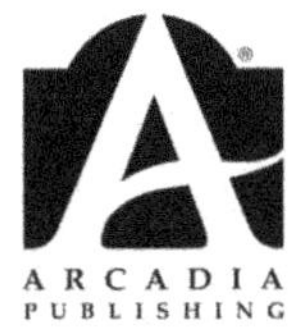

ISBN 978-1-4671-1098-3

Published by Arcadia Publishing
Charleston, South Carolina

Library of Congress Catalog Card Number: 2013938342

For all general information, please contact Arcadia Publishing:
Telephone 843-853-2070
Fax 843-853-0044
E-mail sales@arcadiapublishing.com
For customer service and orders:
Toll-Free 1-888-313-2665

Visit us on the Internet at www.arcadiapublishing.com

To my Mom and Dad, for always believing in me.

CONTENTS

FOREWORD

When I first came to LSU in 1988, I quickly discovered that the campus was one of the most beautiful in America. Italian Renaissance architecture, red-tiled rooftops, and huge, moss-draped live oak trees give the campus a distinctive loveliness. From the campus lakes and shady streets, to the lush magnolias and the perfumed aroma of the sweet olive trees, the campus is indeed a work of art.

But what took a longer period of time for me to discover was the fact that LSU has a colorful and storied history that is as fascinating as the campus is beautiful. In my mind, that's what sets LSU apart. Many campuses are pretty, but how many others are home to ceremonial mounds created by Native Americans more than 6,000 years ago? How many of them boast a $4 million wildlife habitat that houses a live Bengal tiger? And how many of them have a football stadium that doubled as a dormitory for half a century? Only LSU.

LSU's beginnings are steeped in military history and ironic twists of fate. Founded in 1860, the university's first superintendent was William Tecumseh Sherman, who would later fight for the North in the Civil War. The Civil War also caused LSU to close shortly after it was established, but it reopened again after the war. The university's mascot, the Tiger, came from a Civil War battalion of Louisianans known as The Louisiana Fighting Tigers. And for various reasons, including a massive fire, the campus was moved three times before it ended up where it is today. During World War II, LSU produced more officers on active duty than any other institution in the nation except for the military academies; LSU's Memorial Tower and adjacent War Memorial and Parade Ground are testimonials to this military history.

And then there are the political and literary figures who have impacted LSU's history, such as writer Robert Penn Warren and former Louisiana governor Huey P. Long. The long list of distinguished alumni includes political consultant James Carville, Academy Award–winning composer Bill Conti, film critic Rex Reed, former US vice president Hubert Humphrey, and NBA star Shaquille O'Neal.

The story of LSU is indeed entertaining and fascinating. But it could not be effectively told without the aid of the photographs that transport us back in time to see the people and the places who made the university what it is today. Barry Cowan is just the person to weave this story together for us. I hope you enjoy this book as much as I enjoyed the 25 years I spent at LSU, learning this history and living the beauty and the experience that is LSU.

Dr. William L. Jenkins
Former LSU President, Chancellor, Provost, and Dean

ACKNOWLEDGMENTS

Most of the images and information for this book came from the record groups of the university archives and manuscript collections in the Louisiana and Lower Mississippi Valley Collections of the Louisiana State University Libraries Special Collections division at Hill Memorial Library. I appreciate the efforts of those who have come before me in preserving these materials and making them available for use. Special thanks go to Judy Bolton, head of Public Services, and Gabe Harrell, computer analyst in the Digital Services unit, for handling my orders for scanning in a timely manner.

I would also like to thank Jackie Bartkiewicz, editor of the *LSU Alumni Magazine*, for her help and support; Jim Zietz, senior photographer and IT coordinator for digital imaging in the LSU Office of Communications and University Relations, for some of the modern photographs that appear in this book; Kristine Calongne, assistant vice-chancellor of communications in the LSU Office of Communications and University Relations; and president emeritus Dr. William Jenkins. Thanks also to Steve Franz, staff photographer in the Office of Sports Information of the LSU Athletic Department, for the images of modern athletes.

Thanks to the team at Arcadia Publishing, acquisitions editors Simone Monet-Williams and Jason Humphrey, for tolerating my intransigence and tardiness.

Finally, I would like to thank Faye Phillips, retired associate dean of the LSU Libraries and my former boss, for her support and encouragement in getting me involved with writing local history.

Many of the photographs appearing in this book have long credit lines. In an effort to improve the flow of the text and increase the size of the photographs, a key to their sources is listed below.

OCR Office of the Chancellor Records, RG #A0001, Louisiana State University Archives, LSU Libraries, Baton Rouge, Louisiana.

LSUPC LSU Photograph Collection, RG #A5000, Louisiana State University Archives, LSU Libraries, Baton Rouge, Louisiana.

OPRR Office of Public Relations Records, RG #A0020, Louisiana State University Archives, LSU Libraries, Baton Rouge, Louisiana.

OFSR Office of Facility Services Records, RG #A0204, Louisiana State University Archives, LSU Libraries, Baton Rouge, Louisiana.

JFP Office of Public Relations Records, Jack Fiser Photographs, RG #A5000.0020.1, Louisiana State University Archives, LSU Libraries, Baton Rouge, Louisiana.

JES	Jasper Ewing and Sons Photograph Files, Mss. 3141, Louisiana and Lower Mississippi Valley Collections, LSU Libraries, Baton Rouge, Louisiana.
RWL	Richard W. Leche Papers, Mss. 2060, Louisiana and Lower Mississippi Valley Collections, LSU Libraries, Baton Rouge, Louisiana.
FWAP	Fonville Winans Aerial Photographs of Baton Rouge, Fonville Winans Collection, Mss. 4506, Louisiana and Lower Mississippi Valley Collections, LSU Libraries, Baton Rouge, Louisiana.
CEP	Charles East Papers, Mss. 3471, Louisiana and Lower Mississippi Valley Collections, LSU Libraries, Baton Rouge, Louisiana.
THM	Troy H. Middleton Papers and Middleton Room Memorabilia, RG #U107, Louisiana State University Archives, LSU Libraries, Baton Rouge, Louisiana.
DMS	Department of Military Science Records, RG #A0302, Louisiana State University Archives, LSU Libraries, Baton Rouge, Louisiana.
RBL	Russell B. Long Papers, Mss. 3700, Louisiana and Lower Mississippi Valley Collections, LSU Libraries, Baton Rouge, Louisiana.
LSUCR	LSU Centennial Records, RG #A4025, Louisiana State University Archives, LSU Libraries, Baton Rouge, Louisiana.
JMS	James Monroe Smith Photograph Collection, Mss. 3077, Louisiana and Lower Mississippi Valley Collections, LSU Libraries, Baton Rouge, Louisiana.
Beck's	Beck's Studio LSU Campus Photographs, Mss. 2755, Louisiana and Lower Mississippi Valley Collections, LSU Libraries, Baton Rouge, Louisiana.

INTRODUCTION

Louisiana State University began with the name Louisiana State Seminary of Learning and Military Academy, a small school for boys tucked away in Rapides Parish in central Louisiana. Classes began on January 2, 1860, with a handful of students, called cadets because military discipline was the rule, and a curriculum of mathematics, ancient and modern languages, theoretical engineering, and chemistry under Supt. William Tecumseh Sherman.

Just as the Seminary was getting started, the Civil War began. Louisiana seceded from the Union, and Sherman resigned, as he said he would if Louisiana left the Union. He offered his services to the Union Army. The school opened and closed several times as students and faculty left to join the fighting, but closed for good in 1863. During the war, the building was used as a headquarters and hospital by the Union Army. Sherman, now a general, asked that the school be saved from destruction.

After the war ended, only the building survived. David Boyd, a professor before the war, became superintendent and began the rebuilding process. Louisiana's economy was in shambles, but Boyd was determined to get the school restarted. Classes began once more in the fall of 1865. The library was replaced, and by 1869, was one of the best in the South. Many of the volumes were donated by Sherman, or through his influence, and he remained a lifelong friend of the institution. In 1869, the first commencement was held for eight graduates.

Disaster struck on the night of October 15, 1869. A fire broke out in a storeroom near the kitchen and soon the entire building was in flames. All of the library books and some of the scientific equipment were saved, but the commissary stores and other supplies, valued at $20,000, were destroyed. The seminary would have to start over again.

By November 1, 1869, the seminary had found temporary quarters at the Louisiana Institute for the Deaf, Dumb, and Blind in Baton Rouge. "Temporary" being a relative term, the school would remain here until 1887. Quarters here were cramped, with cadets sleeping 8 to 10 to a room and having to share kitchen and dining areas with the inmates of the institute. There was little room for a library or laboratories and cadets drilled in the city streets. On the upside, Baton Rouge offered better availability of food than Rapides Parish, always a sore spot with cadets and faculty, and faculty could live off campus. Several attempts were made to get funding to rebuild the seminary in Rapides, but none was available.

In 1870, the name of the seminary was changed to Louisiana State University. Funds dwindled during the 1870s and the university became a victim of party or factional politics. A rival institution, the Louisiana Agricultural and Mechanical College, opened in New Orleans in 1874. A pet of radical Republicans, the college took funding that might have gone to LSU and was allowed to take advantage of the Morrill land grants where LSU was not. In 1877, the two schools merged to become Louisiana State University and Agricultural and Mechanical College.

The next 10 years would be relatively stable, but finances were still uncertain; the university owed debt that the legislature would not help alleviate. David Boyd, who almost singlehandedly steered the institution through the toughest times it would ever see, was forced out as president in 1880. Financial boom and bust would be a recurring theme right up to the present.

In 1887, LSU was, after many years of requests, able to move into the Baton Rouge Arsenal that had not been used in years. The 200-acre site had serviceable buildings and enough room to build more. The curriculum also grew, allowing, for example, agricultural and veterinary science classes to be held on campus. Between 1900 and 1915, the campus experienced a building boom, adding laboratories, the first purpose-built library, and a dormitory.

By 1915, with increased enrollment and encroachment by the city of Baton Rouge, the campus was experiencing growing pains. Pres. Thomas Boyd wanted to purchase Gartness Plantation south of Baton Rouge to better enable the university to fulfill its role as an agricultural and mechanical college. Gartness was purchased in 1918 and building construction began in 1922. LSU's present campus was formally dedicated on April 30, 1926.

Military discipline had been a part of student life since the beginning. Cadets were awaked with reveille and went to bed at taps. They wore uniforms, learned to fire and maintain weapons, drilled and stood guard duty, and were issued demerits for infractions of the rules. Those rules began to ease in the 1920s, and by 1969, the university dress code was gone along with mandatory ROTC. Female students were not subjected to this but had their own set of rules governing dress, deportment, and off-campus social events.

The 1930s were a time of huge growth, attributable in part to governors Huey Long and Richard Leche and LSU president James Monroe Smith. More buildings were constructed, including additional laboratories, dormitories, and classrooms, almost doubling the size of the physical plant. The academic side grew as well, with additional programs in the sciences, art, literature, and a university press to name a few. The decade ended with scandal involving theft, graft, and embezzlement. After World War II, the university began to move away from a teaching mission to one of scientific research outside of agriculture, helped in large part by grants from the National Science Foundation. World War II veterans, taking advantage of the GI Bill, swelled the campus to double its wartime enrollment and the physical plant grew to accommodate them.

Athletics came of age in the 1890s when the first intercollegiate sports began. Tulane was LSU's archrival for years in baseball and football, but LSU surpassed Tulane as they deemphasized athletics. Over the years, the Tigers have won multiple national and conference championships.

Louisiana State University has persevered through adversity, shone brightly during good times, and will remain, as the last line of the Alma Mater says, forever LSU.

One

The Campuses

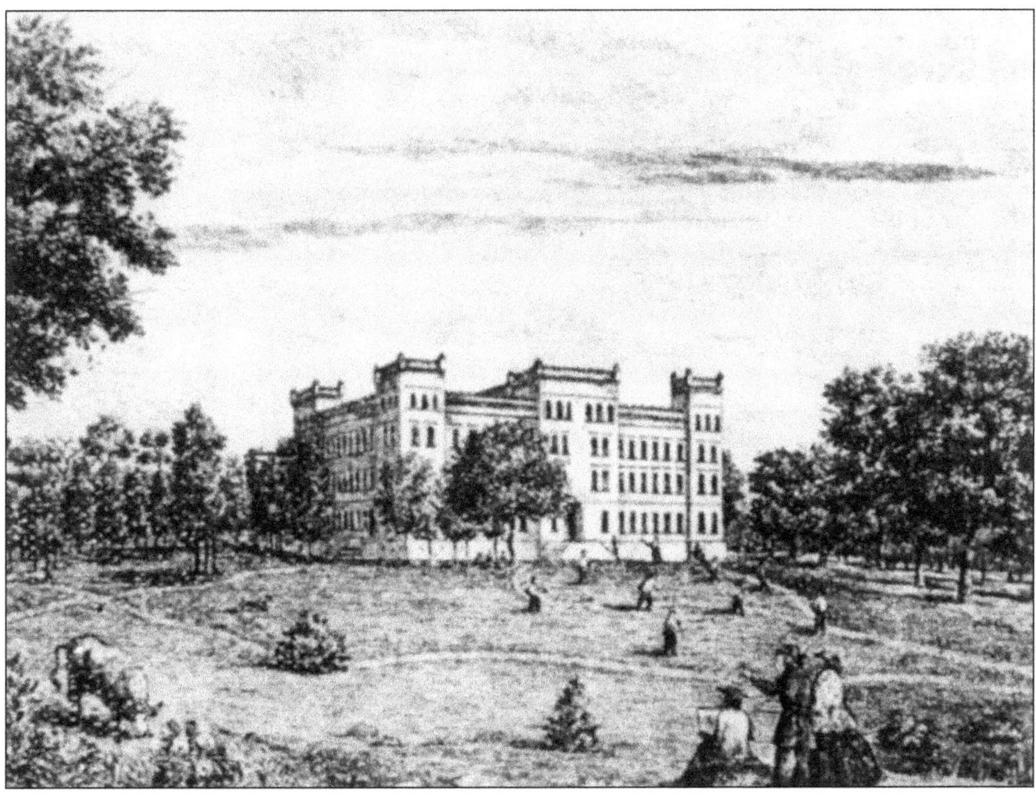

This drawing by Samuel Lockett depicts the first home of the Louisiana State Seminary of Learning and Military Academy. It was designed by A.T. Woods of New Orleans. The cornerstone of the 72-room building was laid on March 12, 1856. As the building was nearing completion in 1858, the bricks were found to be too soft and were cracking under the building's weight. The corner towers were rebuilt, but the rest of the building was reinforced with timbers. It was finally ready in 1859 and upon completion, was one of the largest public buildings in Louisiana. The grounds encompassed 438 acres and the site was purchased from Mrs. E.R. Williams in 1853. In 1855, 80 additional acres were purchased. (LSUPC.)

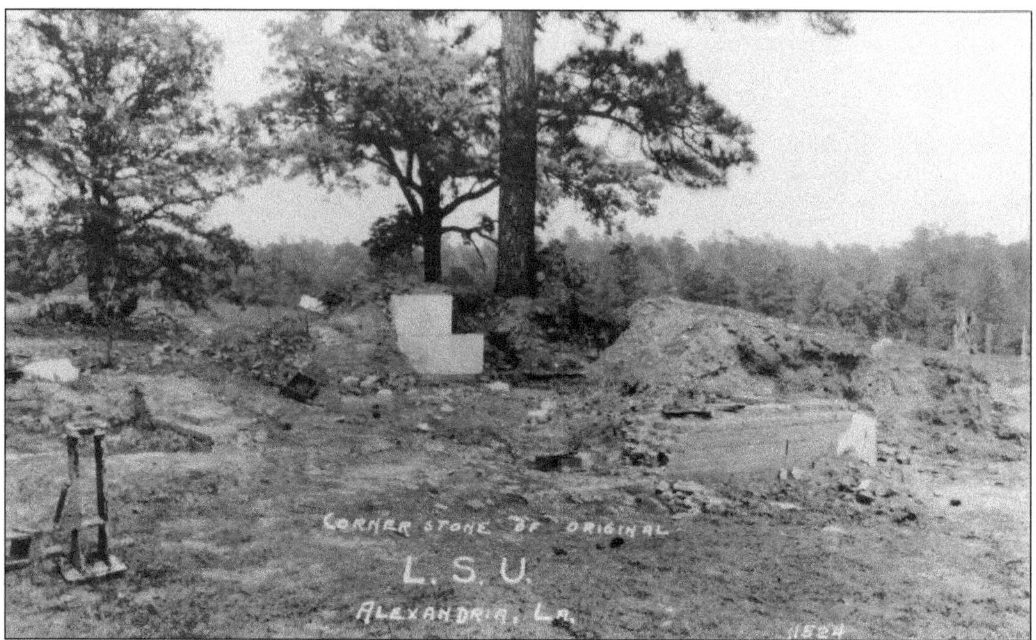

On the night of October 15, 1869, the seminary building was destroyed by fire. By 1926, all that remained was a few bricks and the building's cornerstone, which was later unearthed and moved to Baton Rouge. Pieces of the cornerstone have been cut for use as an entryway in front of the Memorial Tower and contain bronze tablets proclaiming LSU's status as a land, sea, and space grant university. (OPRR.)

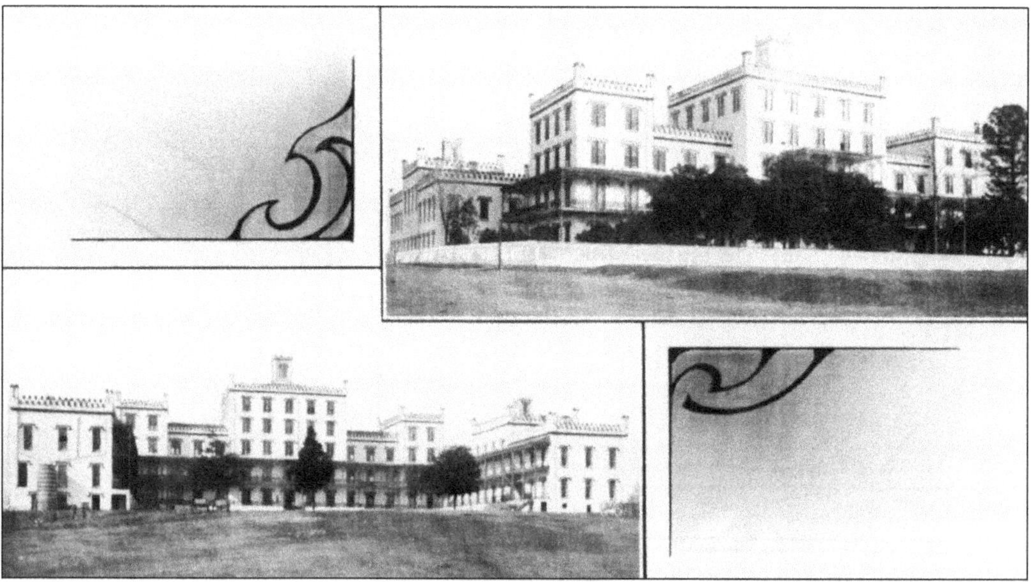

A month after the seminary building was destroyed by fire, the school moved to the Louisiana Institute for the Deaf, Dumb, and Blind in Baton Rouge, shown here, on the corner of South Boulevard and St. Ferdinand Street. The Seminary was allowed use of half of the building, but it was crowded and the kitchen and dining facilities were shared with inmates of the institute. Cadets slept 8 to 10 to a room and had to drill in the streets. This would be LSU's "temporary" home until 1887. (OCR.)

This close-up of the Louisiana Institution for the Deaf Dumb, and Blind shows the iron and stonework on this grand building. The front of the building, shown here, faced the Mississippi River. Constructed in the 1850s, it was condemned in 1940 and razed in 1947. (LSUPC.)

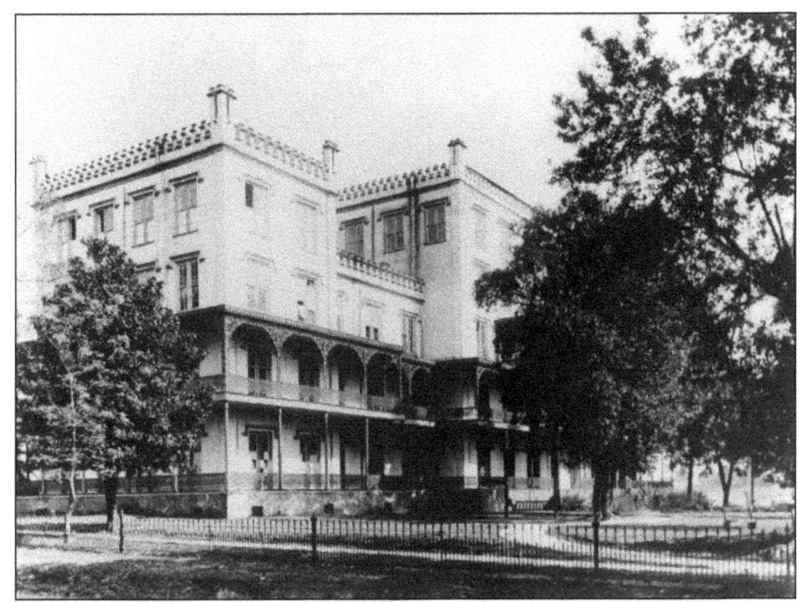

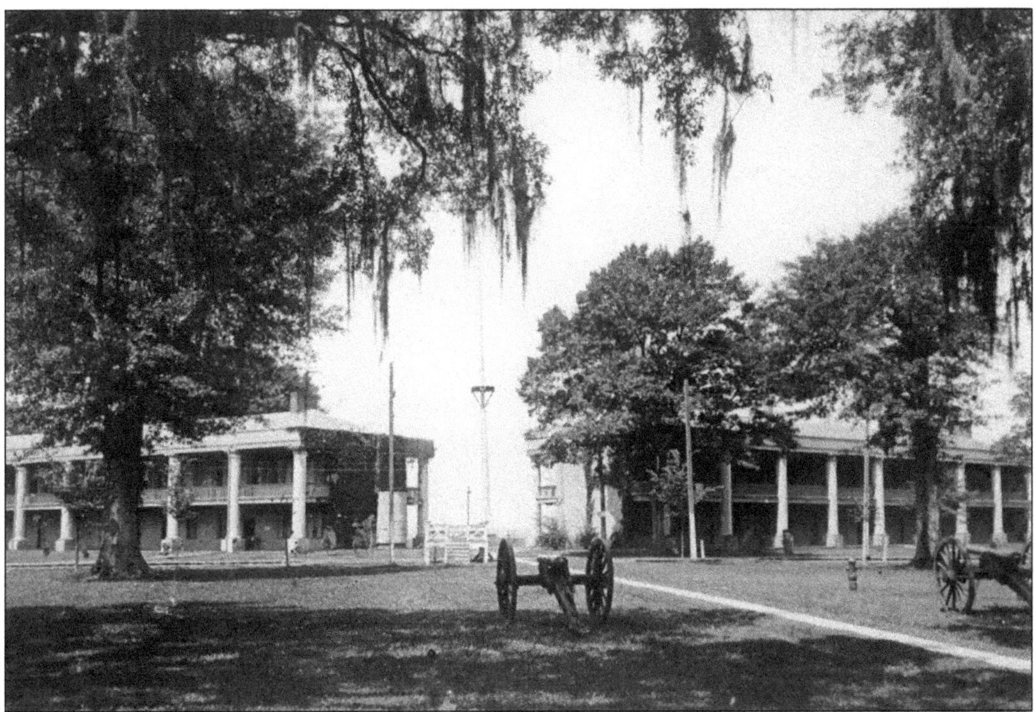

LSU's third home was the former Baton Rouge Arsenal, located on what are now the state capitol grounds. The university moved here in 1887 and remained until the present campus was ready for use in 1925. The Pentagon Barracks, as seen from the president's residence, housed classrooms, cadets' bedrooms, and company arsenals. The arsenal building that was used as a veterinary infirmary and the Pentagon Barracks are the only buildings original to the Baton Rouge military post to survive. The others were demolished to make way for the new state capitol buildings and grounds. The cannons were used in artillery drills. (LSUPC.)

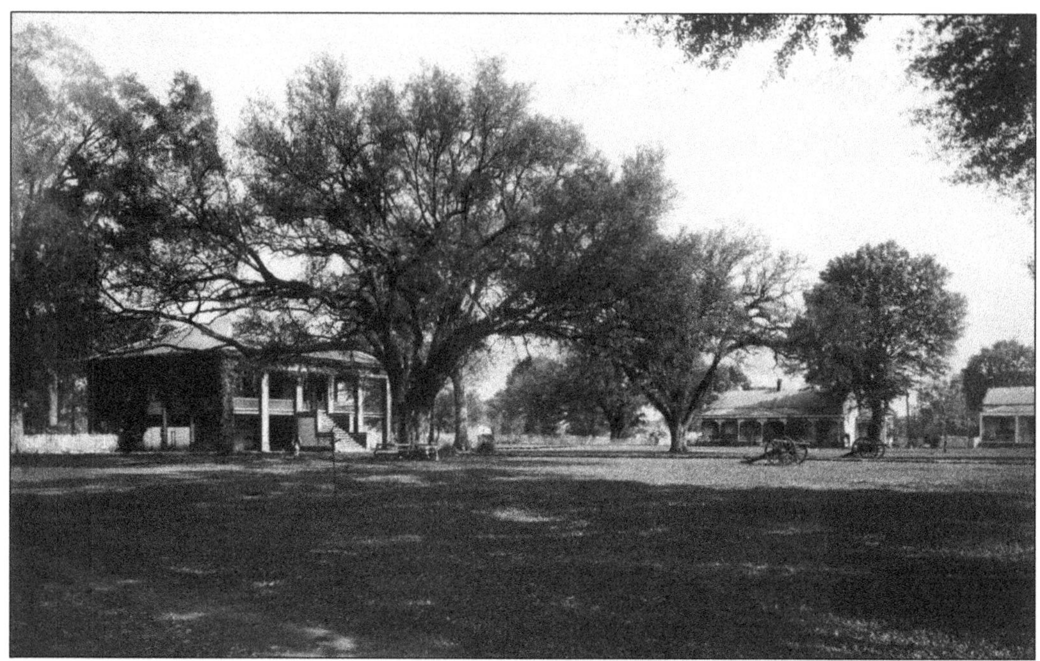

The homes of the president (left) and treasurer (right) were buildings original to the Baton Rouge Arsenal. Both were razed in 1930 to make way for the new state capitol building and grounds. Part of the commandant's house can be seen at far right. (LSUPC.)

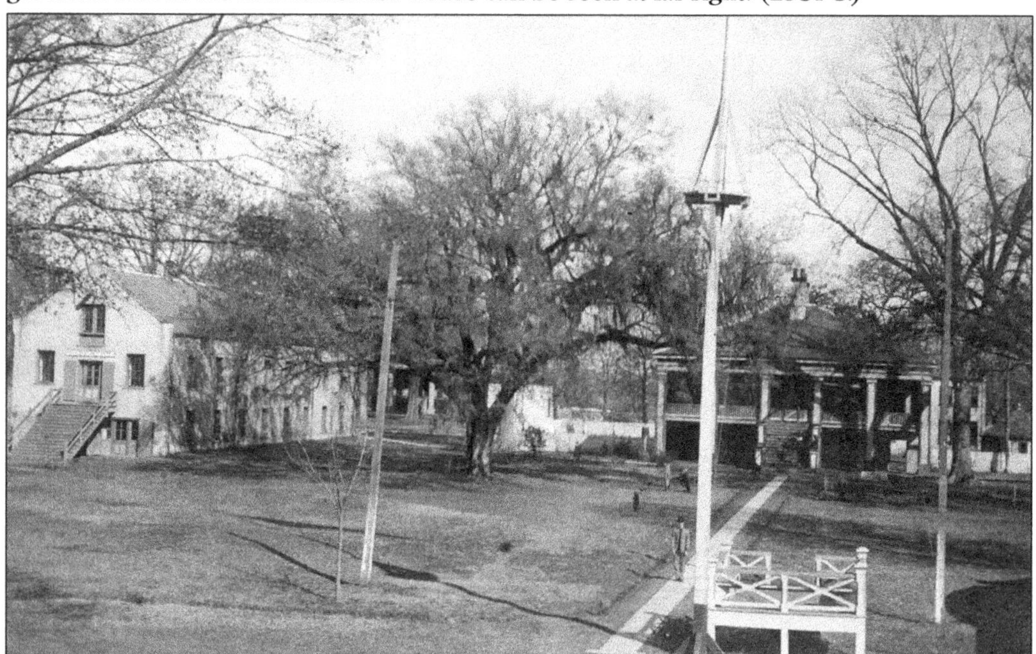

This 1899 view faces east from the Pentagon Barracks toward the chemistry building and the president's residence. The chemistry building later housed the agronomy department. Both of these buildings were part of the Baton Rouge Arsenal, completed in 1825. The president's residence was called the "Boyd Home" because of Thomas Boyd's 31-year tenure as president of LSU. (LSUPC.)

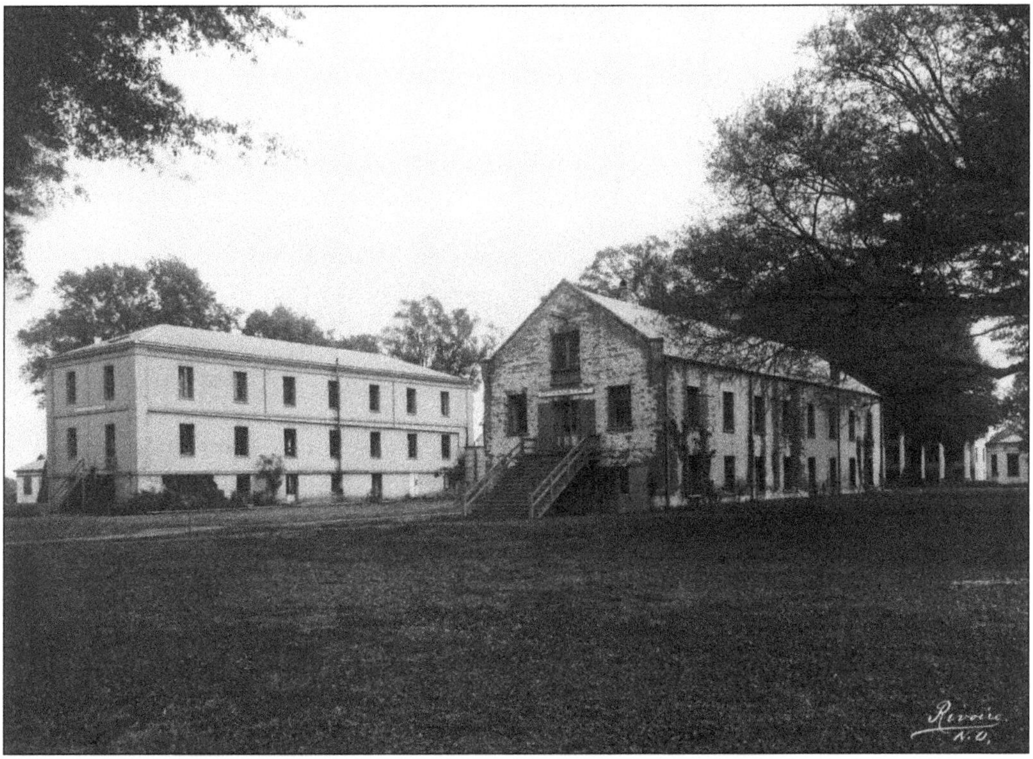

The agriculture (left) and chemistry (right) buildings were holdovers from the Baton Rouge Arsenal. After Irion Hall opened, the chemistry building housed classrooms and laboratories of the agronomy department. (LSUPC.)

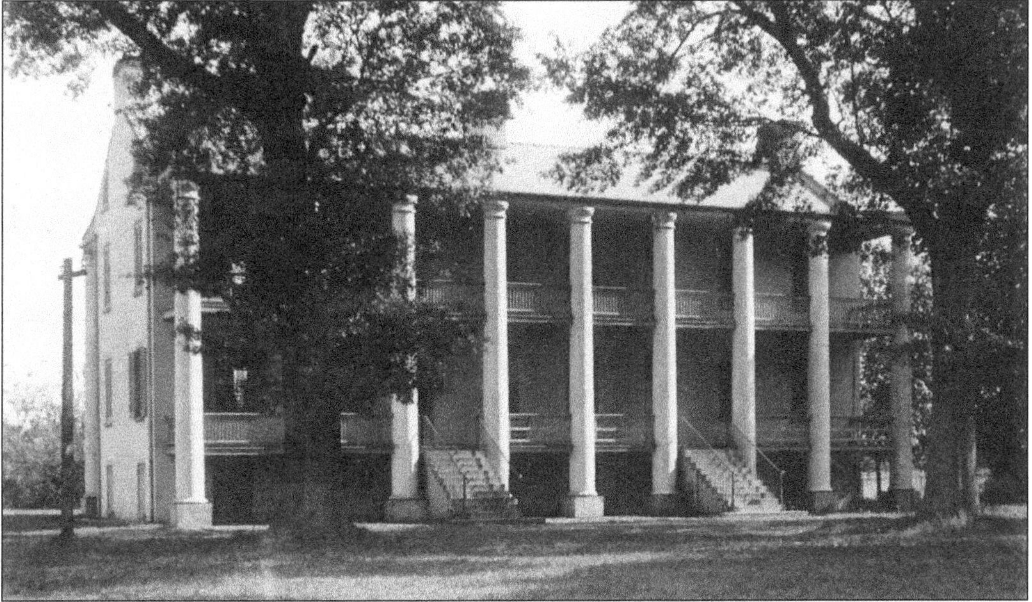

"The Colony" served as a dormitory on the downtown campus. It dated to the 1820s, when the site was the Baton Rouge Arsenal. The building was razed in 1930 to make way for the new state capitol building and grounds. (LSUPC.)

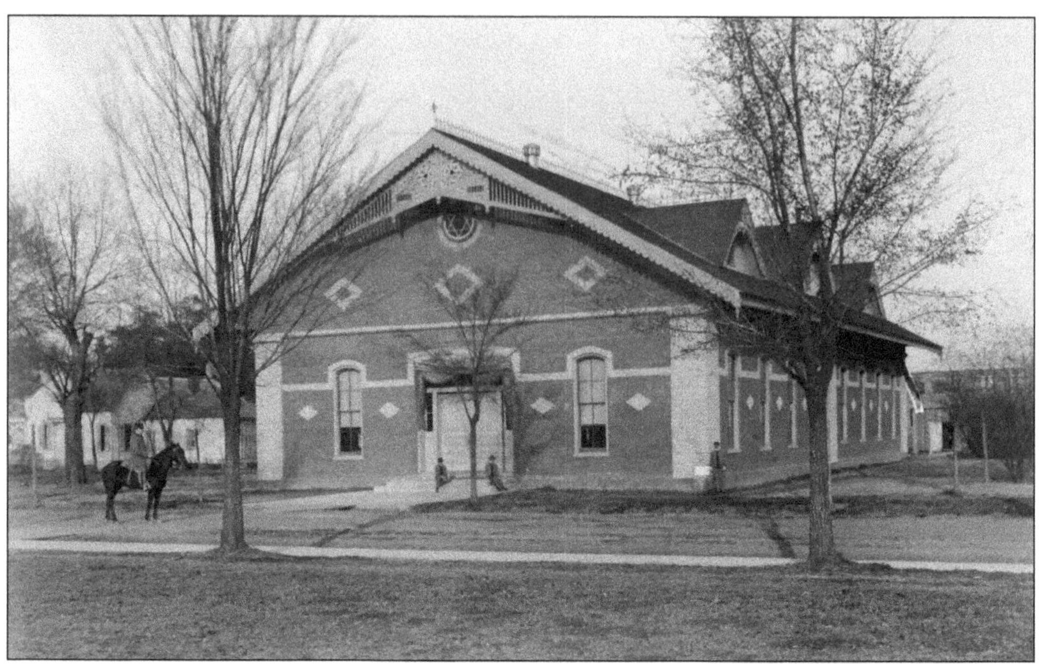

Opened in 1900, Garig Hall was the first purpose-built meeting hall on campus. Baton Rouge businessman William Garig provided the funding, hence the name. This building is significant because it was built with the first private donation of funds for construction that the university ever received. (LSUPC.)

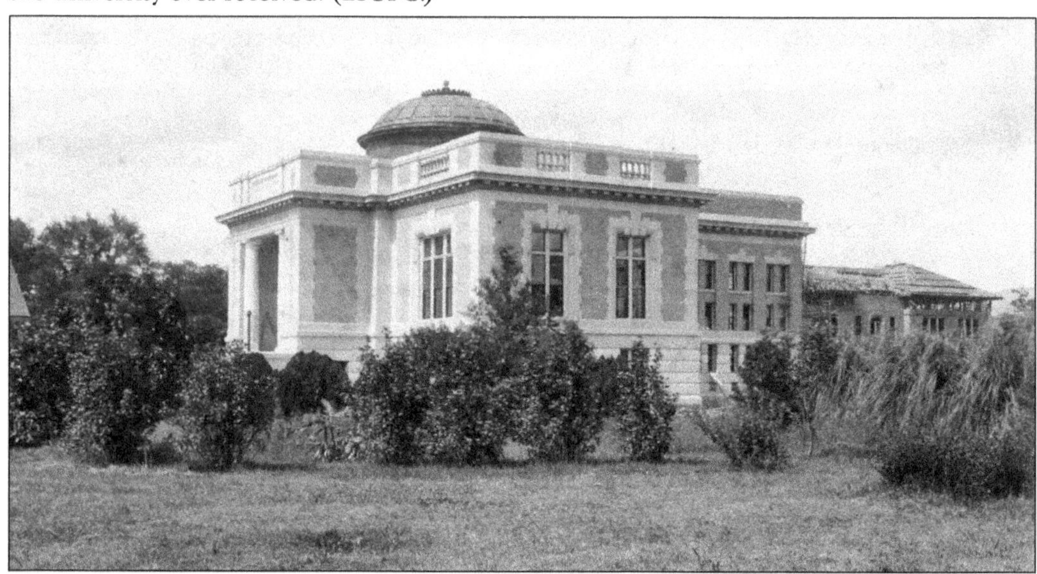

Designed by architect W.L. Stevens of Crowley, Louisiana, and completed in 1903, Hill Memorial Library was LSU's first purpose-built library building. John Hill, a West Baton Rouge Parish businessman, provided $25,000 towards its construction. Hill's contribution was the second donation ever received for constructing a campus building. The library was named in honor of Hill's son, John Jr., an 1873 graduate who was a member of the LSU Board of Supervisors and who died of yellow fever in 1893. The total cost of the library was $34,372.87, plus an additional $12,500 for steel stacks. (LSUPC.)

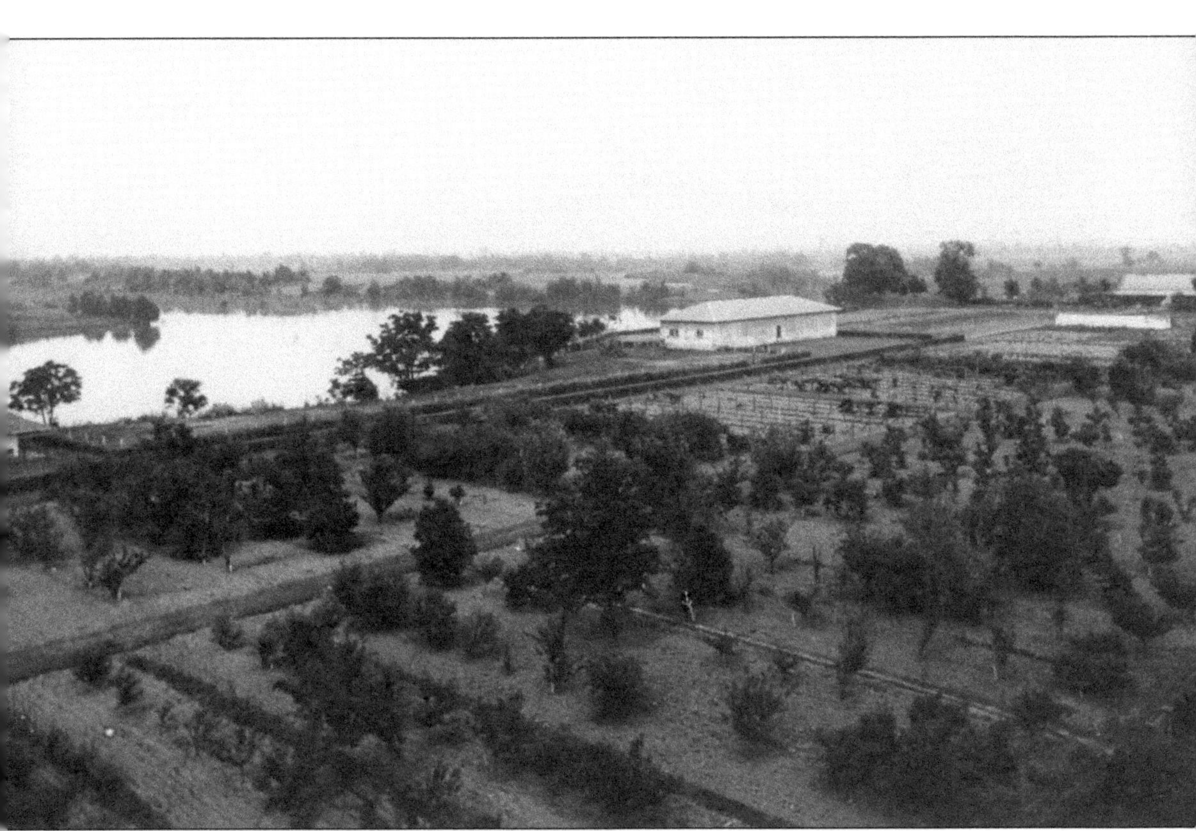

The horticulture garden is seen here near University Lake, now Capitol Lake, at the north end of the campus. The building at center near the lake was a powder magazine and served as the library from 1887 until Hill Memorial Library opened in 1903. (LSUPC.)

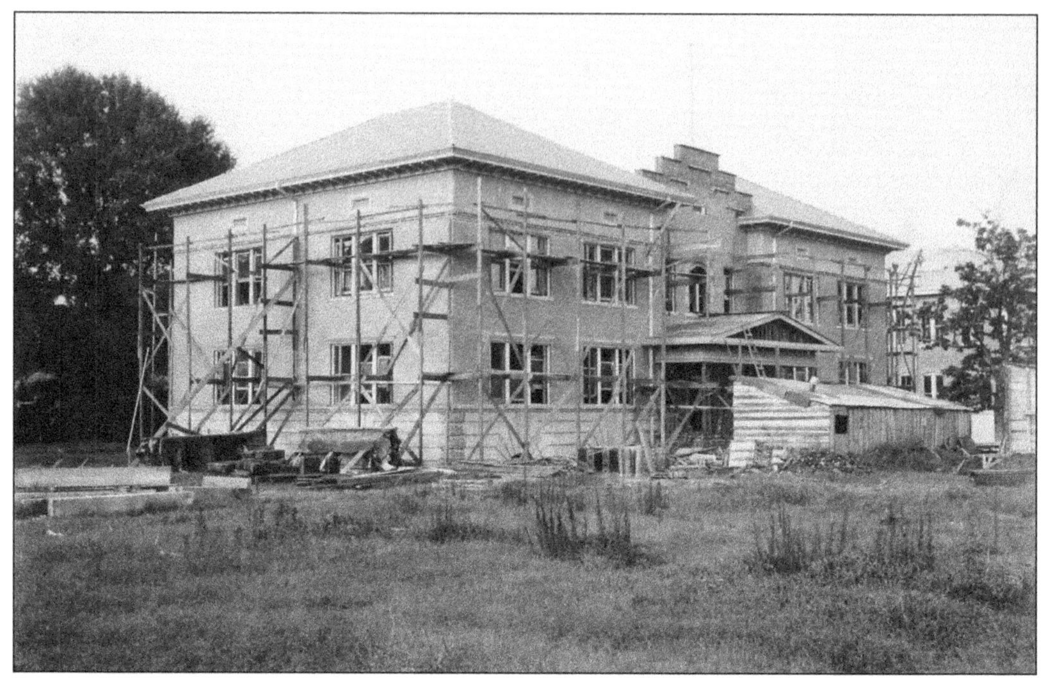

Shown here under construction in 1903, Heard Hall was the new physics and civil engineering building. The physics and electrical engineering departments were on the ground floor, while the departments of civil engineering and mathematics were on the second floor. Designed by Favrot and Livaudais, the building cost $24,947.40. (LSUPC.)

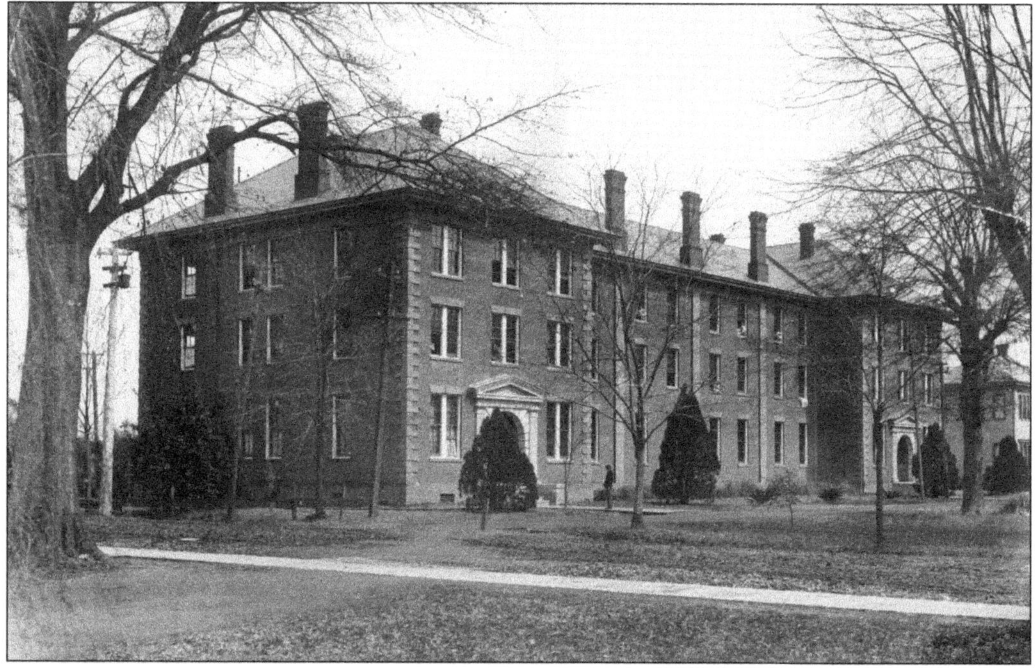

Named for Gov. Murphy J. Foster, Foster Hall was the first new dormitory and dining hall constructed on the downtown campus. It was completed in 1900 and was designed by Favrot and Livaudais. It cost $28,587.96. It burned to the ground in 1926. (LSUPC.)

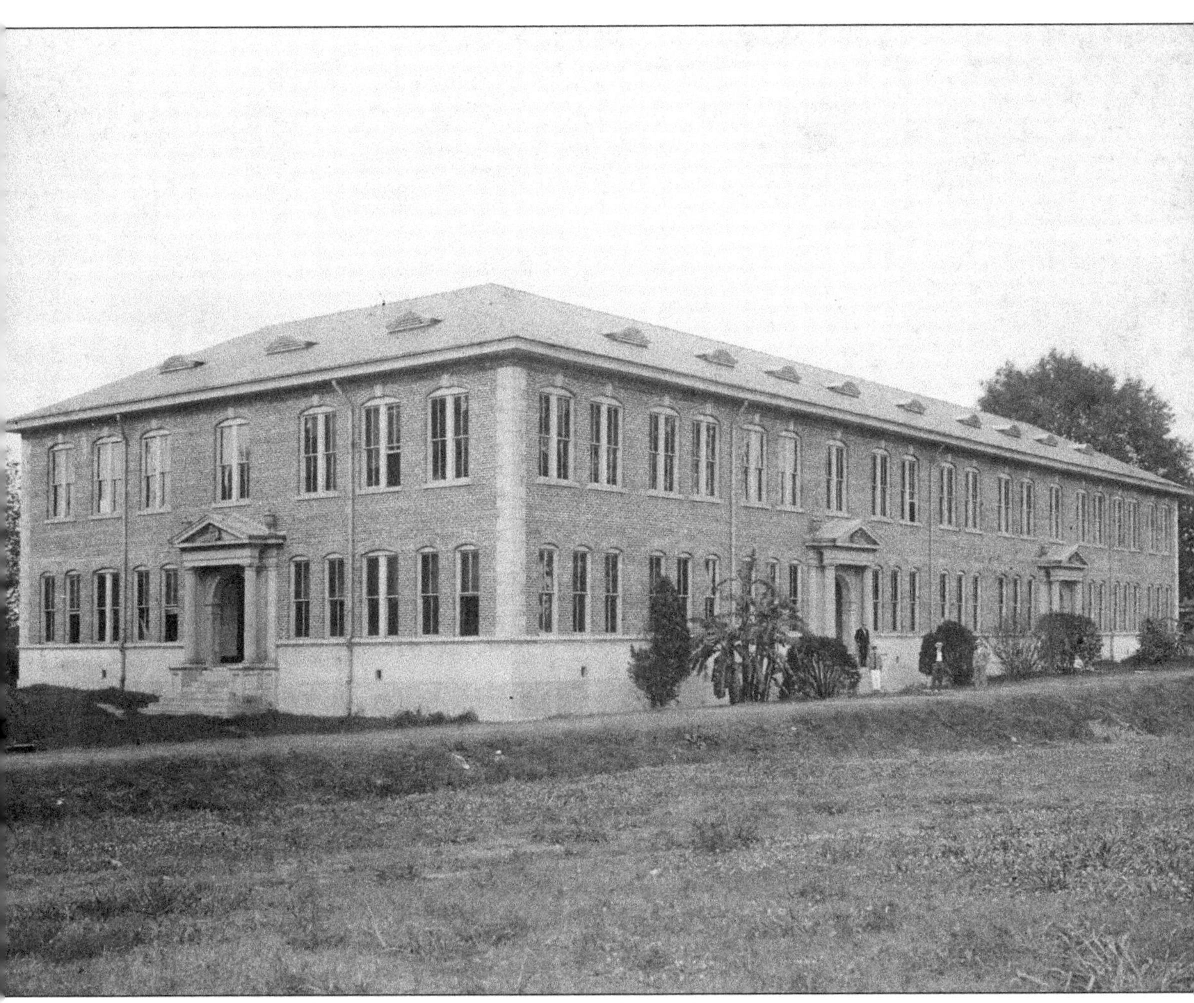

Robertson Hall served as the mechanical engineering building and workshop on the downtown campus. Designed by W.L. Stevens, who also designed Hill Memorial Library, it was built at a cost of $9,825.95. Robertson Hall opened in 1903 and housed the machine shop, forge room, and classrooms. (LSUPC.)

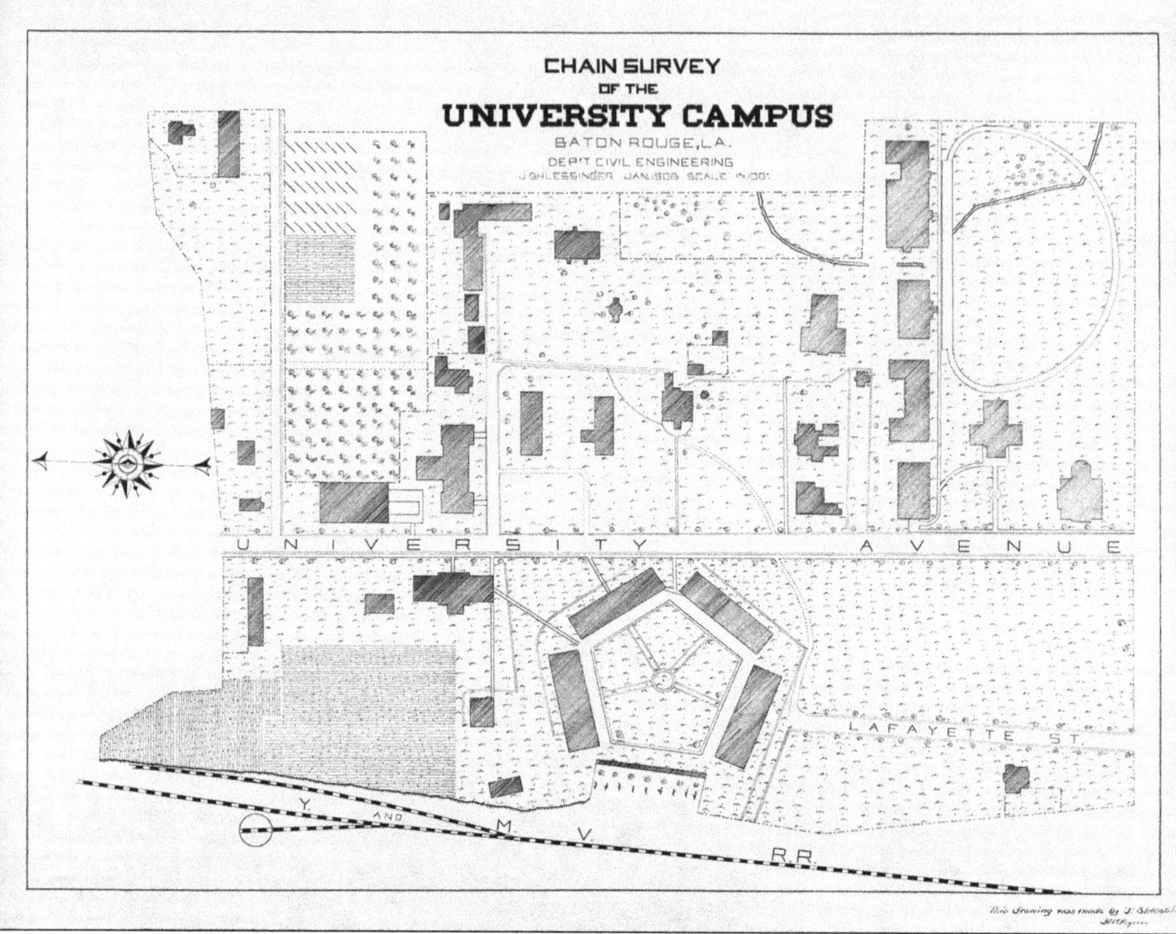

Jacob Schlessinger's survey shows the ground plan of the downtown campus in 1908. Across University Avenue (now North Third Street) from the Pentagon Barracks are, from left to right, the agriculture building, the chemistry building, the president's residence, the commandant's residence, Garig Hall, Hill Memorial Library, and Alumni Memorial Hall. On University Avenue immediately to the left of the Pentagon Barracks is the hospital, and directly across the street is Foster Hall, a dormitory and mess hall. (OFSR.)

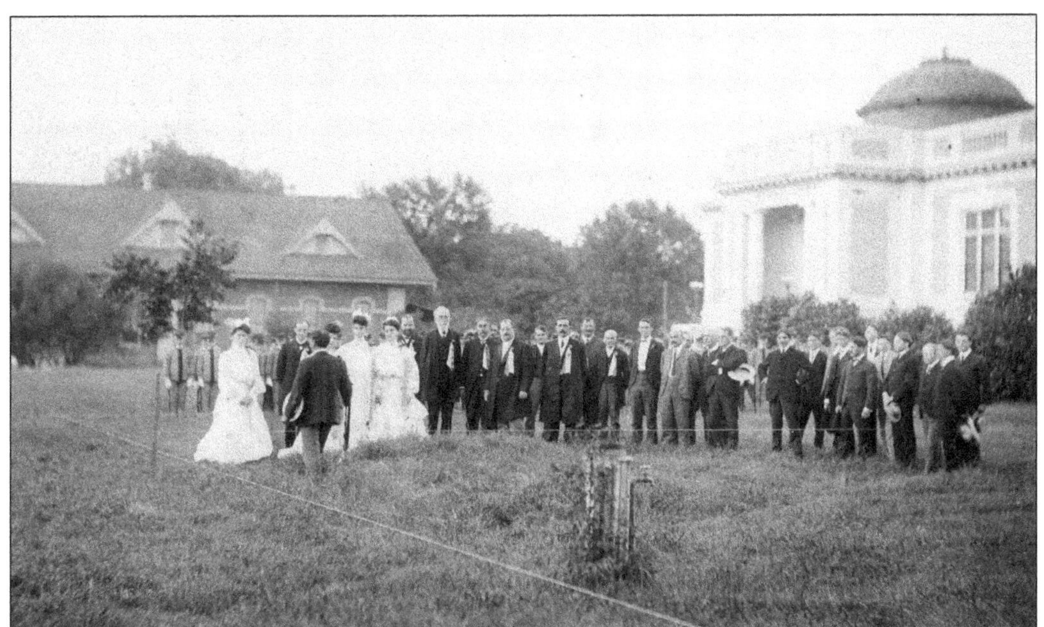

The groundbreaking for Alumni Memorial Hall took place on September 18, 1903, and the cornerstone was laid the following year. The tall, bearded man at center is John Hill, who provided funding toward the construction of Hill Memorial Library, seen in the background. Hill also contributed funds to construct Alumni Memorial Hall and to other campus projects. (LSUPC.)

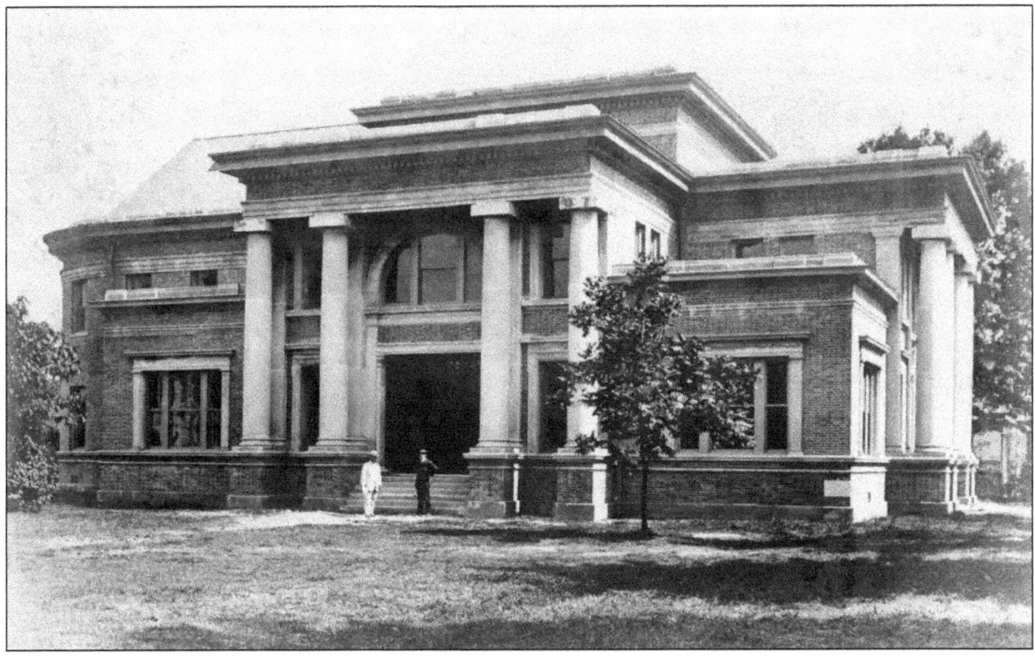

Designed by New Orleans architects Favrot and Livaudais, Alumni Memorial Hall was completed in 1909 at a cost of $40,845.97. The first floor housed the Society of the Alumni, offices for the president, treasurer, and some faculty members, and a large meeting hall. The second floor had small halls set aside for literary societies. (LSUPC.)

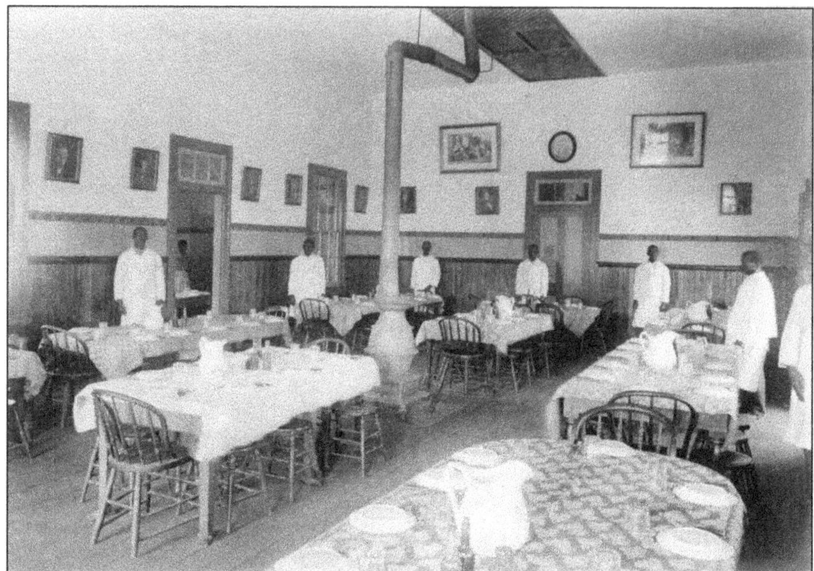

Inside the mess hall, the stewards—as the employees who prepared meals, cleaned, and chopped wood were called—were the only African Americans on campus until the early 1950s. (LSUPC.)

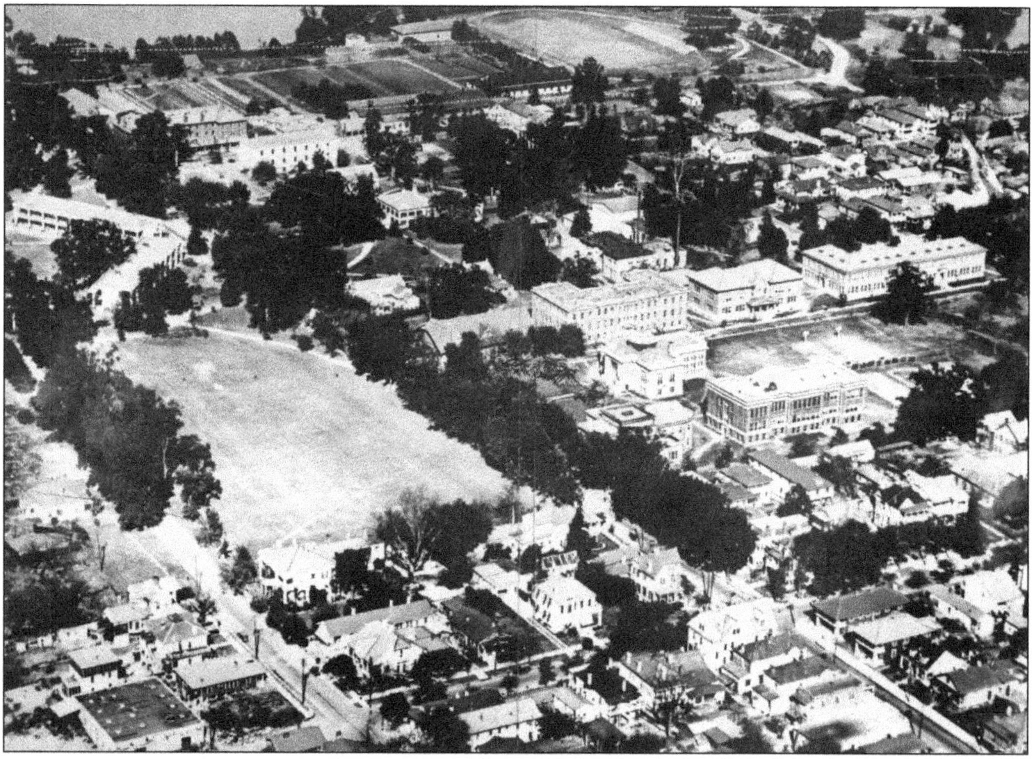

This aerial view from around 1920 shows the downtown campus in its final form. The cleared area at top center is State Field, where the Tigers played football. Peabody Hall (center right) was the last building constructed on the downtown campus. Opened in 1915, Peabody was the home of the Teachers College and the law school. Because of Baton Rouge's steady encroachment, Pres. Thomas Boyd began looking for a new and larger campus that would give the university room to grow and better fulfill its mission as an agricultural and mechanical college. (LSUPC.)

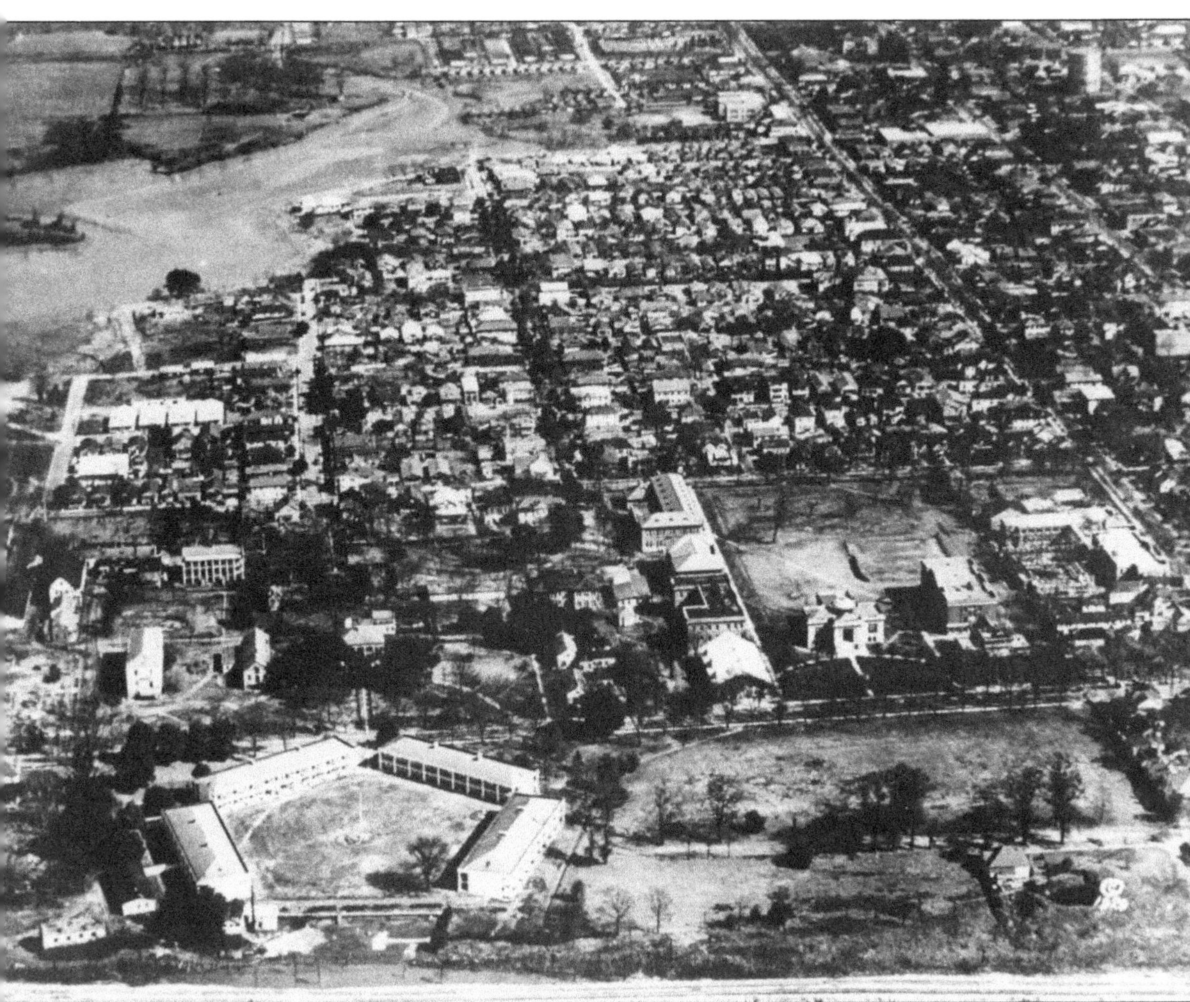

In 1929, Jasper Ewing took one of the last aerial photographs of the downtown campus before it was razed to begin construction of the new state capitol. Some classes were still being held here, even though the new campus south of town had been open since the fall semester of 1925. Female students were housed in the Pentagon Barracks because there was no women's dormitory on the new campus. The Pentagon Barracks remain as apartments for state legislators. At the bottom is the new levee constructed after the great flood of 1927. (LSUPC.)

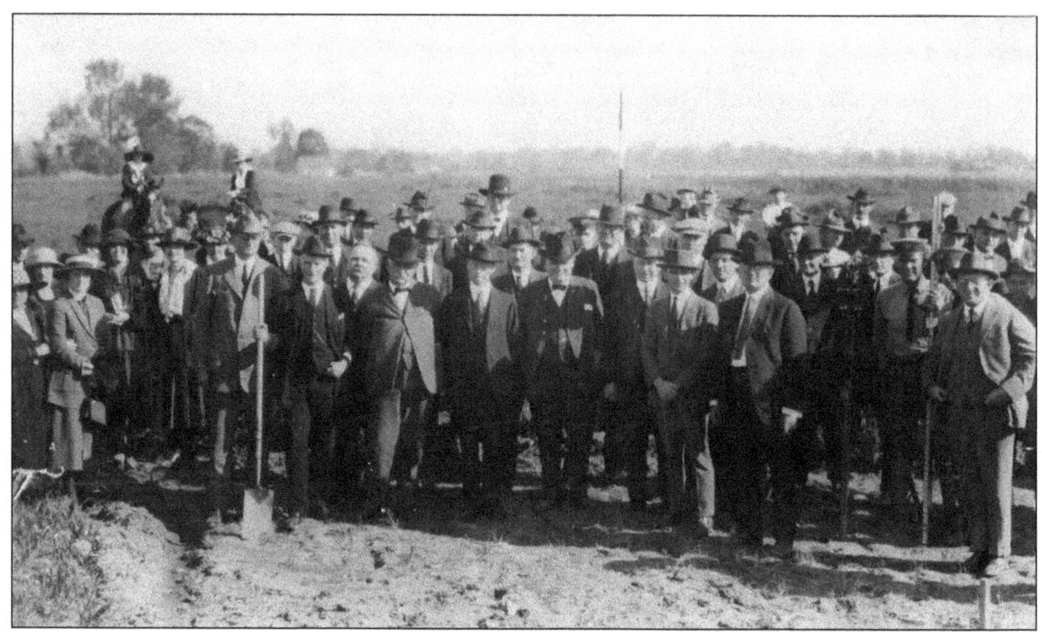

The groundbreaking ceremony for the dairy barn, the first building on the university's present site, took place on March 29, 1922. John M. Parker (with shovel) did the honors. Other dignitaries present included university business manager Robert L. Himes, Rep. Horace Wilkinson, LSU president Thomas Boyd, Prof. Arthur Prescott, Baton Rouge businessman Dalton Reymond, and Prof. Thomas Atkinson (left of the transit). (LSUPC.)

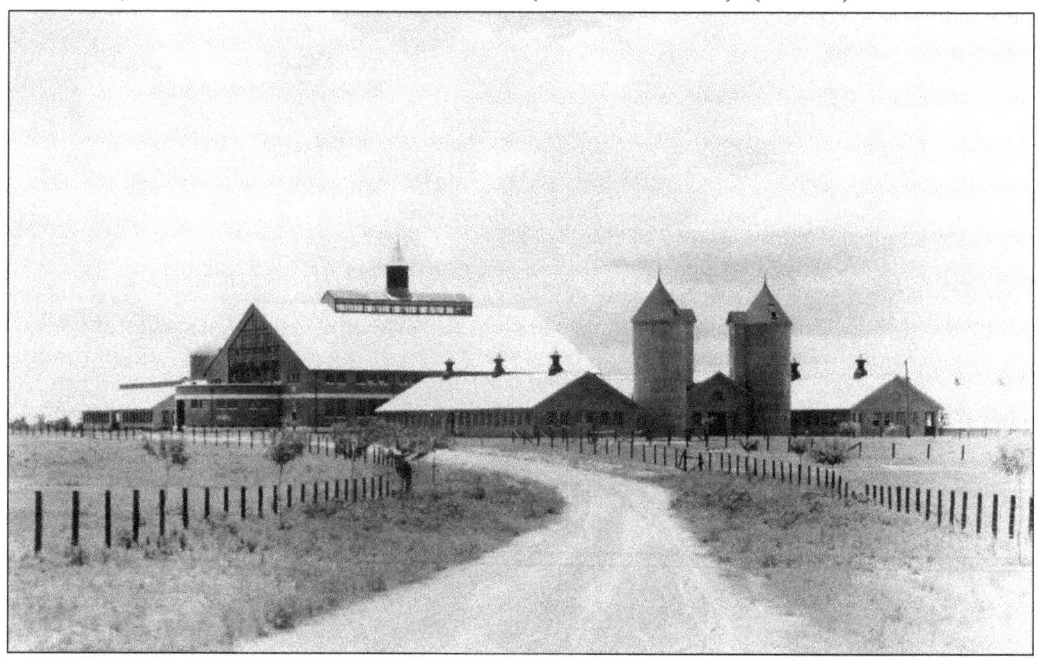

Designed by Theodore Link, the dairy barns and stock judging pavilion were the first buildings completed on the new campus in 1922. The silos no longer exist, but the stock-judging pavilion reopened after renovations as the Department of Theater's Reilly Theater in 2000. (LSUPC.)

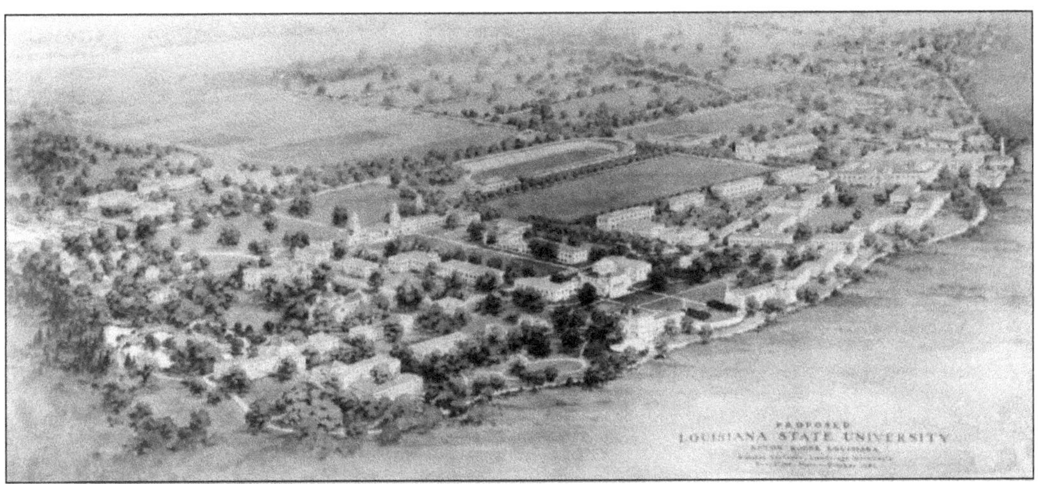

After LSU acquired Gartness Plantation, the prestigious Olmsted Brothers landscape architecture firm was hired to plan the campus, devising the plan in 1921. The firm had already designed the campuses for Ohio State University, Johns Hopkins, and the University of Chicago, and had designed Audubon Park in New Orleans. Some of the Olmsteds' ideas made their way into LSU's final design, such as the sports arena and the large quadrangle. (JFP.)

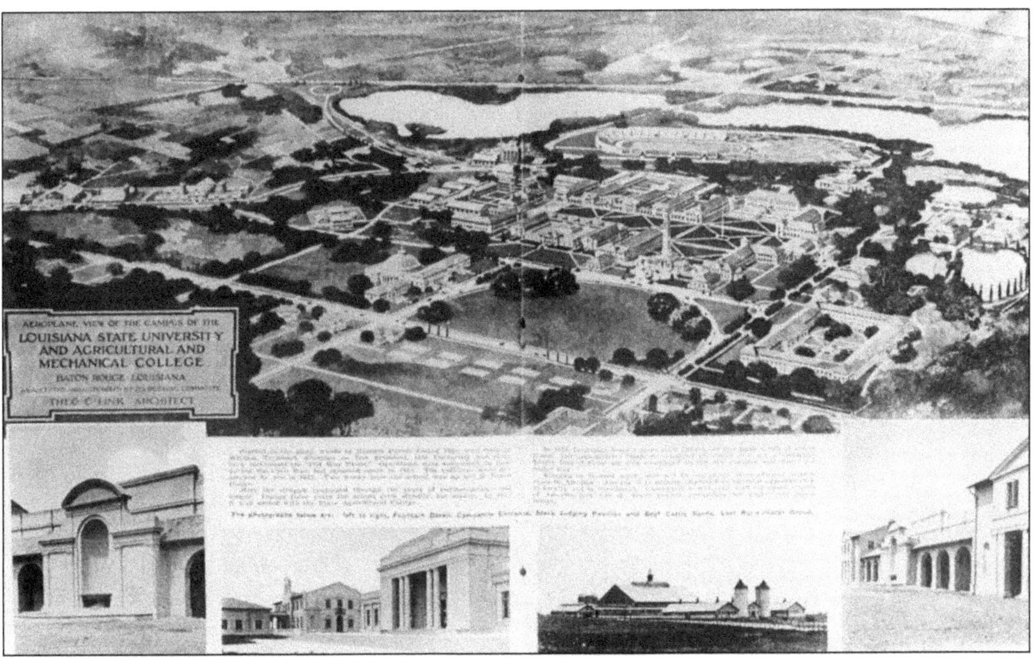

Theodore Link was hired to design the campus buildings, and his preliminary plan from 1922 bears a striking resemblance to what was actually built. He was a well-known architect who had designed St. Louis's Union Station and the Mississippi state capitol. Link died the following year and the architectural firm of Wogan and Bernard continued his designs and supervised construction of the campus buildings. (JFP.)

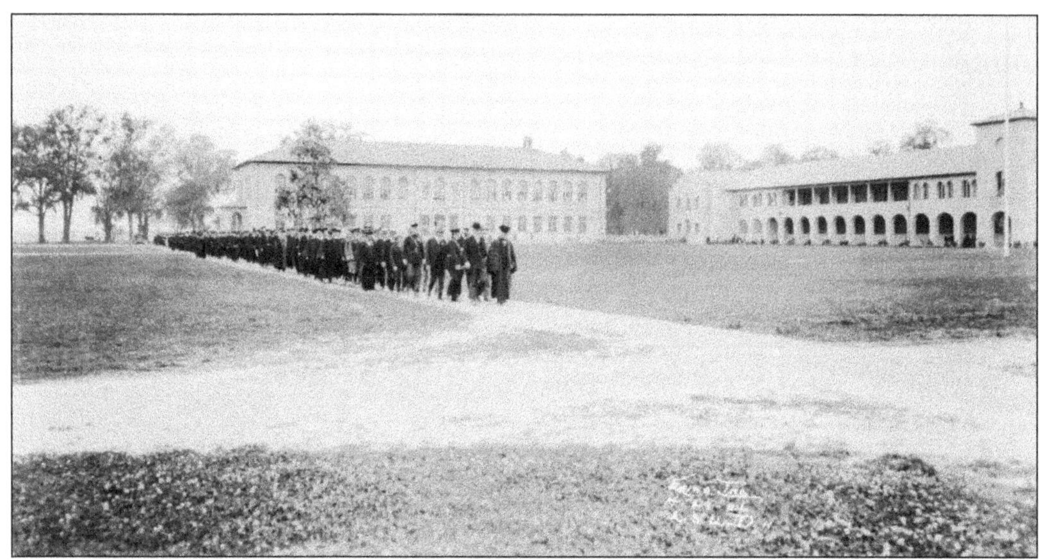

The formal dedication ceremonies for the "greater university" began on April 30, 1926, at 9:45 a.m. with an academic procession from Hill Memorial Library to the Memorial Tower. Pres. Thomas Boyd led the procession, followed by the day's speakers, the LSU Board of Supervisors, delegates, faculty, guests, and alumni. (OCR.)

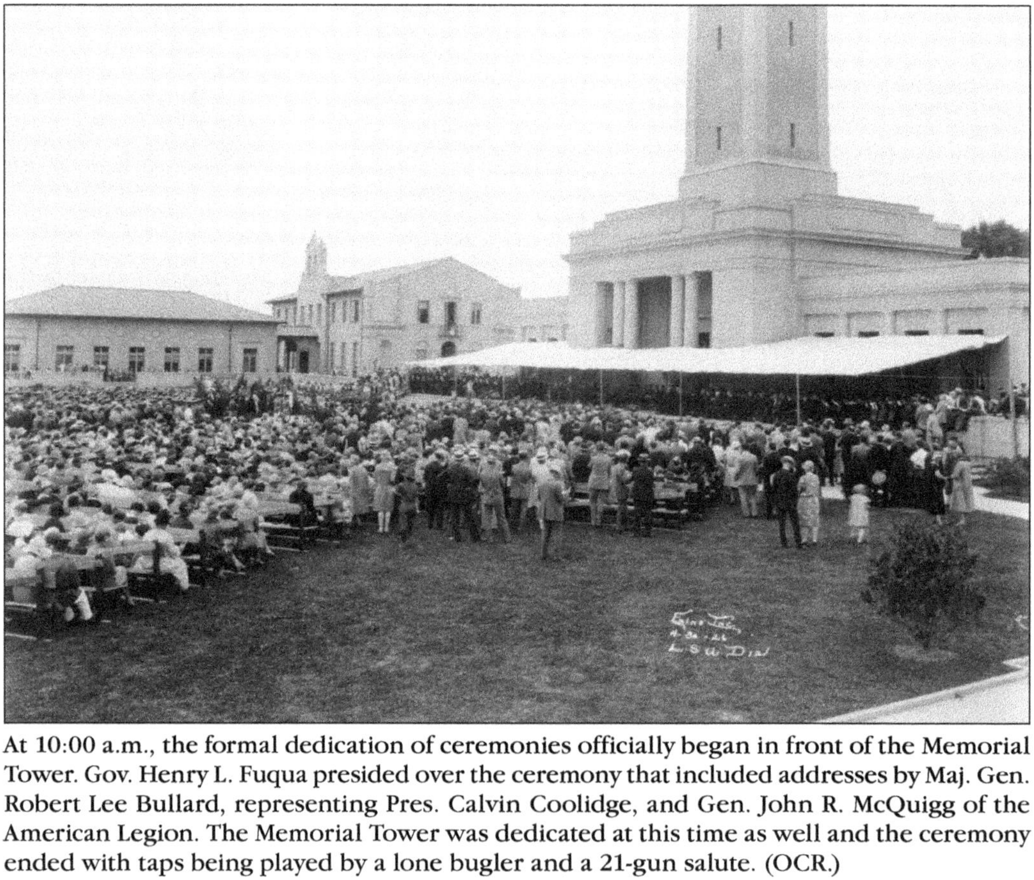

At 10:00 a.m., the formal dedication of ceremonies officially began in front of the Memorial Tower. Gov. Henry L. Fuqua presided over the ceremony that included addresses by Maj. Gen. Robert Lee Bullard, representing Pres. Calvin Coolidge, and Gen. John R. McQuigg of the American Legion. The Memorial Tower was dedicated at this time as well and the ceremony ended with taps being played by a lone bugler and a 21-gun salute. (OCR.)

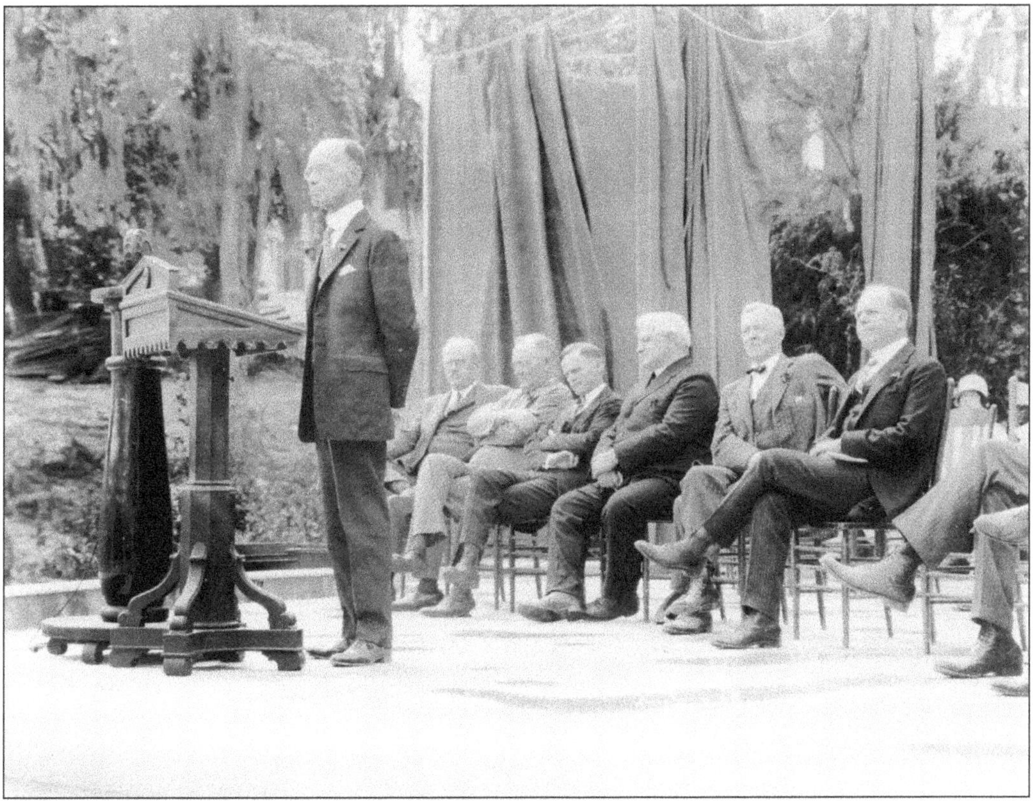

At 2:00 p.m., Thomas Boyd (at the microphone) gave a welcoming address. Dignitaries such as former governor John M. Parker (fifth from left) and Tulane president A.B. Dinwiddie (left) also spoke. Edward J. Gay, member of the Board of Supervisors, presided over the afternoon's events. (OCR.)

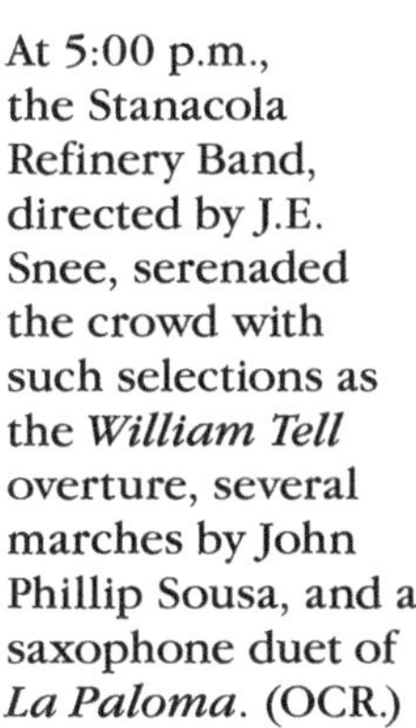

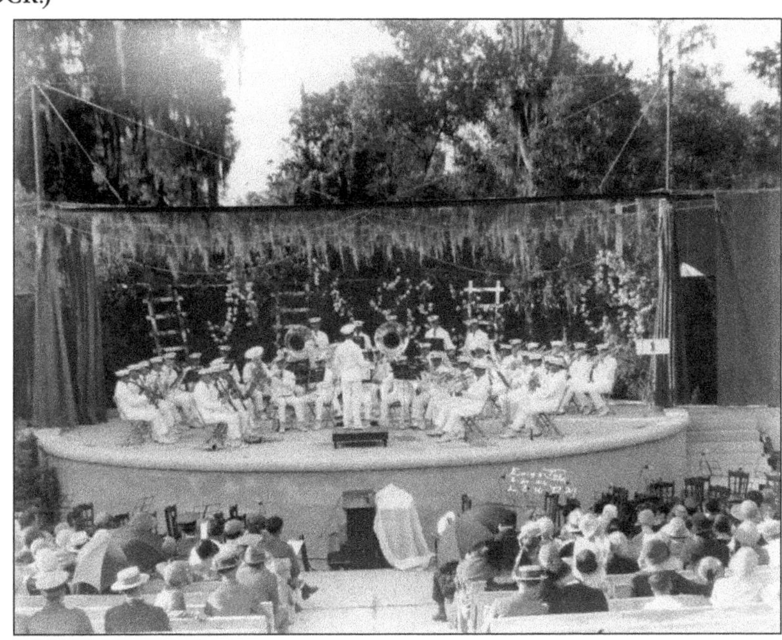

At 5:00 p.m., the Stanacola Refinery Band, directed by J.E. Snee, serenaded the crowd with such selections as the *William Tell* overture, several marches by John Phillip Sousa, and a saxophone duet of *La Paloma*. (OCR.)

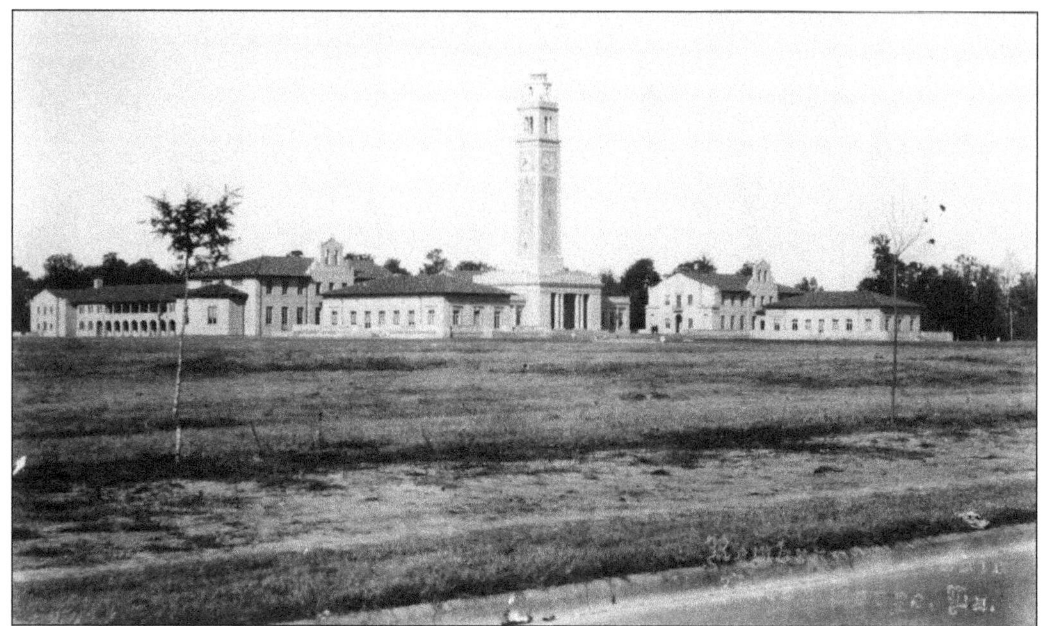

Standing 175 feet high, the Memorial Tower was completed in 1923 as a memorial to the 1,447 Louisianans who were killed in World War I. The center rotunda contains bronze plaques with their names. The tower cost $226,625; $175,000 was raised by the American Legion, and the Louisiana legislature allocated the remainder. Its inspiration came from the clock tower at Vincenza, Italy. (LSUPC.)

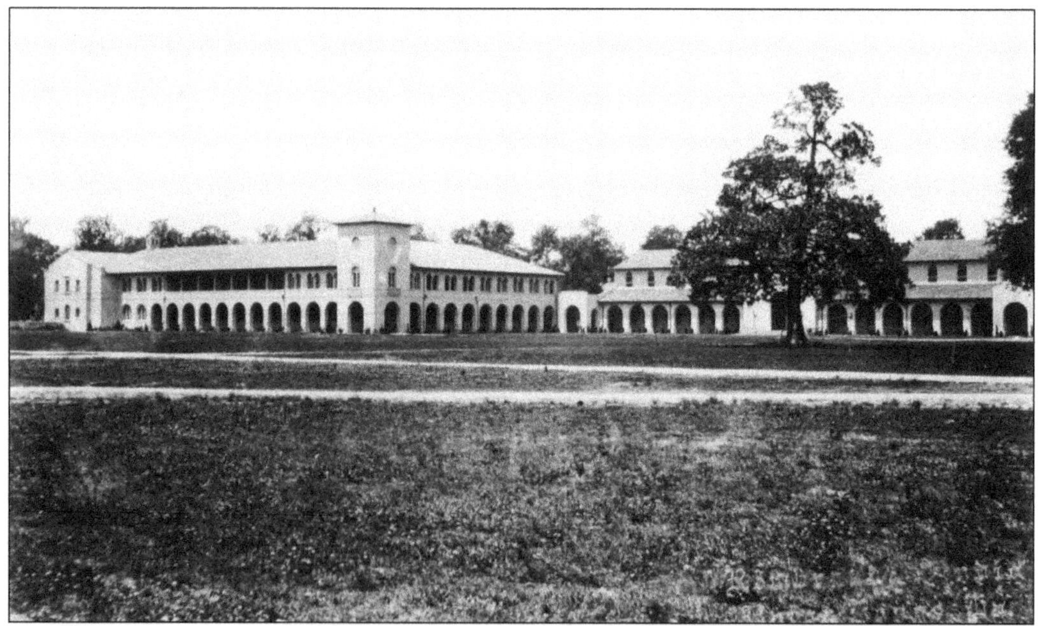

Peabody (left) and Foster Halls are seen here shortly after their completion. Peabody is the home of the College of Education. The open gallery on the second floor was enclosed in the early 1980s after a fire nearly destroyed the building. Foster was the main dining hall on campus until 1950, when campus dining became decentralized. The building now houses a gallery and studio space for the School of Art and the Museum of Natural History. (LSUPC.)

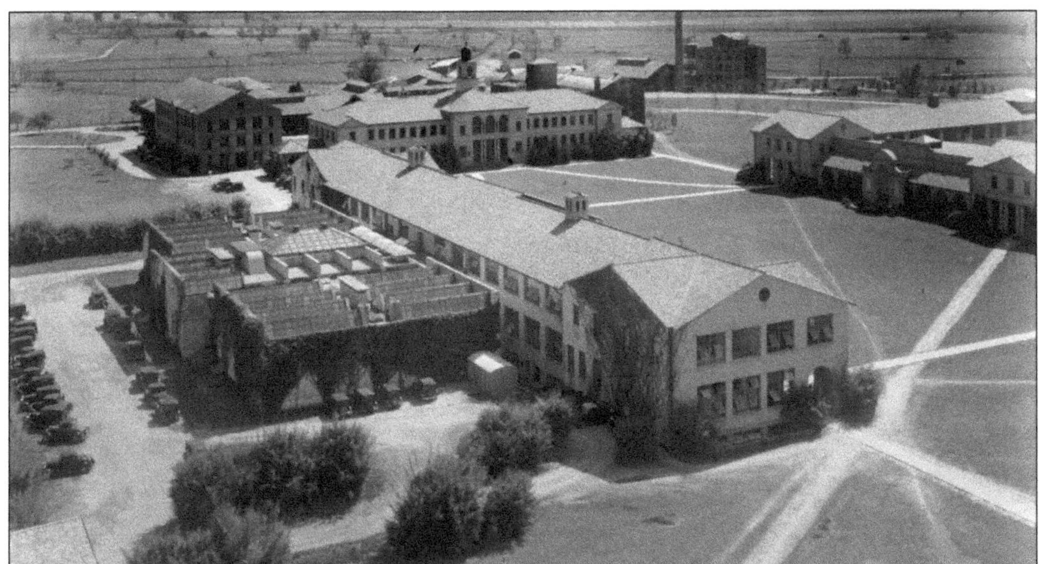

This view from the Memorial Tower shows the chemistry laboratory, now called Charles E. Coates Hall. Designed by Theodore Link and completed in 1924, it now houses classrooms and offices for the School of Library and Information Science and the Department of Philosophy and Religious Studies, among others. The chemistry laboratories are now in the Life Sciences Building and Choppin Hall. Other buildings are the engineering, geology, and agriculture buildings, and the sugar school and power house in the background. All were designed by Theodore Link and completed in 1924. (JES.)

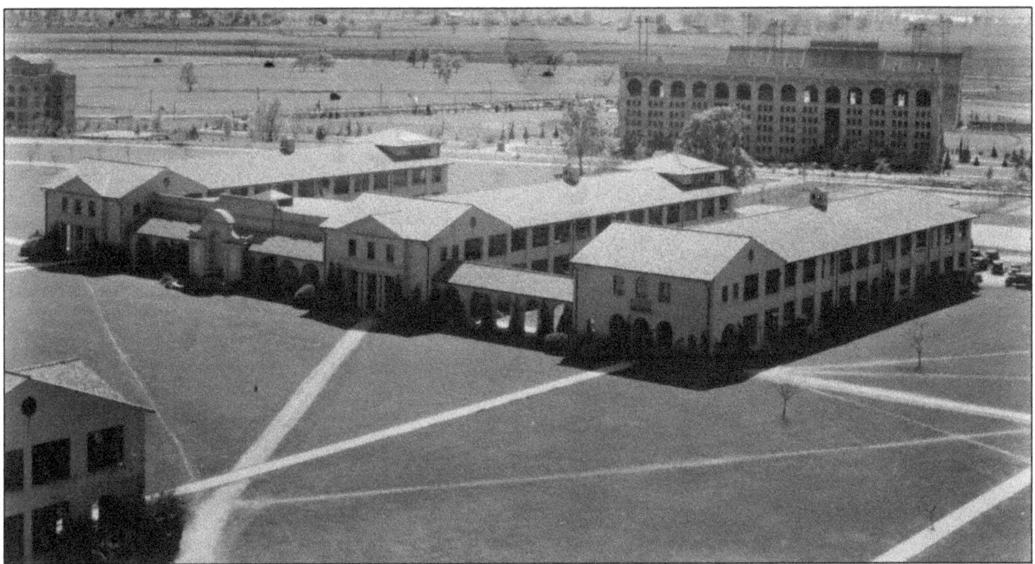

Baton Rouge photographer Jasper Ewing took this photograph from the Memorial Tower in 1934. In the center are the South Agriculture Building (now Audubon Hall), Agriculture Auditorium (Dodson Hall), Center Agriculture Building (Stubbs Hall), and North Agriculture Building (Prescott Hall). At bottom left is the Chemistry Laboratory (Coates Hall). All of the buildings started with functional names and received their present names in the 1940s and 1950s. The campus's Northern Italianate Renaissance architecture is evidenced by the pan tile roofs and arched and columned entryways. (JES.)

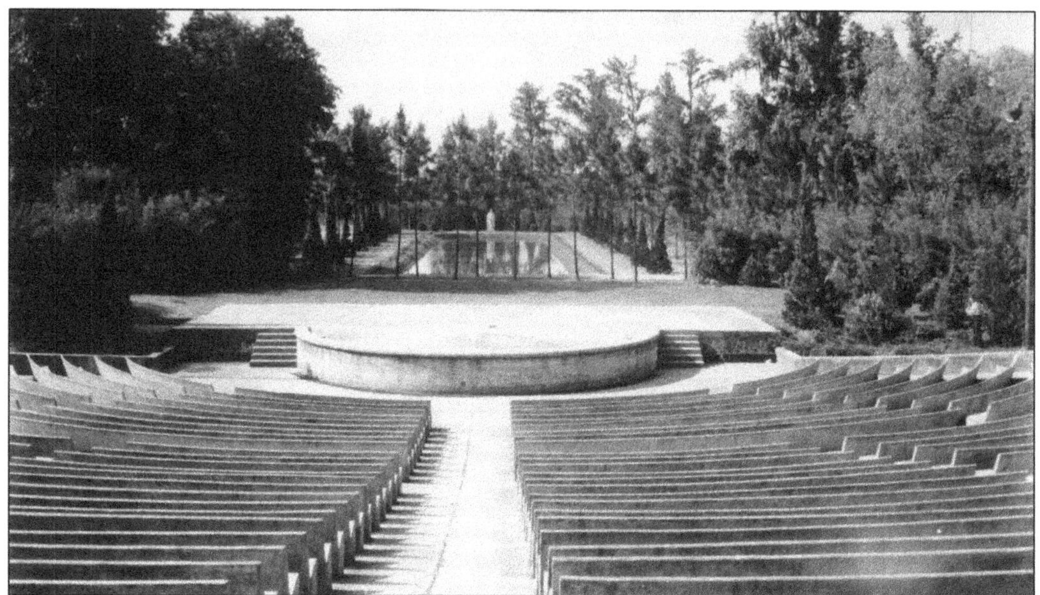

The Greek Theater, sunken garden, and reflecting pool were completed in 1926 and were focal points of the campus when this image was taken in 1934. With seating for 3,500, concerts, pep rallies, and commencement ceremonies were all held here, weather permitting. The statue at the far end of the reflecting pool is of Spanish explorer Hernando de Soto. The reflecting pool was filled in the mid-1960s because of continuous maintenance problems, and the statue was removed. There are two stories about de Soto's fate: one said that the statue was used as part of the fill for the reflecting pool, the other said that it was dumped in the Mississippi River. (JES.)

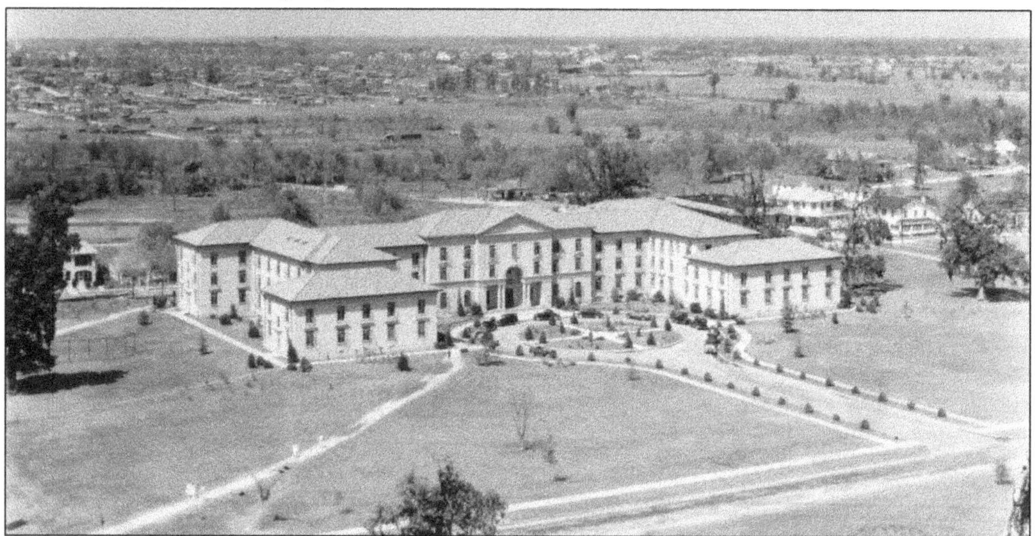

The first dormitory for women, Smith Hall, opened in 1931. Named after LSU president James Monroe Smith, the building was renamed North Women's Dormitory after Smith was convicted for his role in the "University Scandals" of 1939. In 1941, the building became Parker Hall in honor of Gov. John M. Parker. By 1948 it received its permanent name, Pleasant Hall, after Gov. Ruffin G. Pleasant. From the 1960s to the 1990s, Pleasant served as a campus hotel and is the home of the Division of Continuing Education. (JES.)

The Huey P. Long Fieldhouse, designed by Weiss, Dreyfous, and Seiferth and constructed at a cost of $518,000, opened in 1932. It originally had a barbershop, a hair salon for women, a snack bar and coffee shop, post office, and soda fountain. These functions moved into the LSU Union when it opened in 1964. The field house now houses a dance studio, classrooms, and offices of the Department of Kinesiology and the School of Social Work. (JES.)

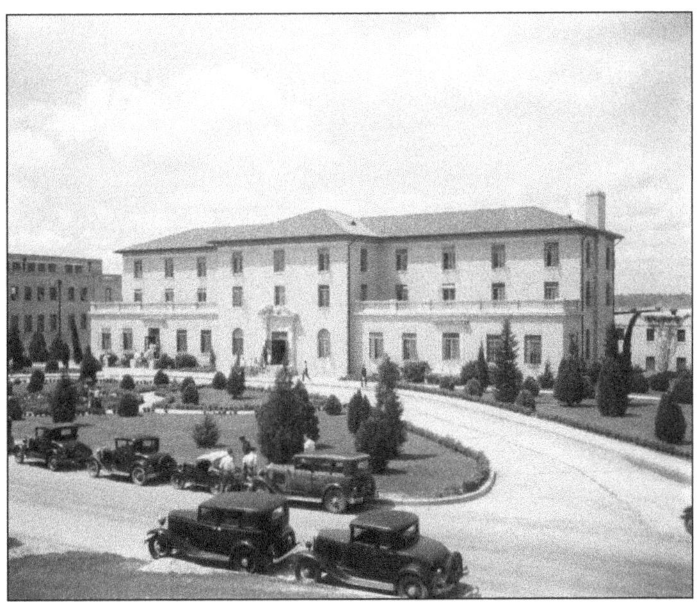

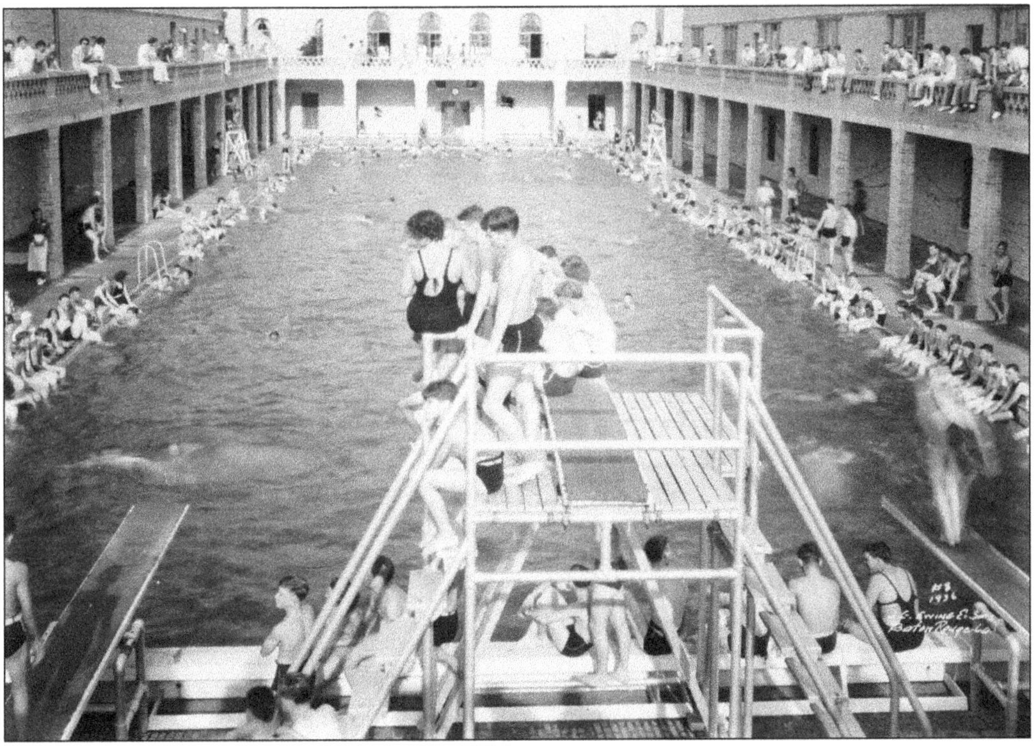

When it opened in 1932, the Huey P. Long Swimming Pool was, at 180 feet by 48 feet, the longest in the United States. The pool hosted swimming lessons, a required course for students into the 1970s, and training for the men's and women's swim teams. The pool was closed for a short time in 1964 after a federal court order compelled the university to allow African Americans to enroll. Students protested, alleging the closure was to keep out black students, and the pool reopened to all students after a few days. The pool closed permanently in 1999 because of maintenance issues. (JES.)

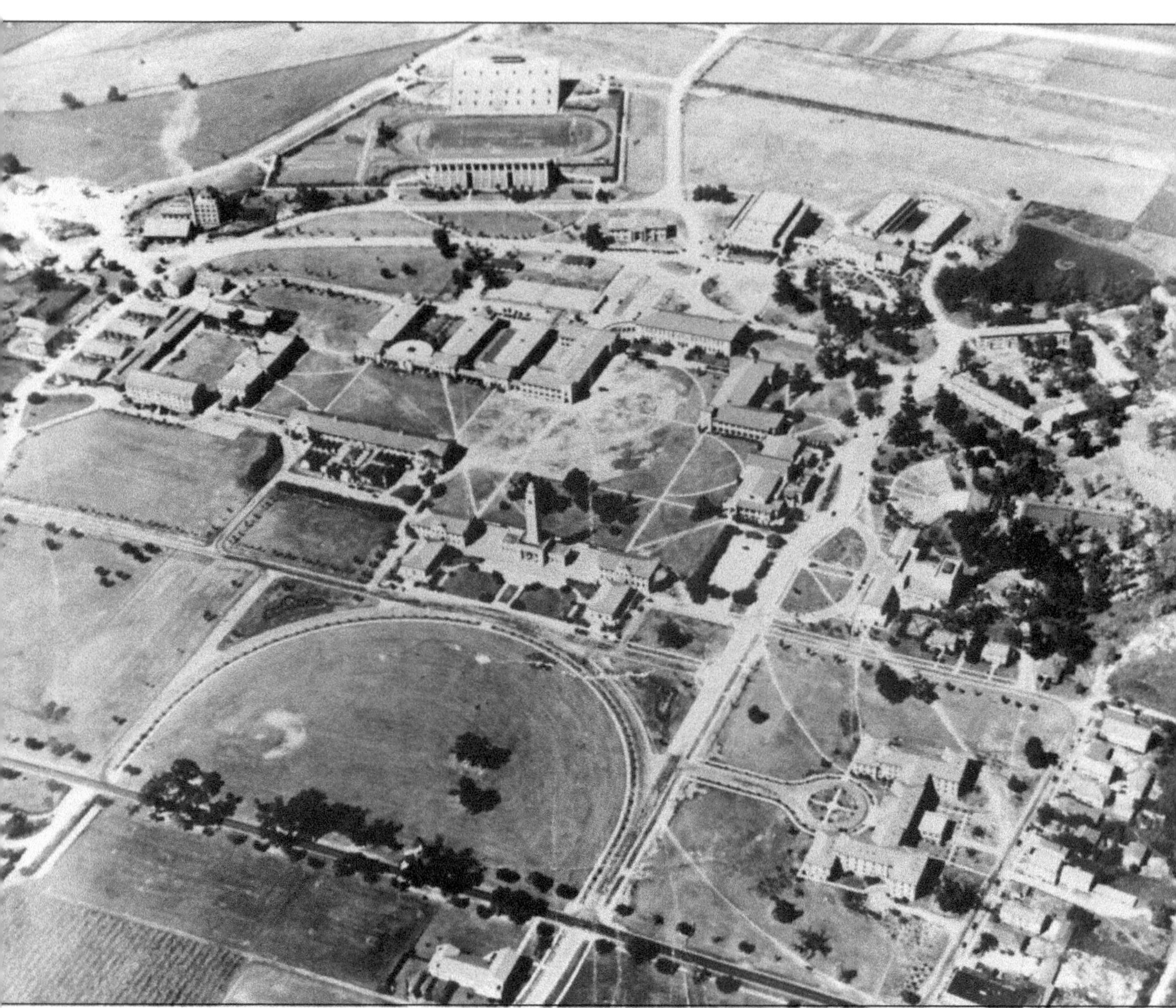

This aerial view from 1935 shows the progressive growth of the campus from its opening in the fall of 1925. The east stadium dormitories are evident, as is alumni hall, which took some of its design elements (and some of the actual building materials) from Alumni Memorial Hall on the downtown campus. Baseball games were played on the parade ground before Alex Box Stadium was completed in 1937. (LSUPC.)

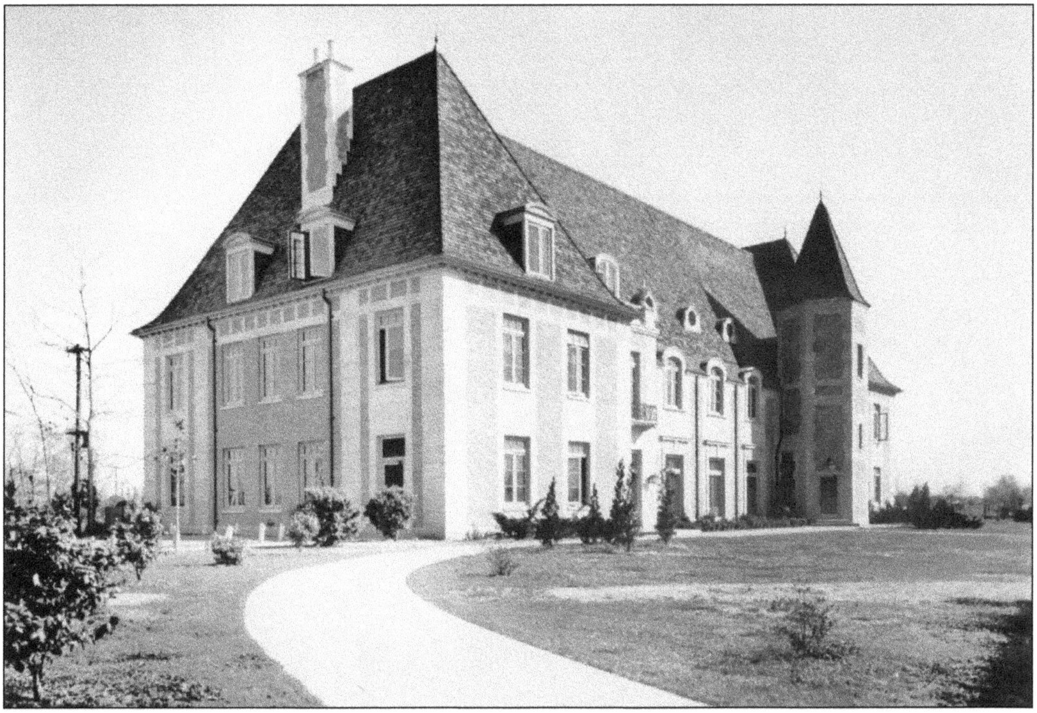

The French House opened in 1936 as a center for the intensive study of French language, literature, and culture. The cornerstone was laid in 1935 and contains a piece of wood from Fort de la Boulaye, the first French settlement in Louisiana, and a Diamond Jubilee issue of *The Reveille*. Designed by the New Orleans architecture firm Weiss, Dreyfous, and Seiferth and with a cost of $120,000, it is a replica of an early Renaissance French country chateau of the type found in the Normandy region. During World War II, the building was an officer's club for the Army Administration School. The French House also served as a women's dormitory, offices for LSU Press, and as the home of the Honors College since 1999. (JMS.)

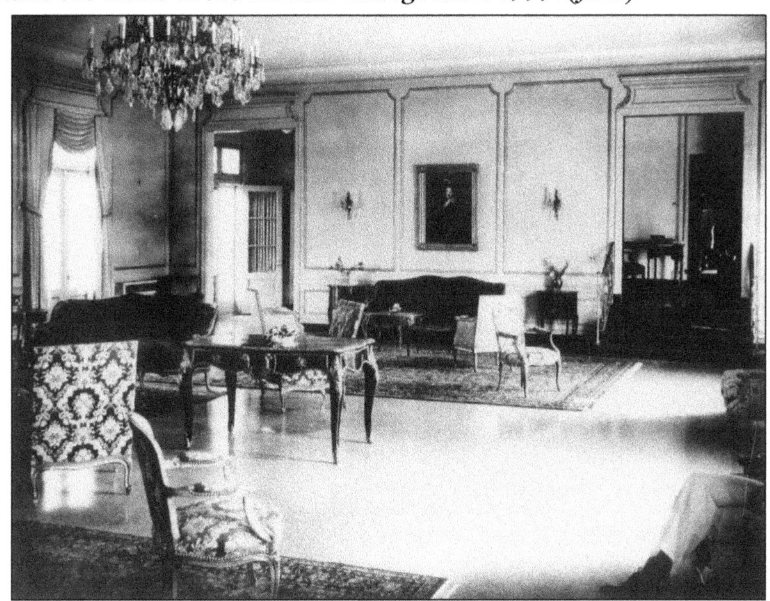

The grand salon was the social center of the French House. Music recitals, literary readings, teas, and other events were held here for the benefit of students who lived at the French House, the campus community, and the general public. (OPRR.)

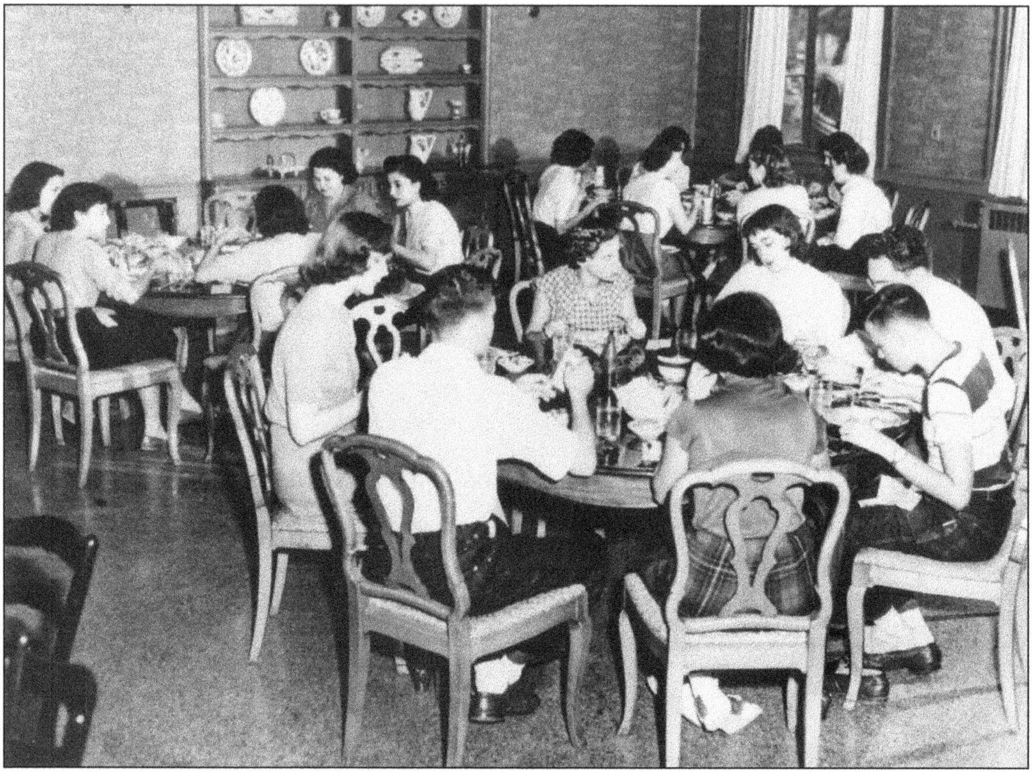

This photograph from the 1940s shows the dining room in the French House, which served French food as part of the immersion program. The university still owns the Quimper pottery in the cabinet seen in the background. (OPRR.)

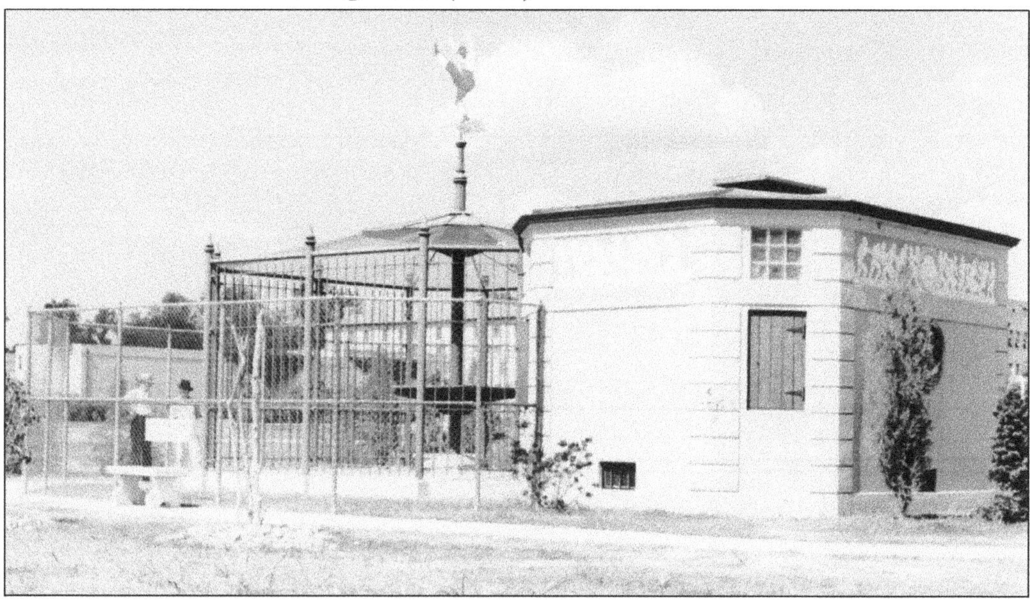

Mike the Tiger's first home on campus was completed in 1937. It was expanded in the 1970s and 1980s, and was replaced with a new and larger habitat in 2005. The frieze along the roofline is still owned by the university. (Beck's.)

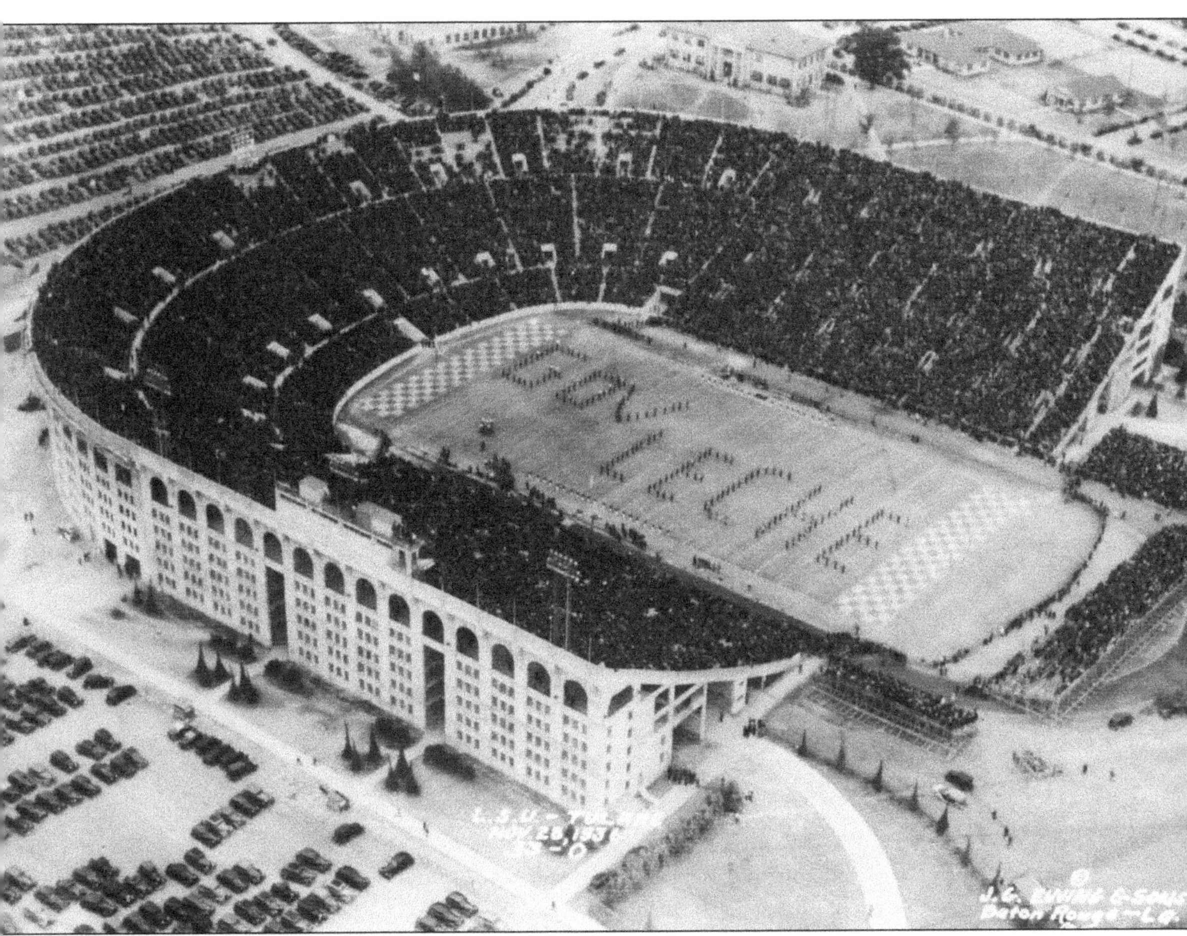

The Cadet Band salutes Gov. Richard Leche in Tiger Stadium for his part in securing funds to construct the north end zone seating and dormitory rooms. The new section increased the stadium's capacity to 45,000 and added more rooms for male students. The annual LSU-Tulane game held on November 28, 1936, was the first to incorporate the new seating. The Tigers won 33–0 in front of a sellout crowd that included Governor Leche and Harry Hopkins of the Works Progress Administration. Leche had a much better relationship with the Roosevelt administration than Huey Long and was able to secure funds from the myriad of Depression-era federal programs. Long was unable to secure these funds because he criticized the New Deal. (LSUPC.)

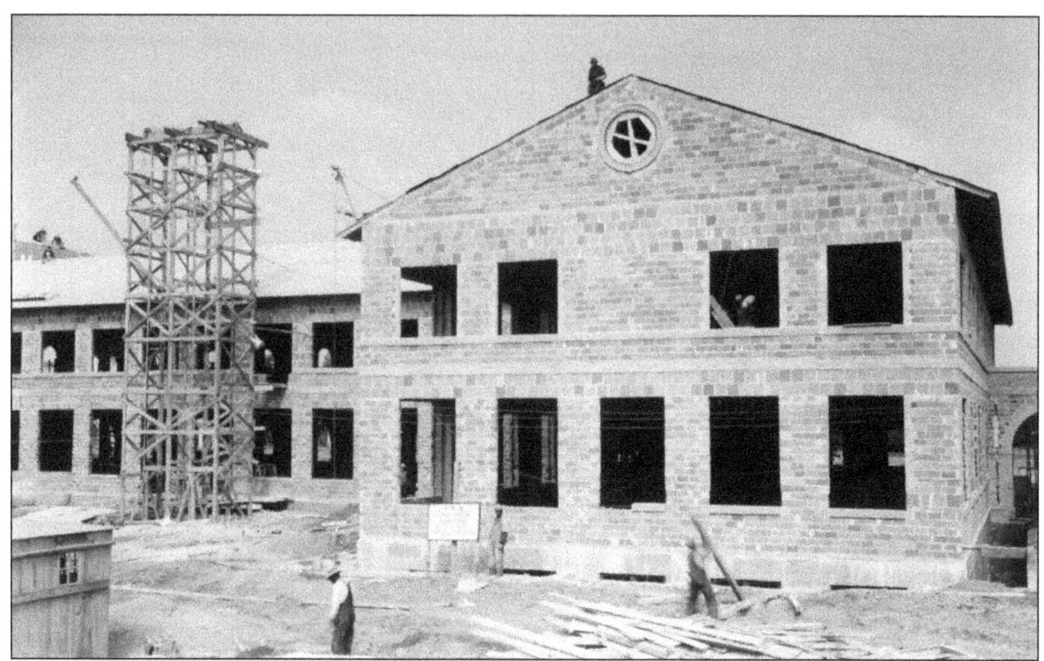

Completed in 1938, Himes Hall was named for Robert L. Himes, who taught business and was LSU's business manager. Construction was funded by the Works Progress Administration and the building housed the College of Commerce, now known as the College of Business. Himes is now the home of the Department of History, Women's and Gender Studies, and the Office of Assessment and Evaluation. (OCR.)

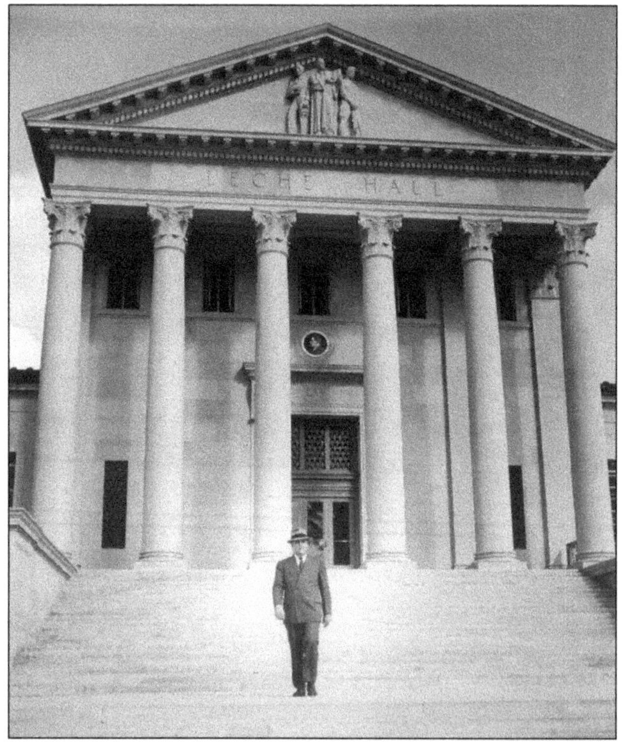

Leche Hall became the new home for the law school and was completed in 1937. Designed by New Orleans architecture firm Weiss, Dreyfous, and Seiferth, the building cost $800,000. The law school was formerly housed in the North Administration Building (now Thomas Boyd Hall). The building's namesake, Gov. Richard W. Leche, is seen descending the steps. The name was changed to the Law Building after Leche was convicted of mail fraud in 1940. (RWL.)

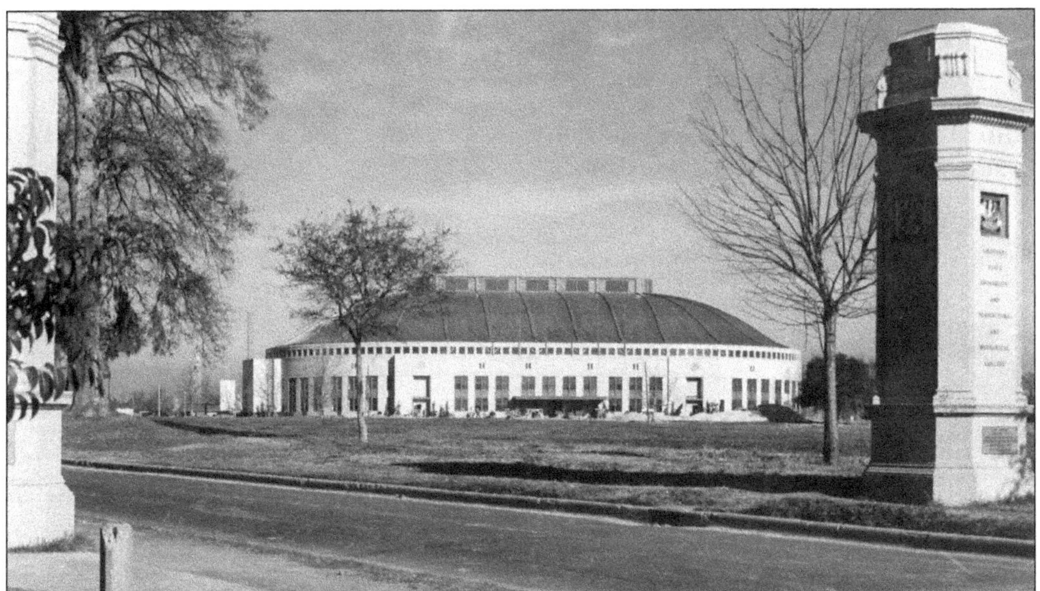

Seen from the south gates of campus on Highland Road, the John M. Parker Coliseum was designed by Edward Neild and cost $1,333,871, paid for by the Public Works Administration. It was the largest copper-domed building in the world when it was completed in 1937. The coliseum was used mostly for livestock shows and rodeos, but concerts and commencement exercises as well as men's basketball games were held here until the Pete Maravich Assembly Center opened in 1971. (RWL.)

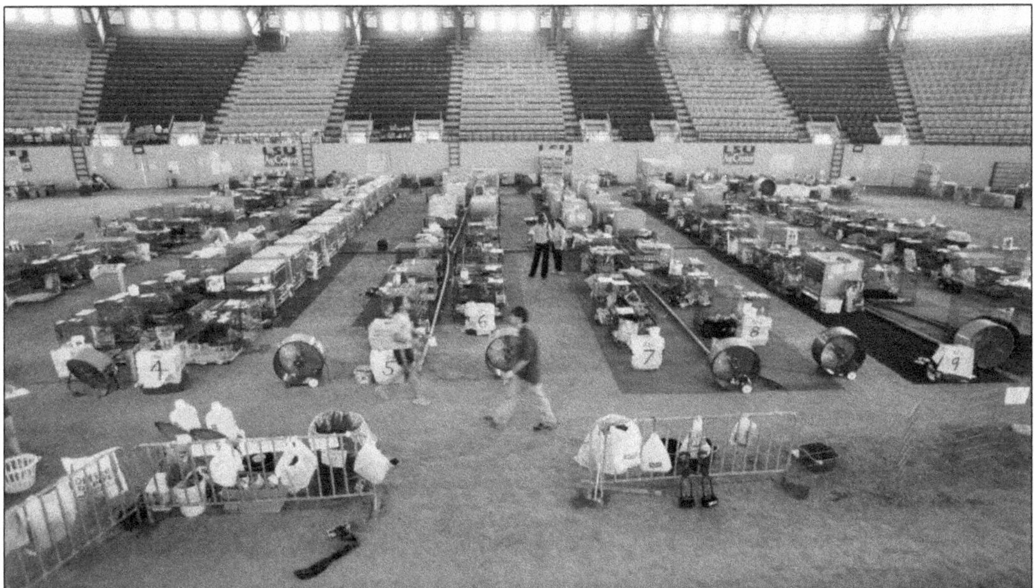

In the aftermath of Hurricane Katrina in 2005, the entire campus mobilized as a field hospital and shelter for both people and animals displaced by the storm. The Parker Coliseum became a shelter for animals rescued from floodwaters. Volunteer veterinarians took care of medical problems while volunteers from throughout the LSU and Baton Rouge communities fed and bathed the animals and cleaned cages. (Courtesy of Jim Zietz, Office of Communications and University Relations.)

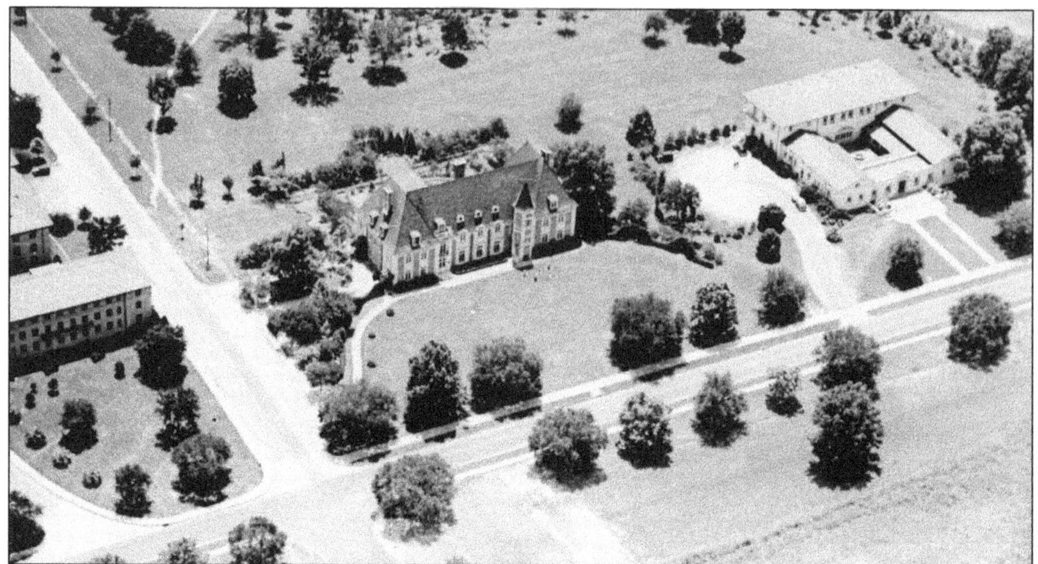

The French House and the Pan-American House (right) are shown in this Fonville Winans aerial photograph from 1947. The Pan-American House, or Casa de las Americas, was completed in 1942 and housed a cultural exchange program between students from Latin America and the United States. Students lived in the house along with a professor of Spanish. (FWAP.)

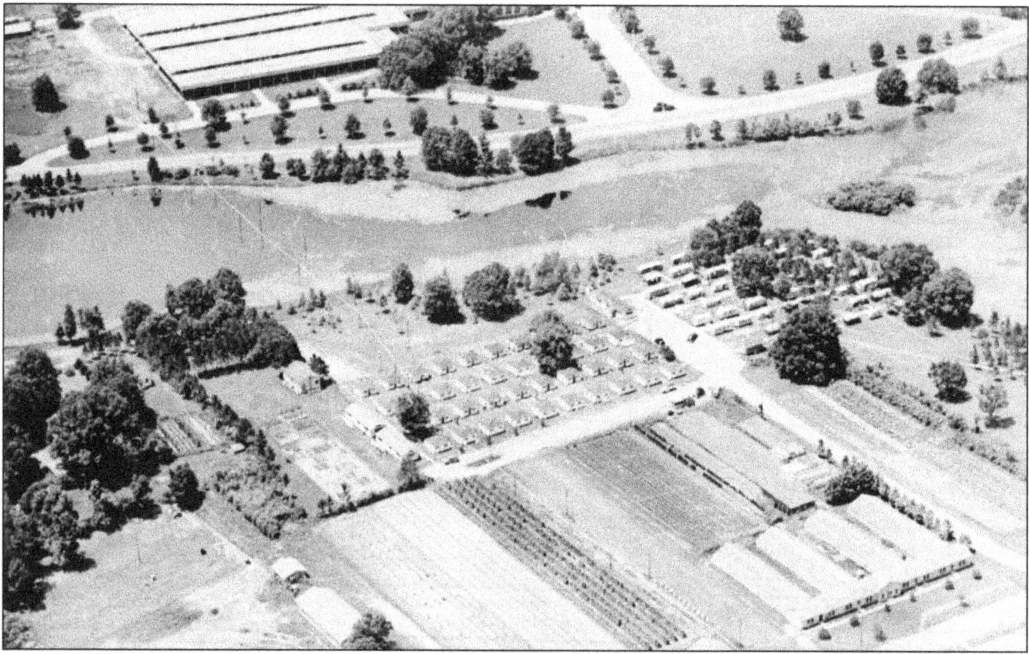

After World War II, the university had to scramble to provide housing for the sudden influx of veterans taking advantage of the GI Bill. The university opened trailer parks (center right in the trees) and clusters of hutments (center) around campus, such as these near the John M. Parker Coliseum. The hutments were military surplus prefabricated housing that were intended to be temporary homes for veterans with families. The student population rose from around 5,000 in 1945 to just over 10,000 by the fall of 1947. The last hutments were removed in 1963. (FWAP.)

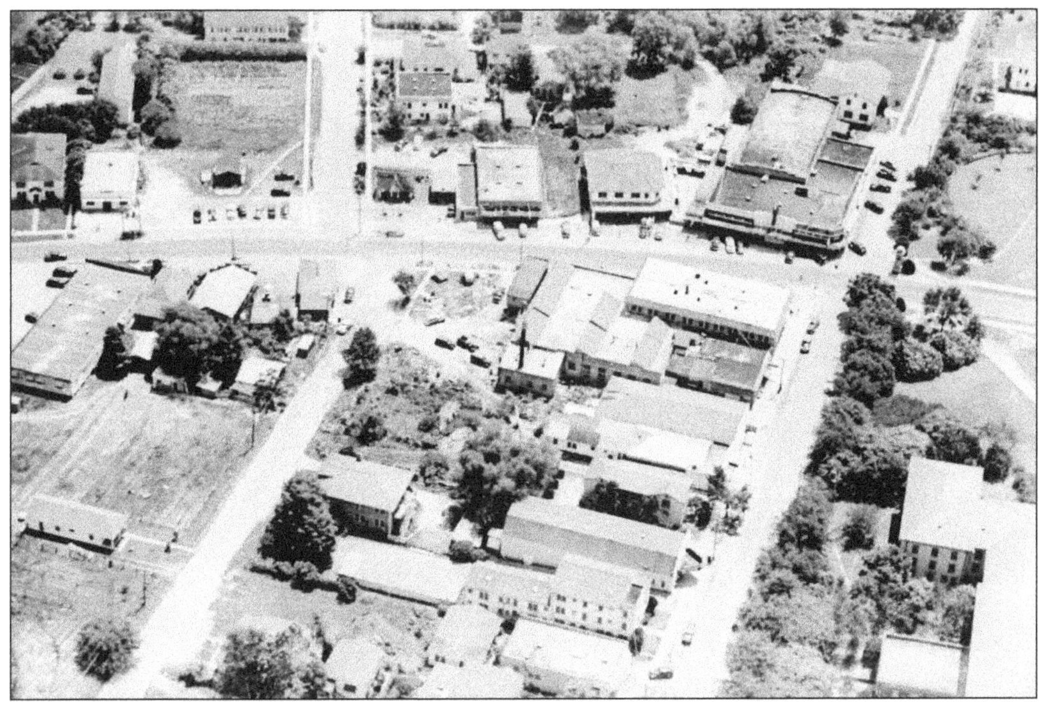

Taken by Baton Rouge photographer Fonville Winans, this 1947 aerial view of Tigertown just north of the campus shows the area around the intersection of Highland Road (running left to right across the center), Chimes Street (running top to bottom at right) and State Street (top to bottom at center). The building at lower right is Pleasant Hall and the building at the northeast corner of Highland at Chimes housed the Varsity Theater and Sitman's Drug Store. Tigertown was the main location of off-campus services, amusements, and housing, but by the 1980s, Tigerland and other areas south of campus saw new development. (FWAP.)

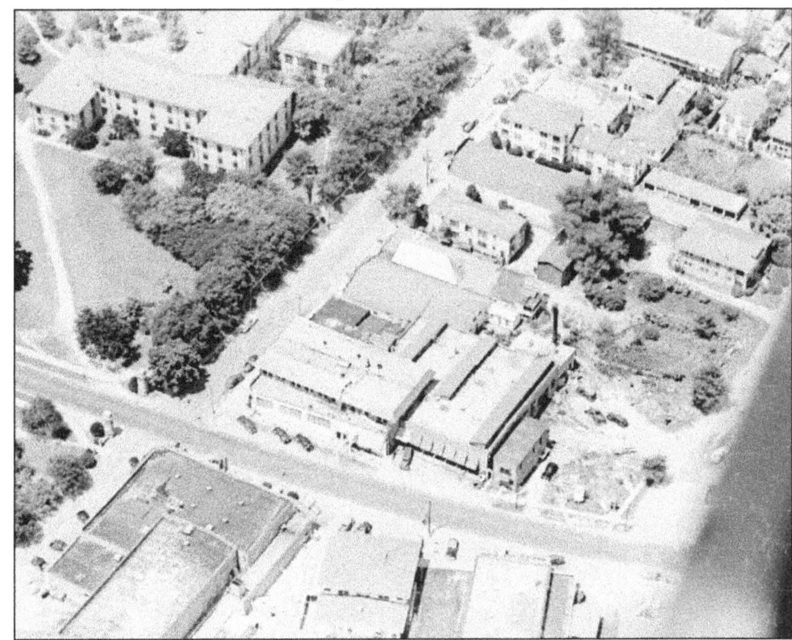

This image shows the same area from the opposite direction. The large building on the northwest corner of Highland Road and Chimes Street housed Baker's Restaurant. (FWAP.)

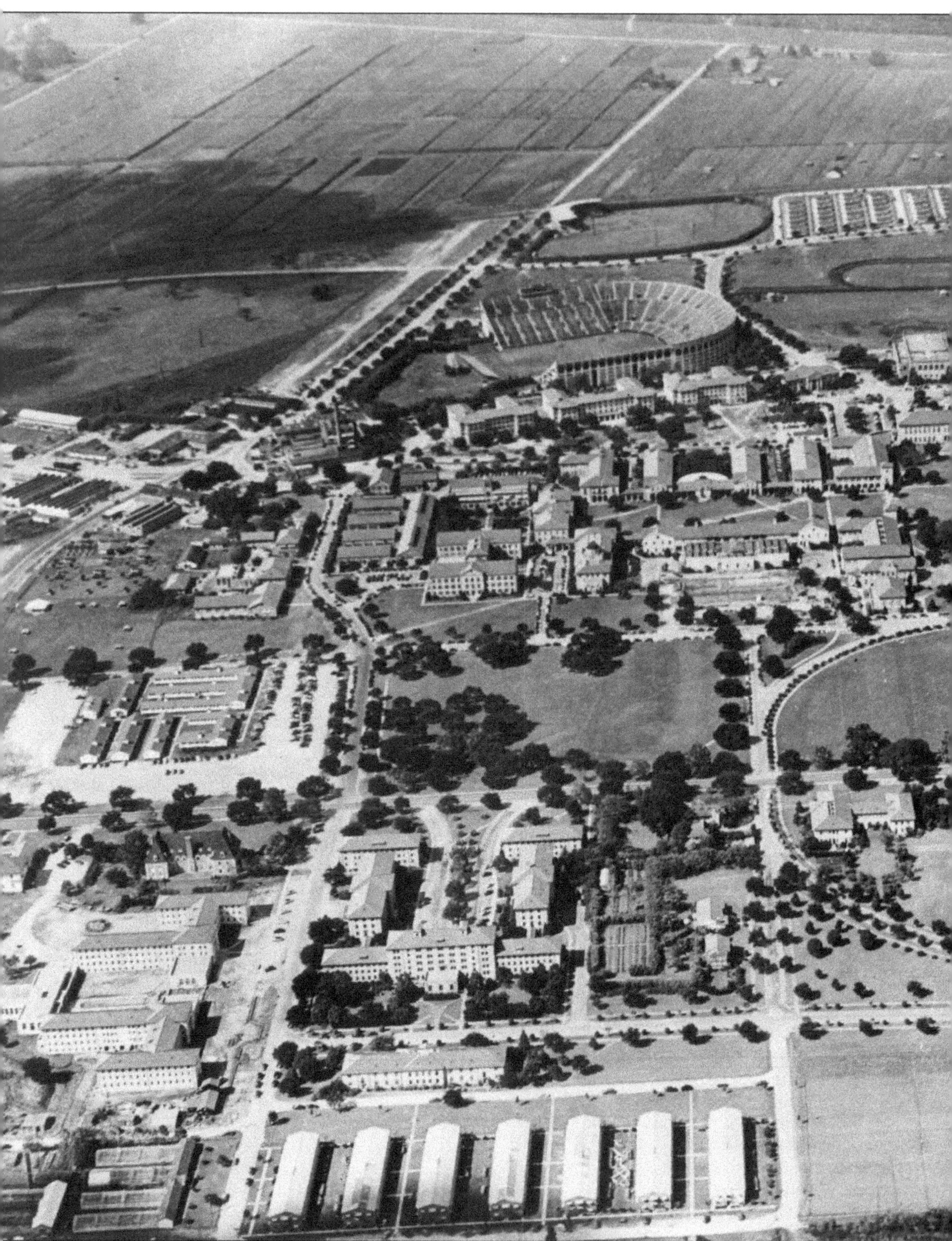

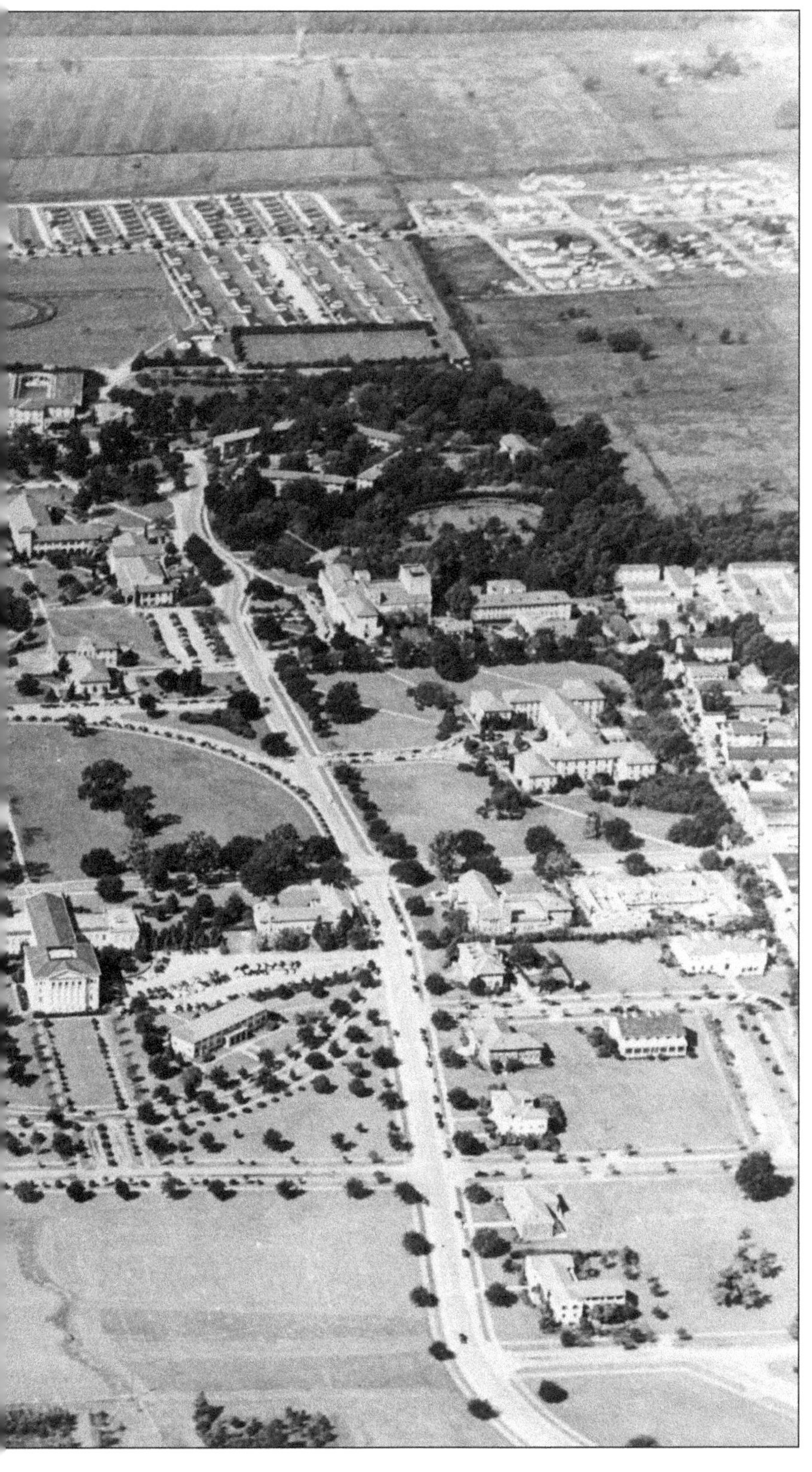

This aerial photograph from 1950 shows the new dormitories required in the immediate postwar period. The seven buildings at the bottom were dormitories for married students and faculty. They were acquired from the Navy and were assembled like an Erector set. They were later renamed McVoy Hall and were razed in the late 1990s to make way for the East Campus Apartments. The small buildings to the right of Alex Box Stadium were hutments for married students. Also seen is the maturing plant life begun in the early 1930s. Except for a few groves of trees, the campus was farm and pastureland devoid of any planned landscaping. (LSUPC.)

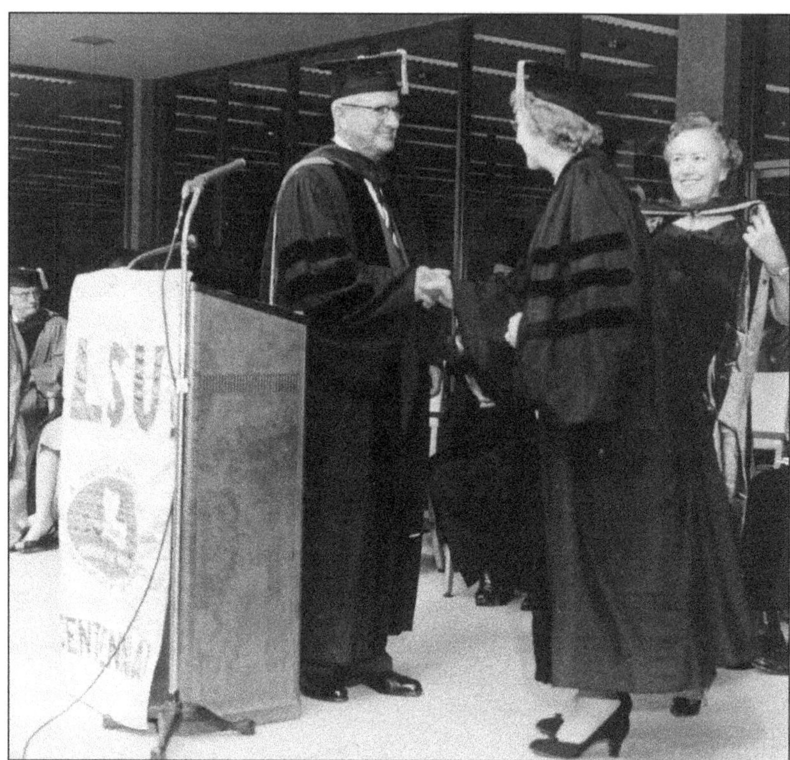

The formal dedication of the LSU Library took place in September 1959 and was the first major event of LSU's centennial celebrated in 1959 and 1960. As part of the dedication, Pres. Troy Middleton is seen here awarding State Librarian Essae Mae Culver an honorary degree. Holding the sash is Ella V. Aldrich Schwing, member of the LSU Board of Supervisors and an ally of the new library. (LSUPC.)

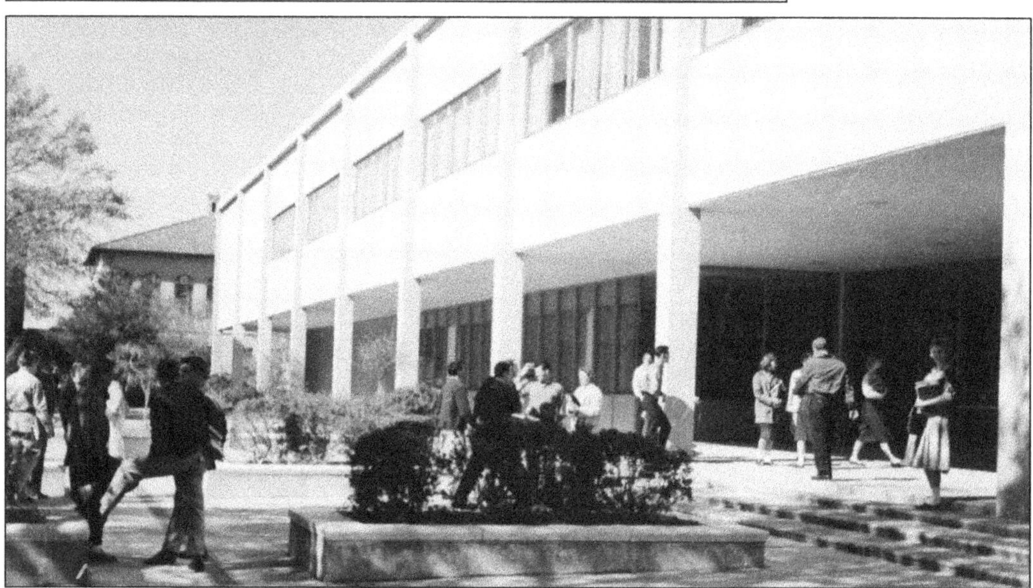

The LSU Library opened in September 1958 and quickly became one of the most popular and populated buildings on campus. Library patrons finally had enough room to study, and all of the libraries' collections were under one roof for the first time since the 1930s. However, the library was also the source of controversy. In a fight for funding between an enlarged Tiger Stadium and a new library beginning in 1950, Tiger Stadium won and the new south end zone seats were called the "library section." Because Pres. Troy Middleton had made the library a priority, it was renamed in his honor in 1979. (OPRR.)

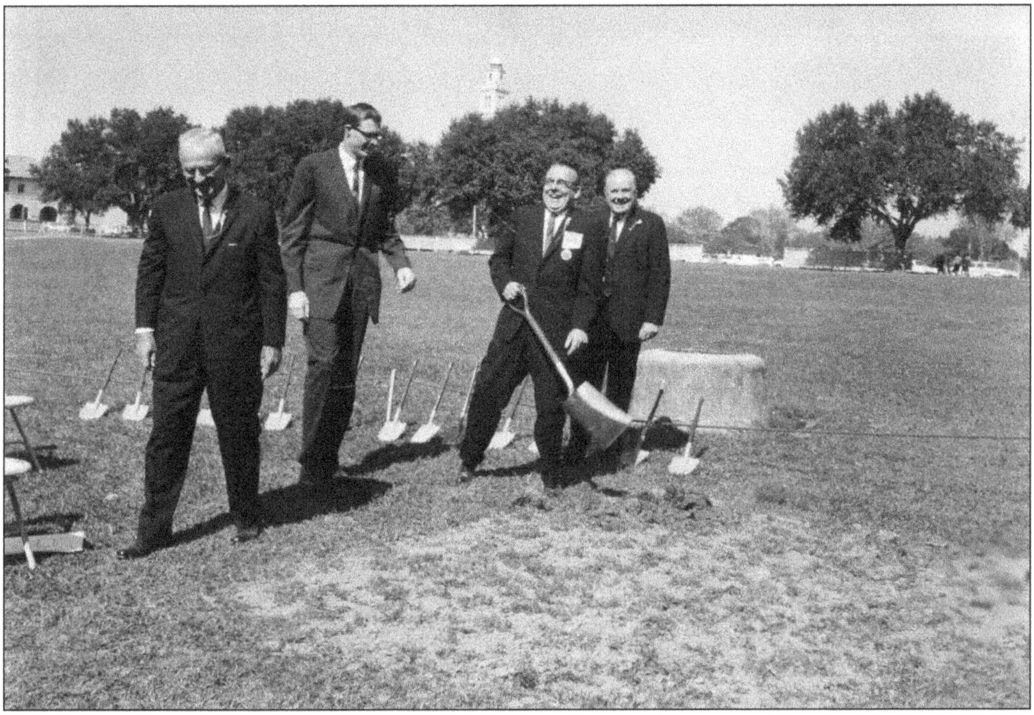

Ground was broken for the LSU Union in 1961. Seen here are Pres. Troy H. Middleton (left) and Dean of Student Services John A. Hunter (second from right). The other men are unidentified. (*Gumbo* Photographs, RG #A5000.0305, Louisiana State University Archives, LSU Libraries, Baton Rouge, Louisiana.)

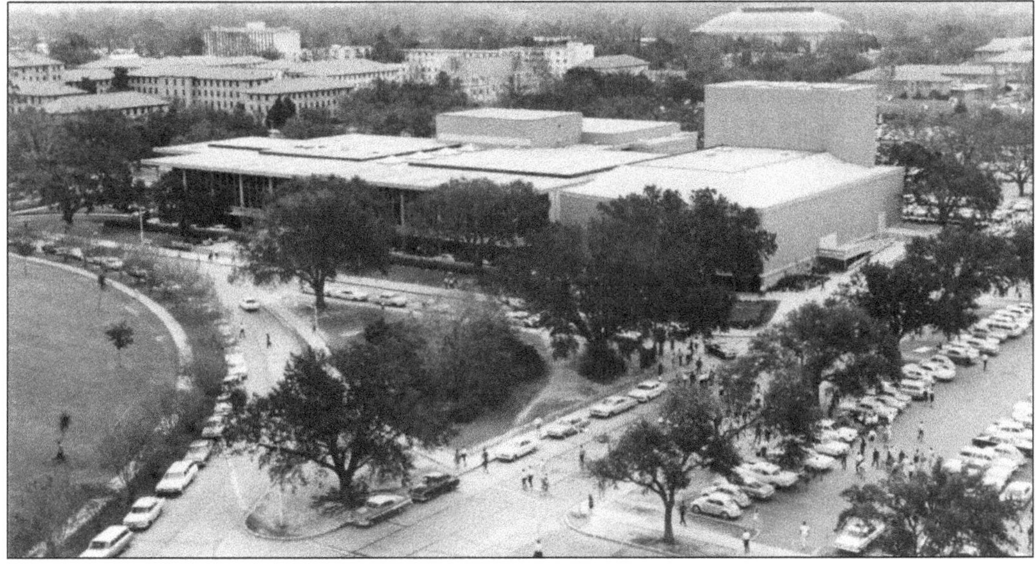

An idea since the late 1930s and finally opened in 1964, the LSU Union quickly became one of the most popular places on campus. It contained such amenities as a dining hall serving full meals and light snacks, a gaming area with a bowling alley and pool tables, meeting rooms, a bookstore, offices for campus organizations, ballrooms, and a theater. Designed by John Desmond, the building comprised 200,000 square feet and cost $5.5 million. (OPRR.)

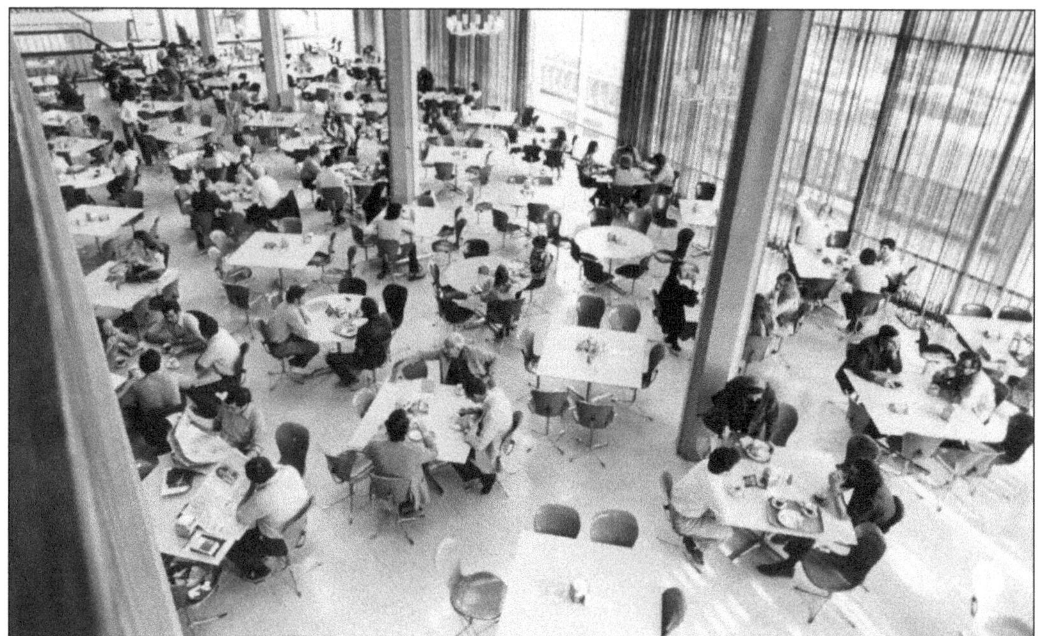

The floor-to-ceiling windows in the Union dining room provide a bright and airy place for lunch or a cup of coffee. The Union won the American Institute of Architects' First Honor Award for the Gulf South Region. (OPRR.)

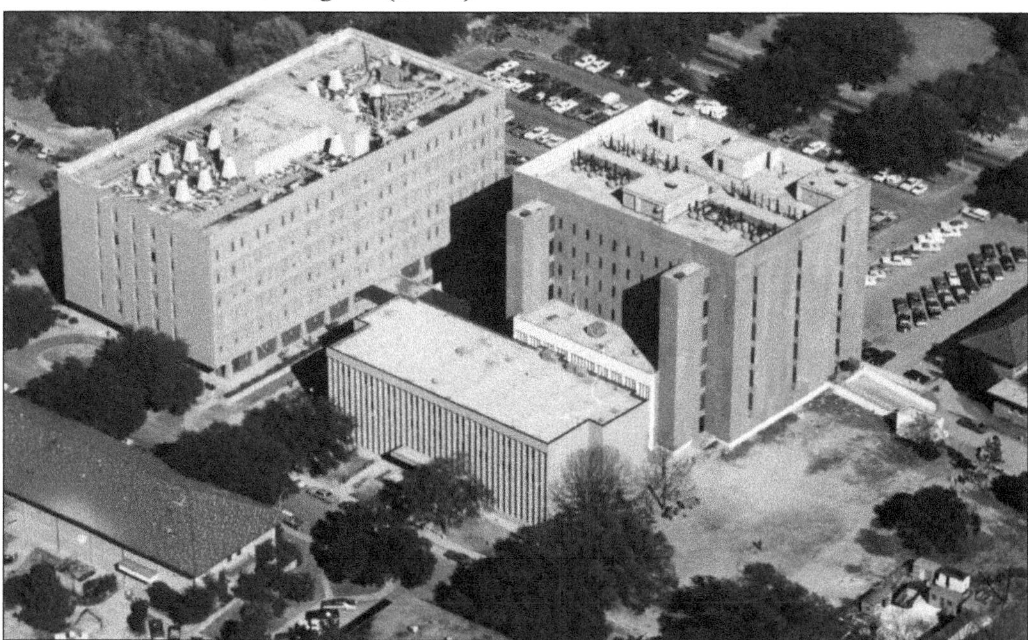

This aerial photograph shows buildings that are part of the College of Science. The Life Sciences Building at left opened in 1969 and houses the departments of zoology and physiology, microbiology, plant biology, plant pathology, and entomology. Arthur R. Choppin Hall, at right, opened in 1977 and houses various laboratories. At center is Virginia Rice Williams Hall, also opened in 1977, which contains auditoriums and classrooms. Modern architecture began on campus in the 1950s and had reached full fruition by the early 1980s. (OPRR.)

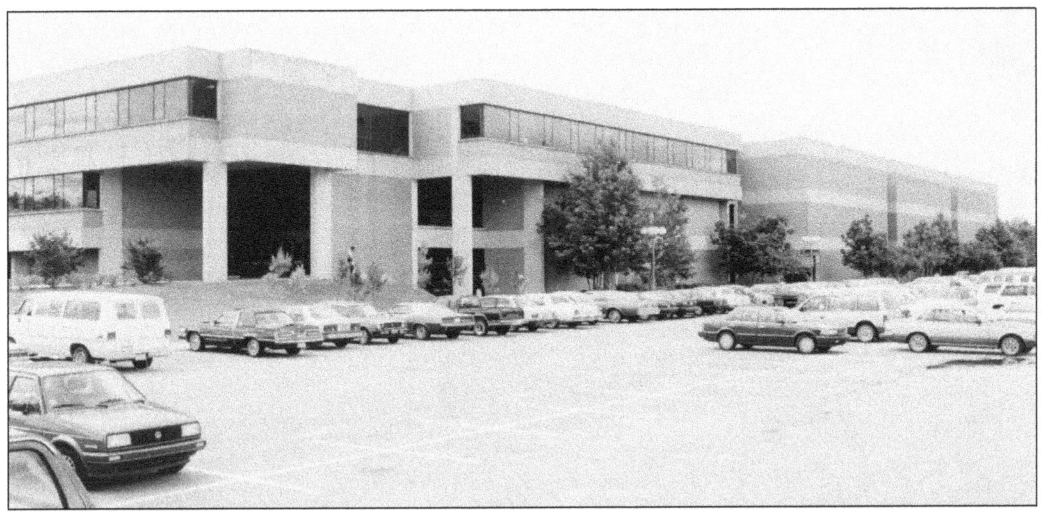

The Center for Engineering and Business Administration, or CEBA, opened in 1979. Designed by Desmond-Miremont, the building cost $16 million. Funding began in 1969, when the LSU Foundation collected $3 million in private donations. The legislature appropriated $12.5 million and the Athletic Department contributed $100,000. The 310,000-square-foot building contains two open-air courtyards, offices, classrooms, and laboratories. CEBA is now called Patrick F. Taylor Hall. (OPRR.)

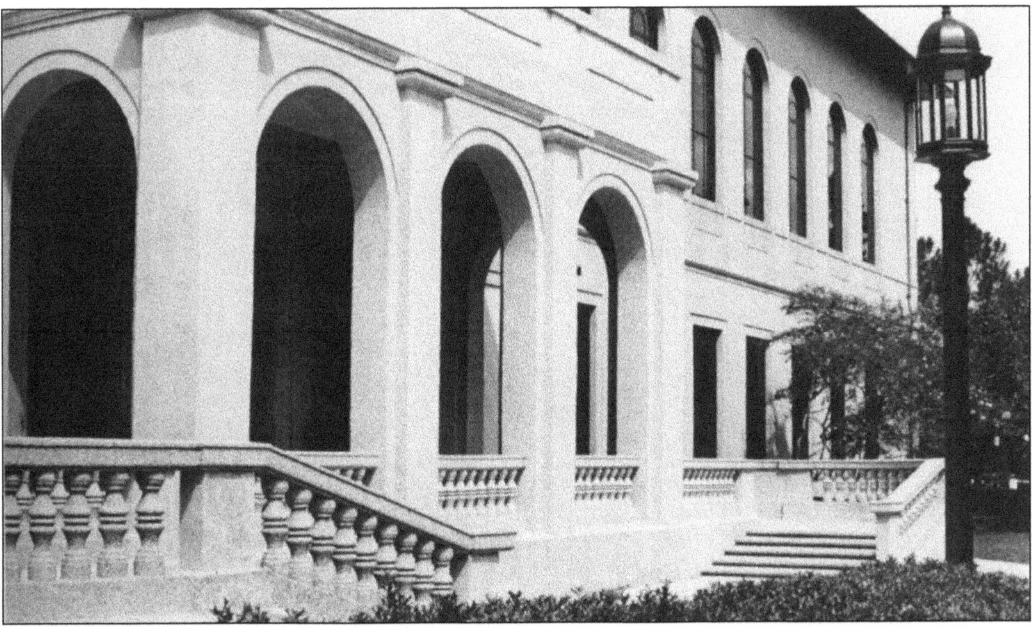

Hill Memorial Library was completed in 1925 and served as the main library on campus until Middleton Library opened in 1958. From 1959 to 1983, Hill was used as storage for the Libraries' little-used items and the microfilming and photography units. It also served as studios for the School of Architecture and offices for LSU Press. From 1983 to 1985, the building was renovated to house the LSU Libraries' Special Collections department. The library now contains the University Archives, the Louisiana and Lower Mississippi Valley Collections of manuscripts and political papers, and rare books. The building also features a reading room, a gallery, and a lecture hall. (*Gumbo* 1987.)

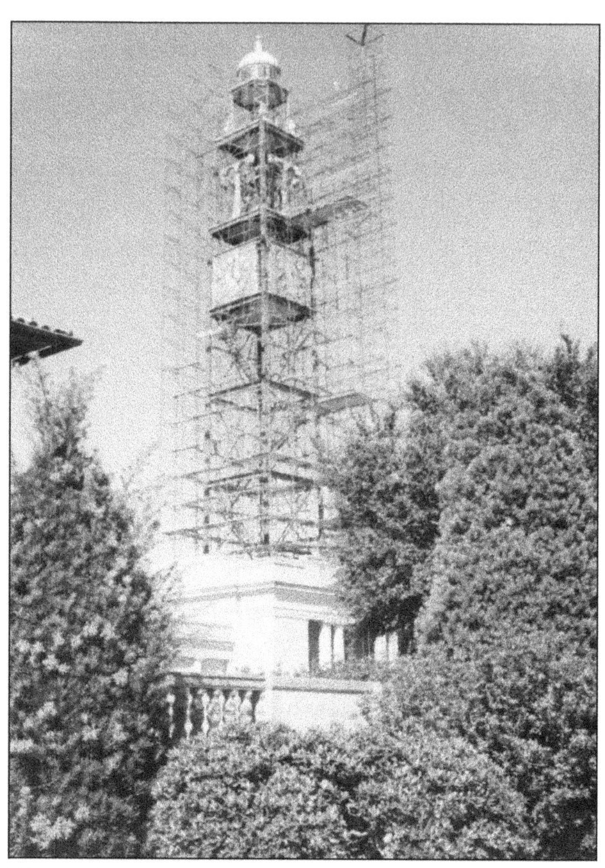

In time for LSU's centennial in 1960, the Memorial Tower's stucco "skin" was removed to facilitate rust removal and apply rustproofing to the steel structure. The wings were also remodeled to house the Anglo-American Art Museum. (LSUPC.)

Estimated to be 5,000 years old, the Indian Mounds are some of the oldest structures made by humans on earth. The south mound, seen here around 1965 from the Huey P. Long Fieldhouse, has experienced subsidence over the years. (OPRR.)

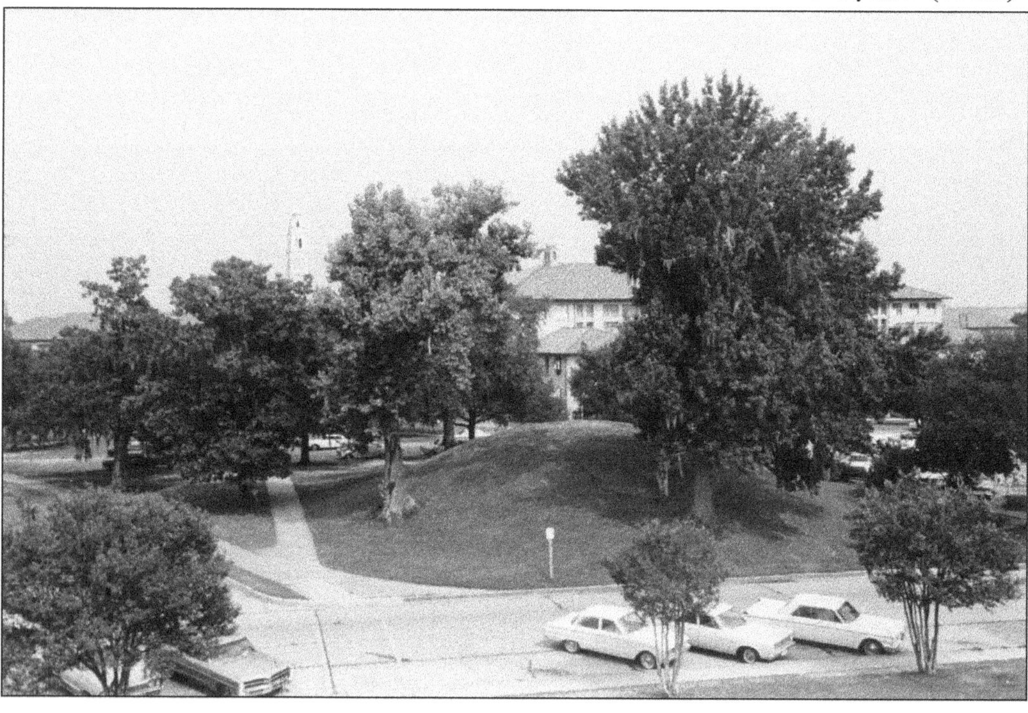

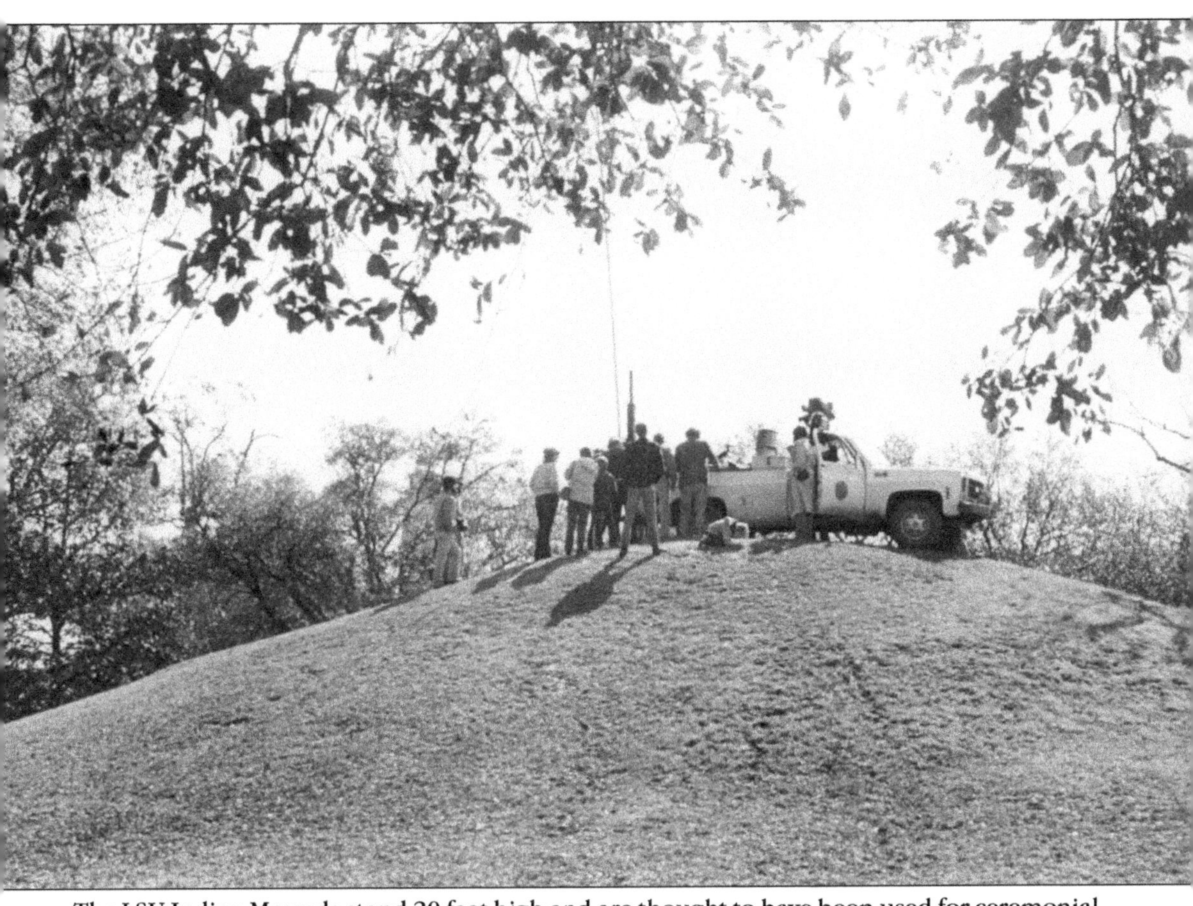

The LSU Indian Mounds stand 20 feet high and are thought to have been used for ceremonial purposes. This image from 1982 shows the north mound undergoing core sampling. The sample was analyzed and carbon dated. (OPRR.)

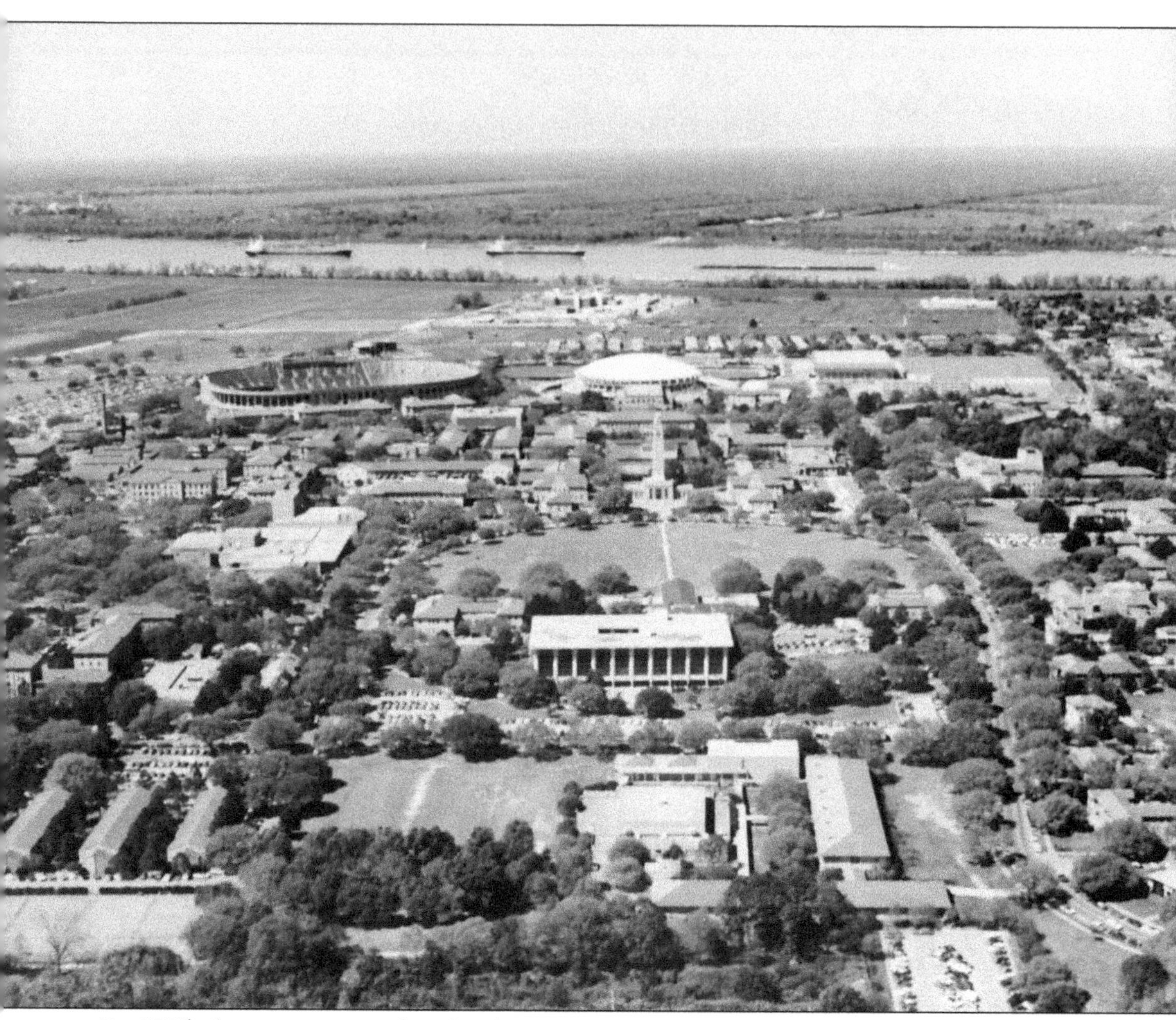

By 1976, the campus—and its landscaping—had reached maturity. At the bottom of the photograph is the University Laboratory School, constructed in 1951. Above that is the LSU Law Center and library added in 1969, nearly doubling the law school's capacity. Nearest to the Mississippi River is the complex for the School of Veterinary Medicine. The oak trees and general landscaping conceived in the 1930s has the equivalent of 25 acres of annuals, perennials, and ornamental plants. (OPRR.)

Two

Academics and Administration

The first faculty at the seminary was hired in 1859. The Board of Supervisors elected William Tecumseh Sherman superintendent and professor of engineering. Anthony Vallas (1809–1869) was named professor of mathematics and natural philosophy. Vallas had been forced to leave his native Hungary in 1850 and became an ordained Episcopalian minister. He was living in New Orleans when he became a faculty member. Francis W. Smith (1838–1865) was elected professor of chemistry and commandant of cadets. David Boyd became professor of ancient languages and English. Smith and Boyd were both Virginians and graduates of the University of Virginia. Dr. Powhatan Clarke (1837–1917) was appointed surgeon and assistant professor of ancient languages. Not shown is E. Berté St. Ange, professor of modern languages. St. Ange had been an officer in the French marines with a reputation as a duelist and had taught at the University of Louisiana in New Orleans. (OCR.)

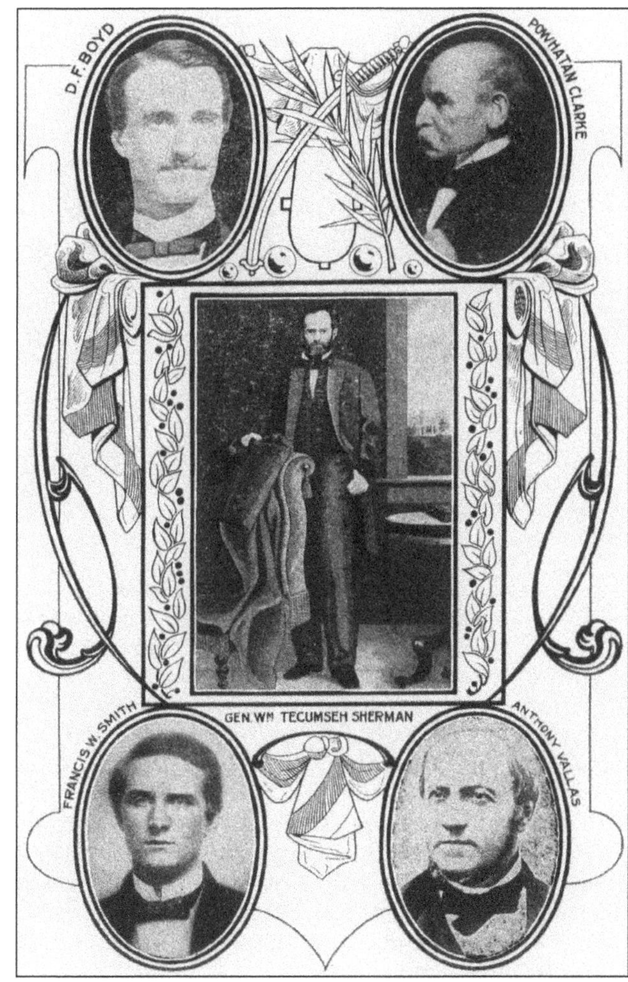

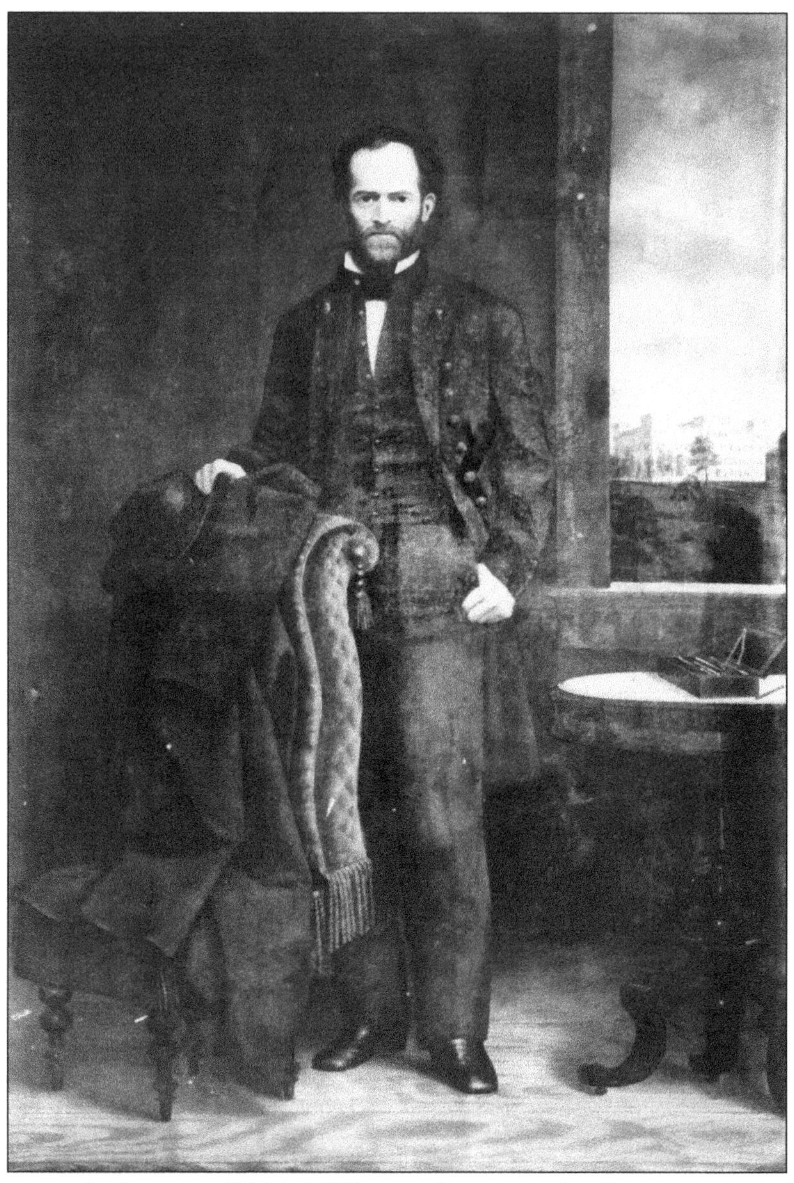

William Tecumseh Sherman (1809–1891) was chosen as the first superintendent of the seminary in 1859. He was an 1840 graduate of West Point and served in the Army, mainly in administrative posts, until 1853, when he left to become a banker and lawyer. Sherman saw little success in either field and applied for superintendent of the seminary. Soon after his arrival, he began readying the school by securing books, uniforms for the cadets, furniture for the seminary building, and rifles and accoutrements for drill. Sherman resigned after Louisiana seceded in 1861 and offered his services to the Union Army. During the Civil War, he remained interested in the seminary's welfare and requested that it be spared during Gen. Nathaniel Banks's Red River expedition in 1863. Sherman also helped David Boyd, with whom he maintained a lifelong friendship, gain parole after being taken prisoner by the Federal Army. After the war, Sherman helped the seminary get back on its feet by donating books and maps from his own library and used his influence to secure books and equipment from the Smithsonian. (OCR.)

David French Boyd (1834–1899) started at the seminary in 1859 as a professor of ancient languages and English. He left for service in the Confederate Army in the Civil War and returned in 1865 as superintendent. Boyd worked tirelessly for the good of the institution: he was instrumental in changing the name to Louisiana State University in 1870, stayed on during the 1870s despite little or no financial support from the state and no salary, and pressed for the merger of LSU with the rival Louisiana Agricultural and Mechanical College in 1877. Boyd resigned in 1880, pushed out by a new Board of Supervisors, but returned as president for the last time from 1884 to 1886. During this time, he secured the Baton Rouge Arsenal for use by the university. He returned to teach in 1897 and stayed until his death two years later. (LSUPC.)

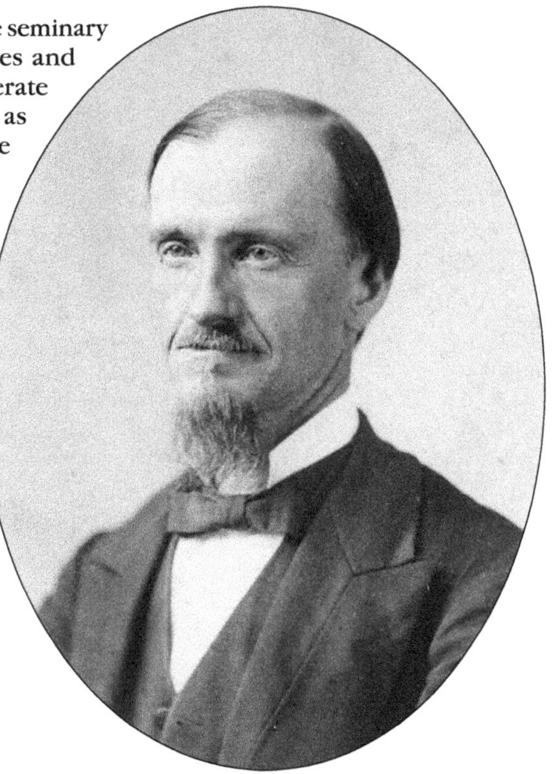

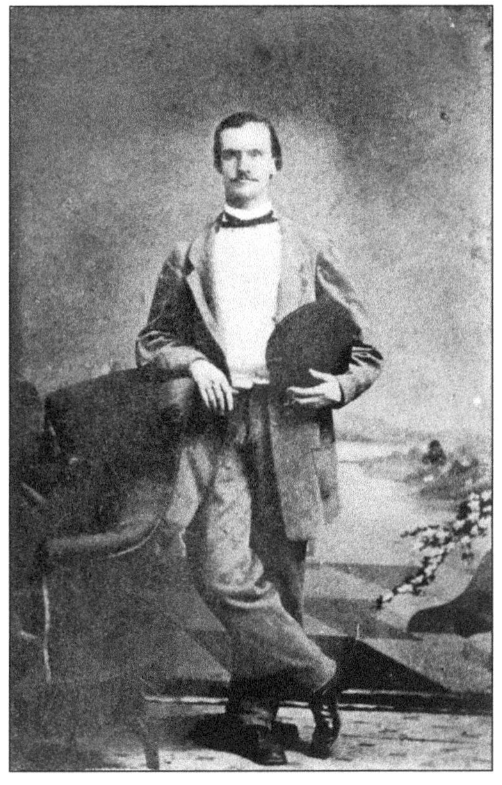

This photograph of David Boyd was taken in 1866 while superintendent of the seminary. In the early post–Civil War years, Boyd outfitted the seminary building to make it habitable after being used as a hospital by the Union Army, and acquired books, maps, scientific instruments, and geological and botanical specimens. William Tecumseh Sherman donated some of the book and maps. (LSUPC.)

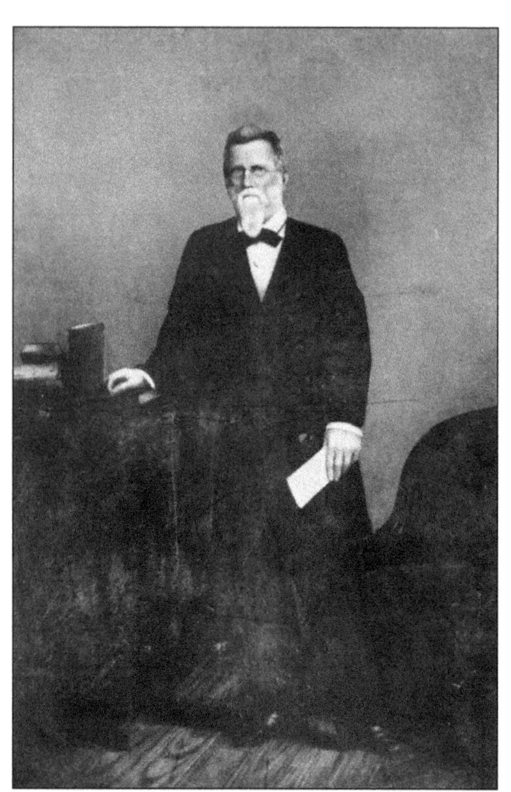

George Mason Graham (1807–1891) was called "the father of LSU" because of his lifelong support of the university. Originally from Virginia, Graham moved to Louisiana in 1828 and built Tyrone Plantation on Bayou Rapides in Rapides Parish in 1842. During the Mexican War, he was a captain in a Louisiana infantry unit and became brigadier general of the Rapides and Avoyelles Parish militia units in 1847. In 1853, Graham was named to the Board of Trustees (now Board of Supervisors) for the newly authorized State Seminary of Learning and served almost continuously until 1885. He is responsible for the seminary being a literary and scientific institution with a military form of government and discipline similar to the Virginia Military Institute. Graham oversaw construction of the seminary building, hiring the first faculty in 1859 and creating the first curriculum. (OCR.)

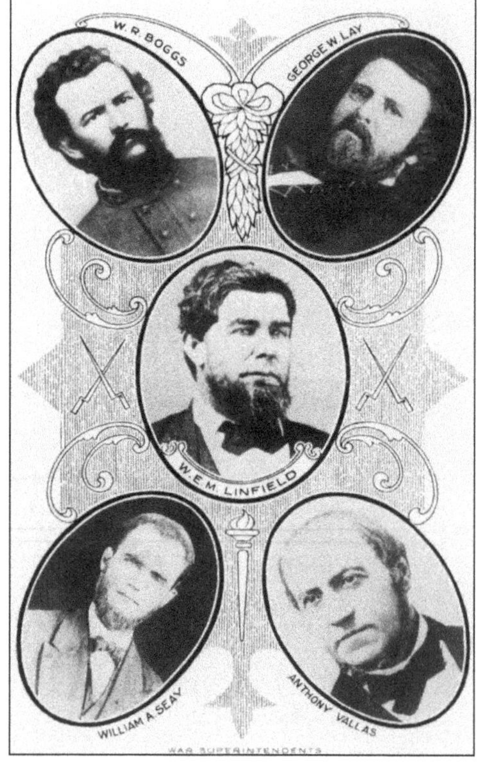

From 1861 to 1863, the seminary had five different superintendents. Col. George M. Lay, an 1842 West Point graduate, was appointed in April 1861 and resigned in May after the outbreak of war. Capt. William R. Boggs, an 1853 West Point graduate, was appointed but was in the Confederate Army and so could not serve. Anthony Vallas was acting superintendent and a professor during this time. The seminary closed in June 1861 and reopened in April 1862. Rev. W.E.M. Linfield, a Mexican War veteran and a Methodist minister, was made superintendent pro tem. He found it difficult to control the students, most of whom wanted to go to war. On April 1, 1863, the students rioted, destroying the dishes and kitchen furniture, and Linfield resigned. William A. Seay, who had replaced David Boyd as professor of ancient languages and English, was then elected superintendent pro tem. He kept the Seminary running until April 23, 1863, when Nathaniel P. Banks's army invaded the area and the students were sent home. Seay closed the seminary for good on May 1, 1863. (OCR.)

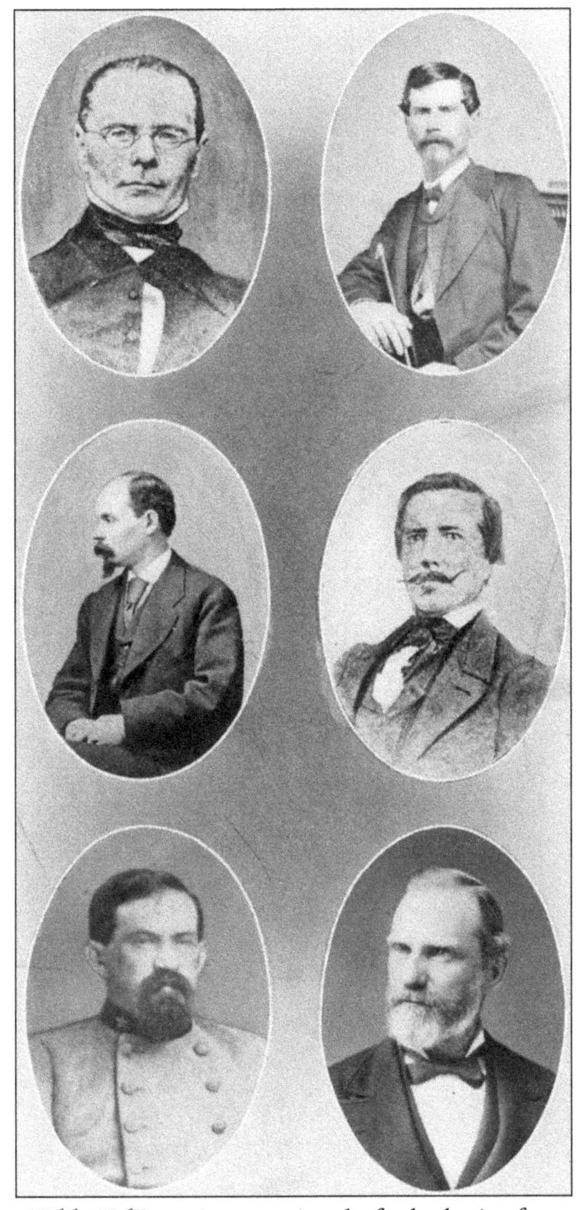

The faculty from the 1866–1867 session consisted of, clockwise from top left, Father Jean Pierre Bellier, professor of modern languages; James M. Garnett, professor of Greek; Raphael Semmes, professor of moral philosophy; John A.A. West, professor of mathematics and natural philosophy; Richard M. Venable, professor of engineering; and Dr. John R. Page, surgeon. Not shown is David Boyd, who had become superintendent in 1865. Bellier arrived at the seminary in 1865 and had been a priest in Alexandria, Louisiana. Garnett taught at the seminary from 1866 to 1867. Semmes, the former Confederate admiral, also left in 1867. A West Point graduate, West taught from 1865 to 1867 and resigned to practice medicine. Venable, a popular, easy-going member of the faculty, also taught from 1865 to 1867. Page had been a surgeon in General Lee's Army of Northern Virginia and spent part of 1866–1867 collecting specimens for a proposed scientific museum at the seminary. Salaries were $2,000 per year and the superintendent received an extra $750. (OCR.)

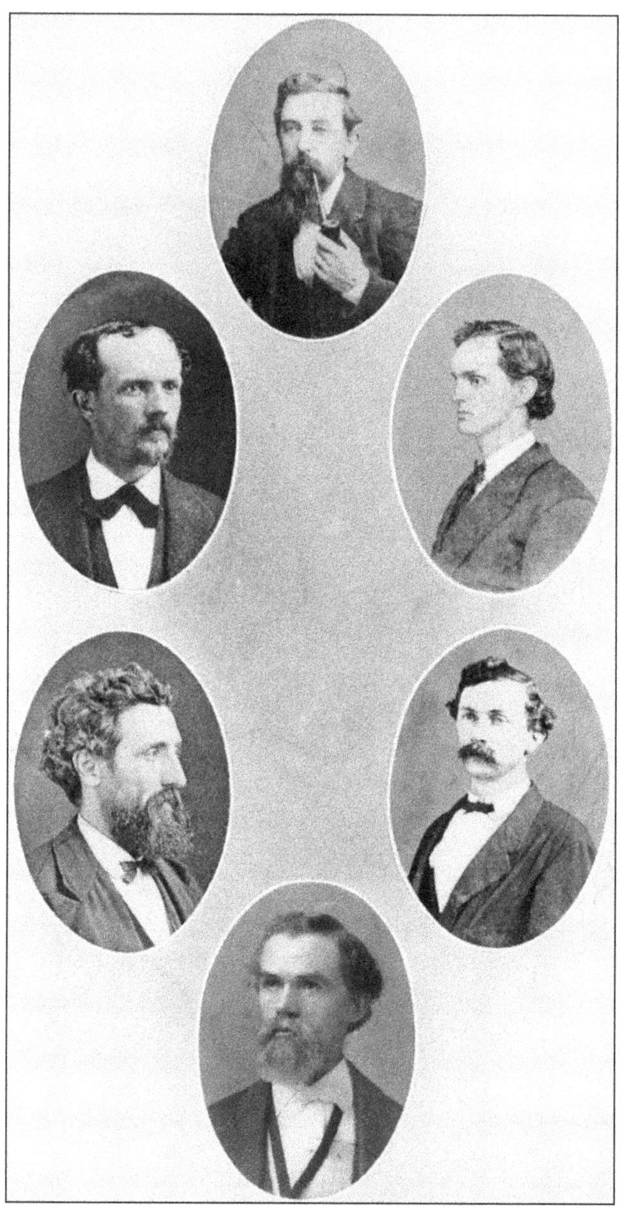

The faculty of 1869–1870 consisted of, clockwise from the top, John P. McAuley, professor of Latin; Edward A. Cunningham, professor of natural philosophy; Samuel Lockett, professor of engineering and instructor of artillery tactics; Rev. Edward P. Palmer, professor of moral philosophy; Frederick V. Hopkins, surgeon and professor of chemistry; and James Maury Boyd, assistant professor of ancient languages and English. McAuley taught from 1868 to 1873 and left when the state appropriations ran out. He studied for the priesthood after leaving but returned in 1877. Cunningham, a faculty member from 1870 to 1872, also served as commandant of cadets and was a strict disciplinarian. Lockett and Hopkins both started in 1868 and began a topographical and geological survey of Louisiana the following year. Hopkins abandoned the project soon after it began, but Lockett finished the survey and published his findings in 1876. Palmer, a Presbyterian minister, also taught Hebrew. James Maury Boyd, a cousin of David Boyd, died at the seminary in 1869. (OCR.)

Stephanos Athanasiades was professor of Greek from 1869 to 1875. Originally from Jerusalem and educated in Athens, he brought Modern Greek pronunciation to the curriculum. After appropriations ran out in 1873, Athanasiades sued the university for wages owed for his last two years of employment. (LSUPC.)

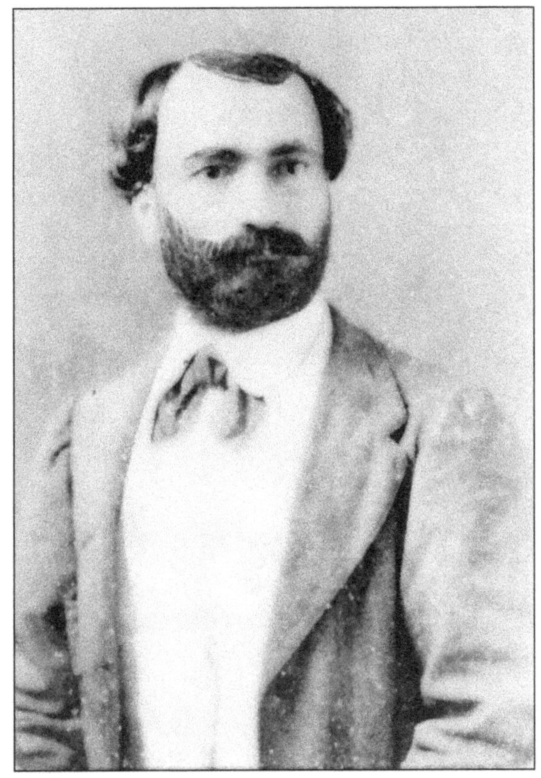

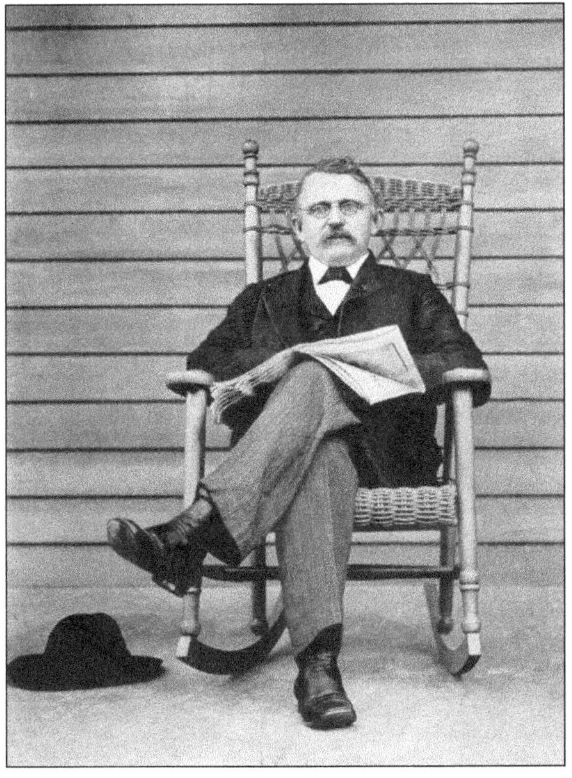

William C. Stubbs (1843–1924) came to LSU in 1885 and held a dual role as professor of agriculture and head of the state experiment station at Kenner, Louisiana, for the Louisiana Sugar Planters Association. He organized state experiment stations in Baton Rouge and in Calhoun in the Ouachita Parish. Stubbs was director of the sugar experiment station from 1885 to 1905 and was instrumental in the development of the modern sugar industry in Louisiana. (LSUPC.)

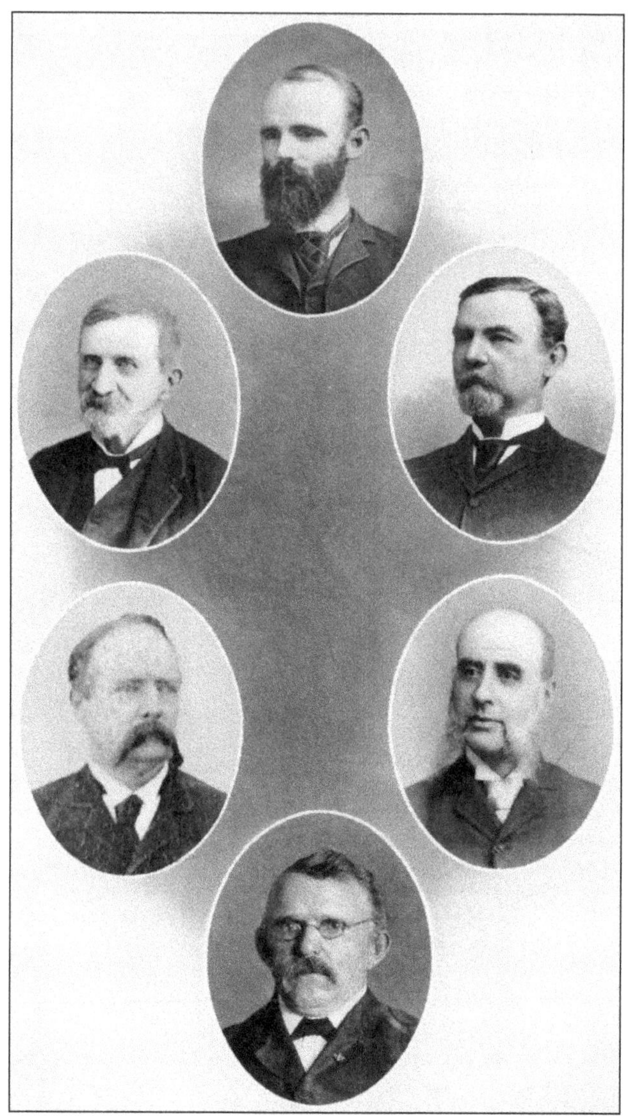

The faculty of 1886–1887 consisted of, clockwise from the top, William H. Magruder, James W. Nicholson, Leonard W. Sewell, William C. Stubbs, John H. Randolph, and Richard S. McCulloch. Magruder served as professor of ancient languages from 1883 to 1886. He was released after the Board of Supervisors decided to eliminate the teaching of Latin and Greek. Nicholson had taught mathematics since 1877 and had been acting president in 1883 and in 1886. Sewell had taught modern languages and literature at the Louisiana Agricultural and Mechanical College and arrived at LSU in 1877. Here, he taught modern languages and English and was placed in charge of the library until his dismissal in 1888. Stubbs arrived in 1885 and was simultaneously employed by LSU as a professor of agriculture and the Louisiana Sugar Planters Association as a chemist. He developed the first agricultural courses at LSU. Stubbs was a recognized expert in sugar cultivation and was director of the experiment stations until his retirement in 1905. Randolph arrived in 1880 as professor of mechanical engineering and resigned in 1890. McCulloch served as professor of chemistry from 1877 to 1888. He was supposedly an expert on sugar cultivation, but was not as knowledgeable as Stubbs. (OCR.)

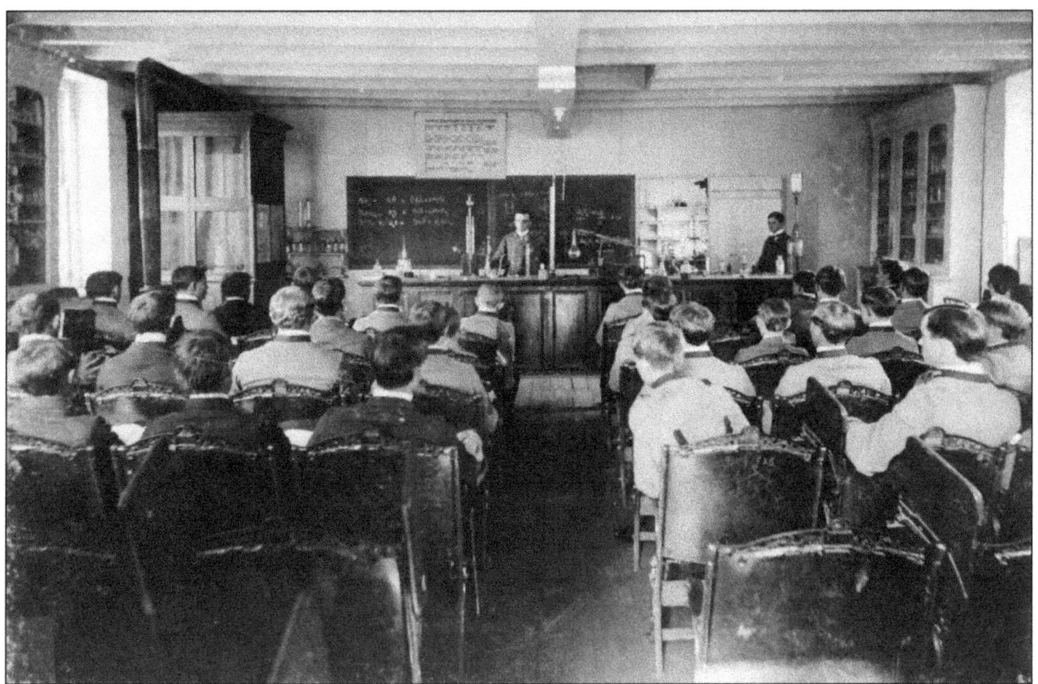

Chemistry has been a part of the curriculum since the very beginning in 1860. When Charles E. Coates arrived from Johns Hopkins in 1893, he brought new ideas for teaching chemistry and chemical engineering. (LSUPC.)

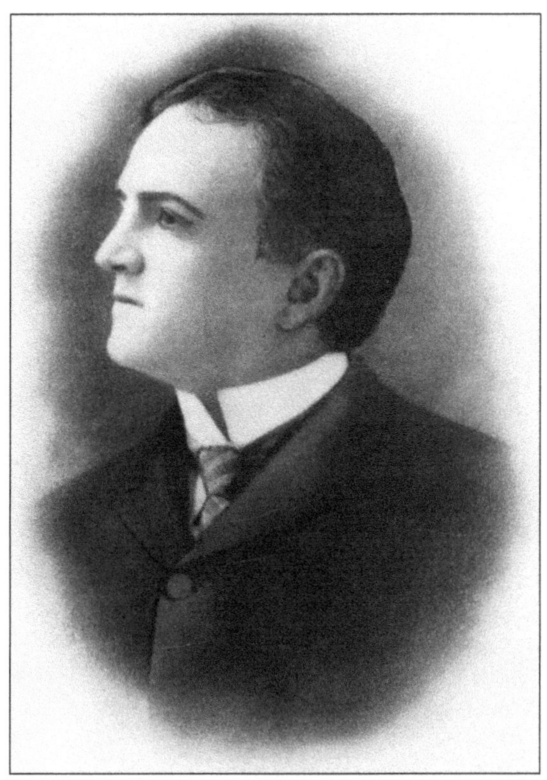

Charles E. Coates (1866–1939) was one of the leaders in teaching chemical engineering in the United States and was known worldwide for his research in sugar chemistry. Educated at Johns Hopkins University and in Germany, Coates came to LSU in 1893 as a professor of chemistry. He became head of the Department of Chemistry and dean of the Audubon Sugar School and College of Pure and Applied Science (now the College of Science). He retired in 1937. Coates also coached LSU's first football team in 1893. Coates Hall is named for him. (OPRR.)

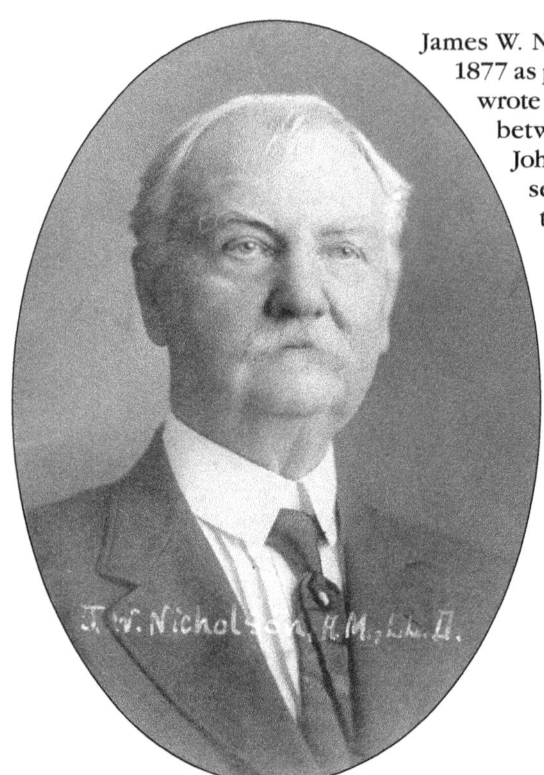

James W. Nicholson (1844–1917) joined the faculty in 1877 as professor of mathematics and mechanics. He wrote several widely used textbooks on mathematics between 1867 and 1910. After William Preston Johnston resigned as president in 1883, Nicholson served as acting president or president for the next two years and improved scientific education. Through his efforts, the legislature awarded LSU a $10,000 grant, most of which was used to outfit a chemistry laboratory. In 1887, he was elected president again and remained in that position until 1896. During this time, agricultural experiment stations were begun, the university moved to the former Baton Rouge Arsenal, and the curriculum was enlarged. (LSUPC.)

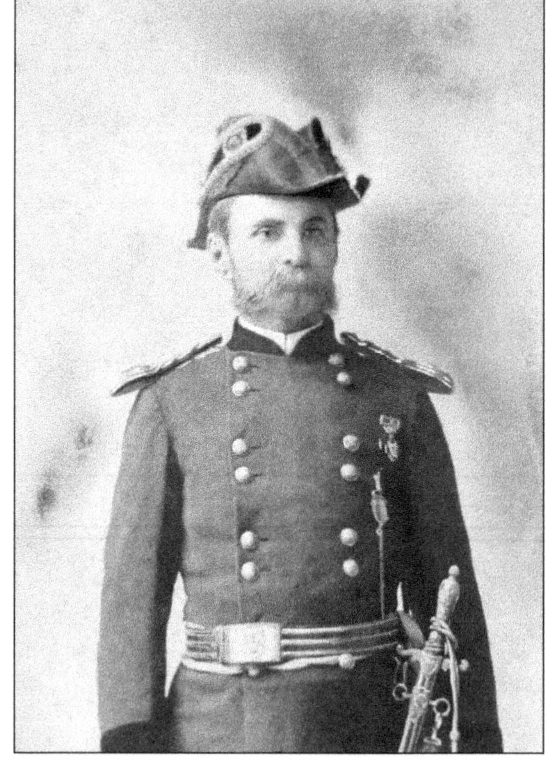

Dr. J.W. Dupree (1842–1906) was LSU's surgeon and taught anatomy and physiology. He was also in private practice in Baton Rouge. Dupree had been a surgeon with the Pointe Coupee Artillery during the Civil War. In 1883 and 1884, a smallpox outbreak swept the South and Dupree established a vaccine station on campus to produce synthetic vaccine extracted from calf lymph nodes. He made his own cattle available for the process and sent vaccine throughout Louisiana and to other southern states where smallpox was particularly virulent. (LSUPC.)

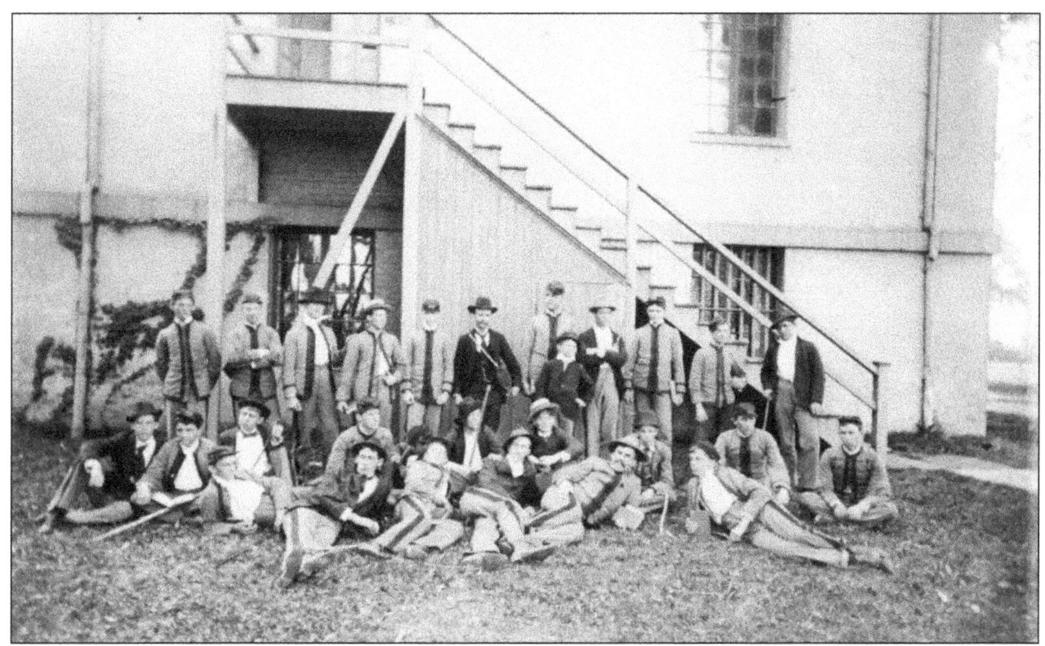

William R. Dodson's botany class is shown outside the agriculture building on the downtown campus in this undated photograph. Dodson (center) is wearing a suit with a haversack slung over one shoulder. Dodson (1867–1951) came to LSU in 1894 as professor of botany; in 1905, he became director of the agricultural experiment stations after William Stubbs retired. (LSUPC.)

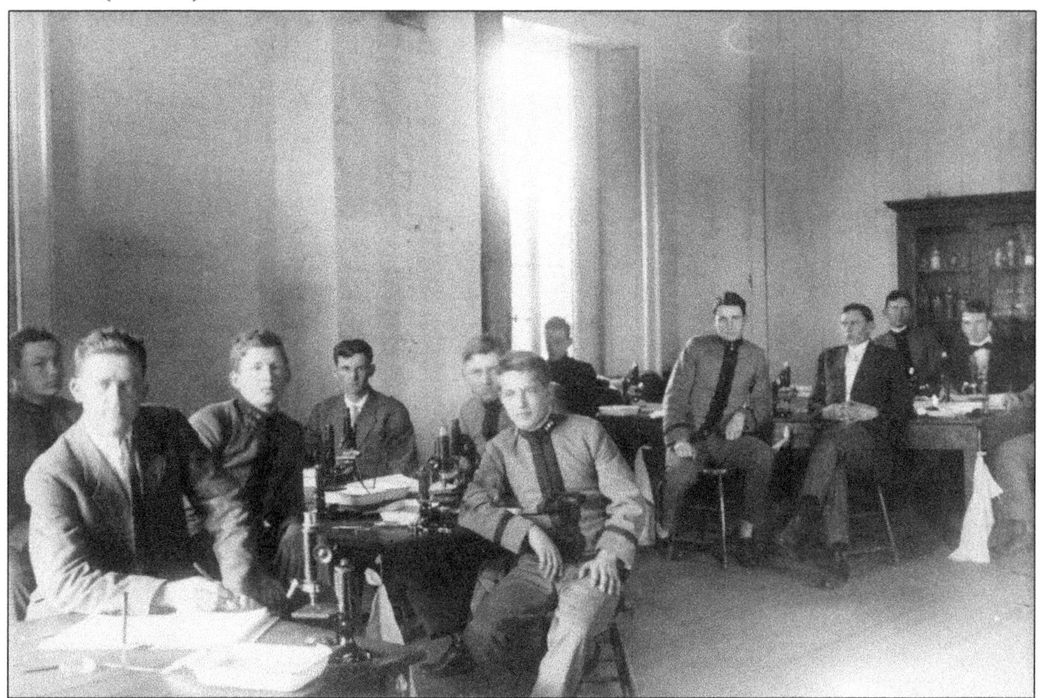

These zoology students from around 1913 are using microscopes. Zoology became an important part of the agriculture curriculum by the 1880s. (LSUPC.)

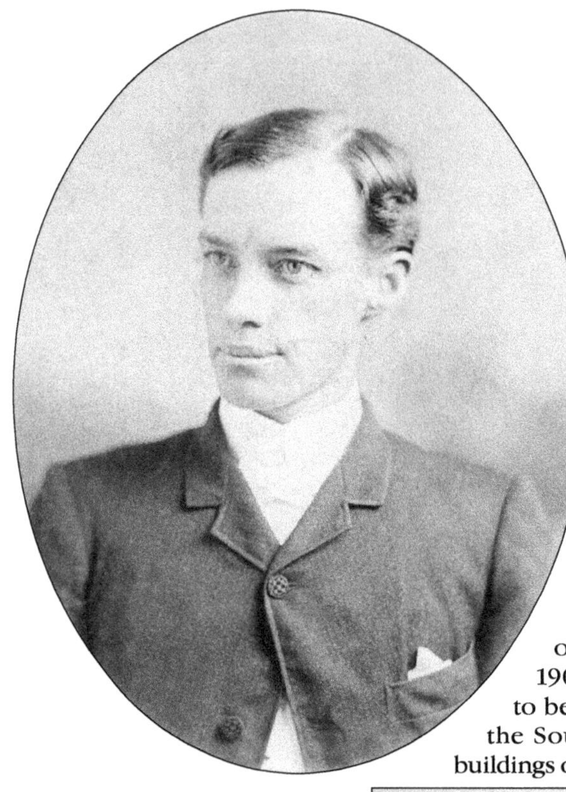

Thomas D. Boyd (1854–1932) was David Boyd's younger brother and an 1872 graduate of LSU. He became a professor of mathematics in 1874, professor of drawing and commandant of cadets in 1877, professor of history and English literature in 1883, and briefly served as acting president in 1886. From 1888 to 1896, Boyd was president of the Louisiana State Normal School in Natchitoches. He returned to LSU in 1896 as president and, despite attempts to retire, remained in office until 1927. During his presidency, the curriculum was expanded, the system of colleges that is in use today began in 1908, the downtown campus was expanded to become one of the larger physical plants in the South, and the land was acquired and the buildings of the present campus were begun. (LSUPC.)

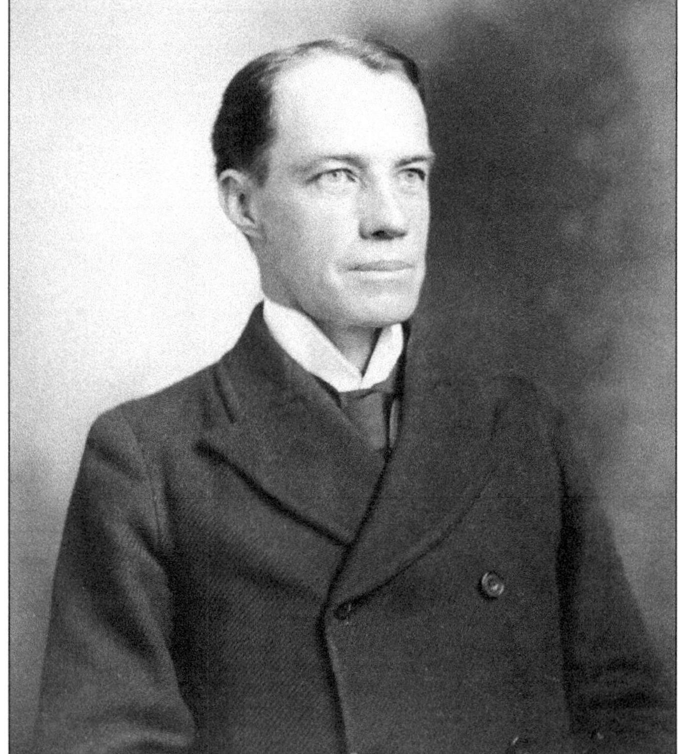

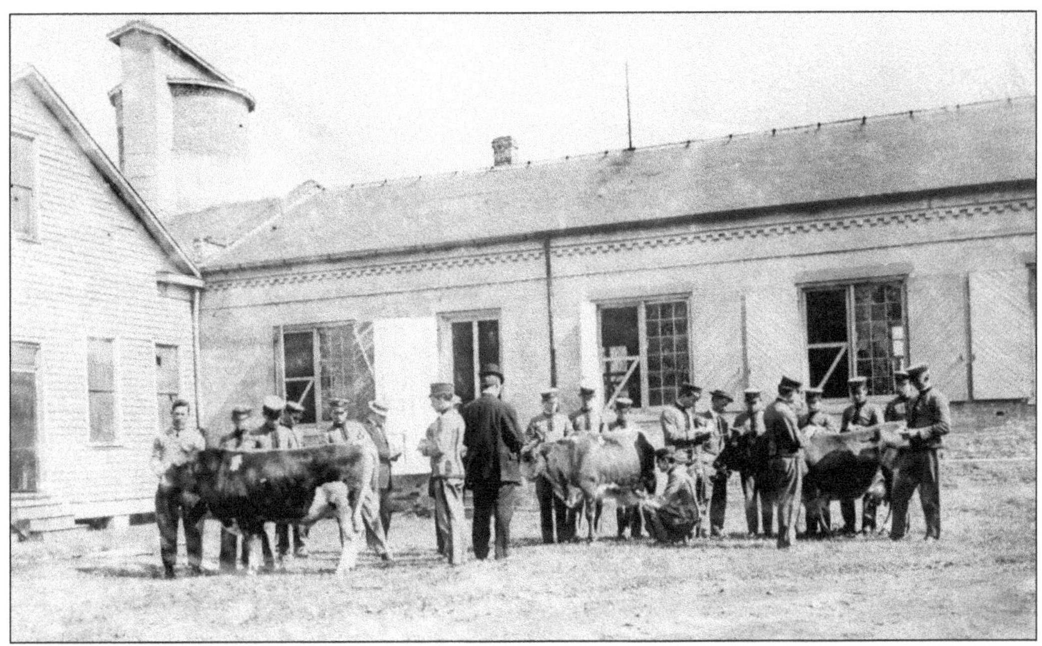

This 1913 image shows agriculture students examining cattle behind the creamery building. By the 1890s, agriculture had become a large part of the university, helped by its move to the downtown campus and the Morrill land grant acts. (LSUPC.)

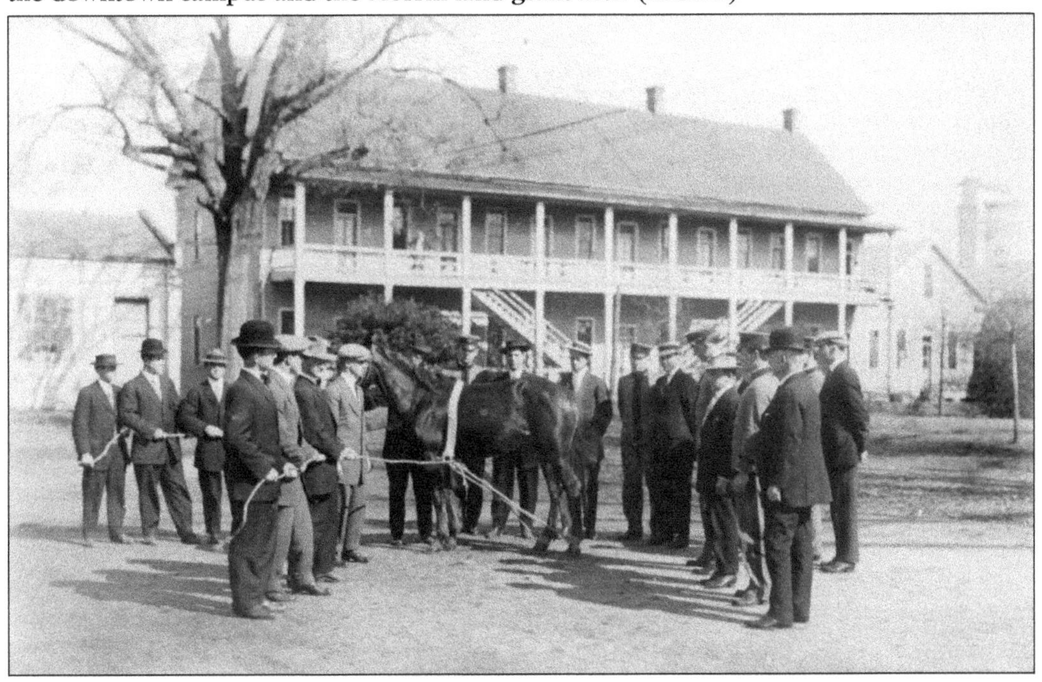

Veterinary science students are seen here in 1913 learning to hobble a horse. William Dalrymple is at right wearing a bowler hat. Dalrymple (1856–1925) came to LSU in 1889 as a professor of veterinary science shortly after graduating from the Glasgow (Scotland) Veterinary College. In 1897, he became the veterinarian for the agricultural experiment stations and wrote books on veterinary obstetrics and livestock sanitation. (LSUPC.)

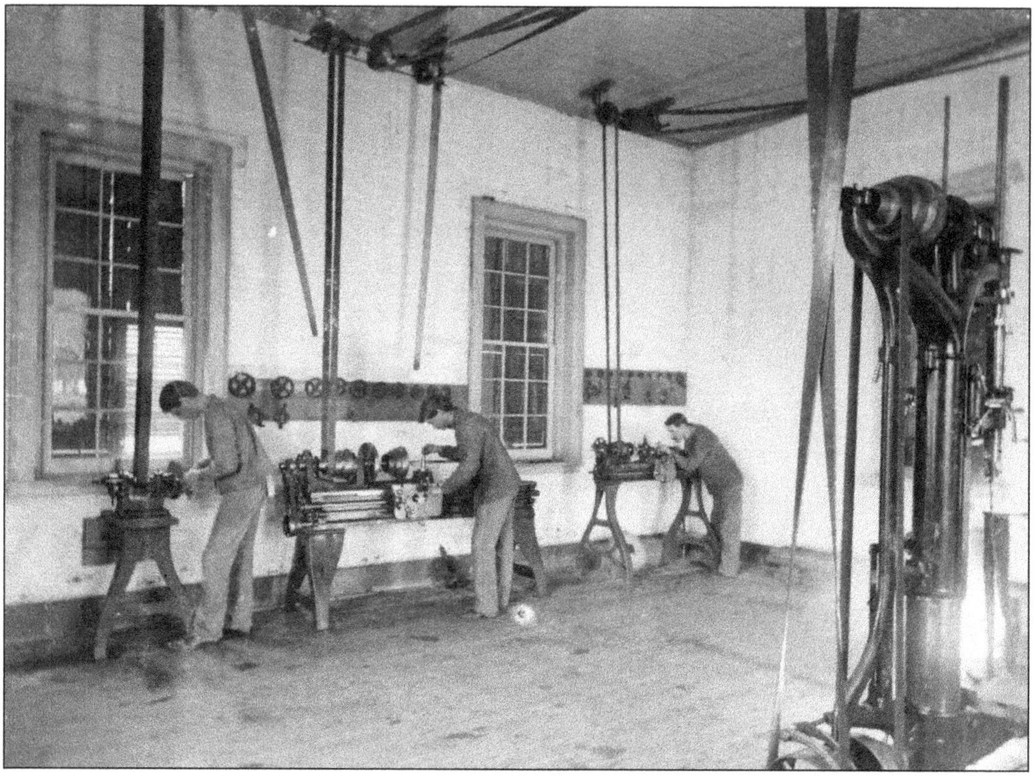

Learning to use machine tools was a part of the mechanical engineering curriculum. Seen here in Robertson Hall in about 1903, these cadets are using lathes and a grinder. The machine at right is a drill press. A stationary engine drove all of the machines, powered by a series of belts and pulleys, just as they would have in a factory at that time. The handles hanging from the shaft near the ceiling were brakes to stop the machines. (LSUPC.)

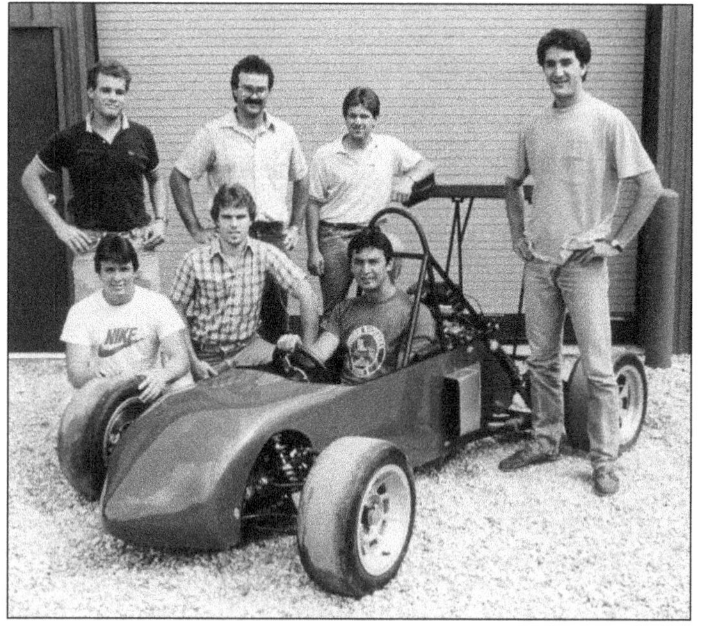

This Formula SAE car was constructed by students in the Department of Mechanical Engineering in 1985. Formula SAE began in 1979 and LSU has been in the competition since the early 1980s. With guidance from a faculty advisor, students construct the car themselves based on design specifications provided by the Society of Automotive Engineers. (OPRR.)

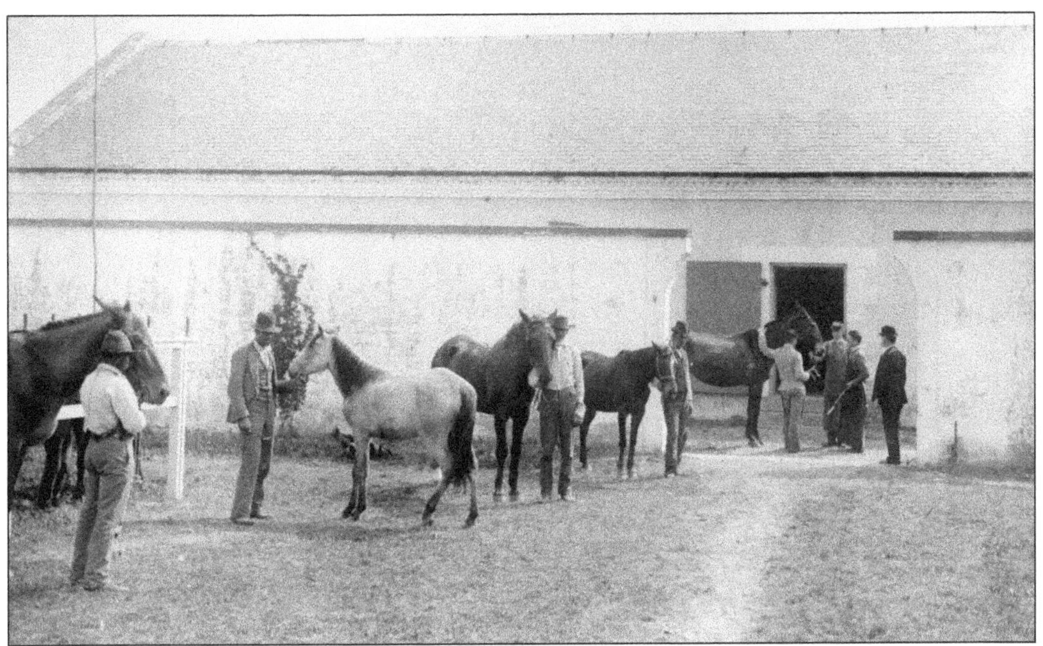

The powder magazine was used as the veterinary infirmary on the downtown campus. Students in the agriculture course learned about veterinary health, but courses in veterinary medicine would come much later. The African American men holding the horses worked for the university as janitors and stewards. (LSUPC.)

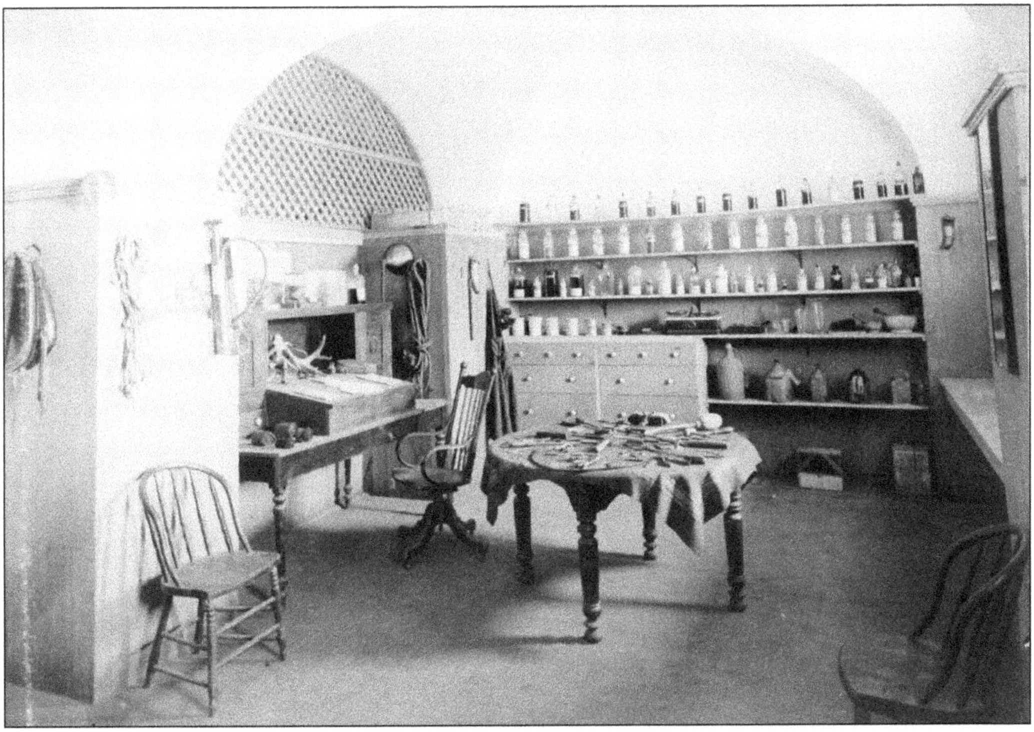

Inside the veterinary infirmary, the solid construction is evidence of the building's former use as a powder magazine. Note the horse collars, medicines, ropes, and other tools. (LSUPC.)

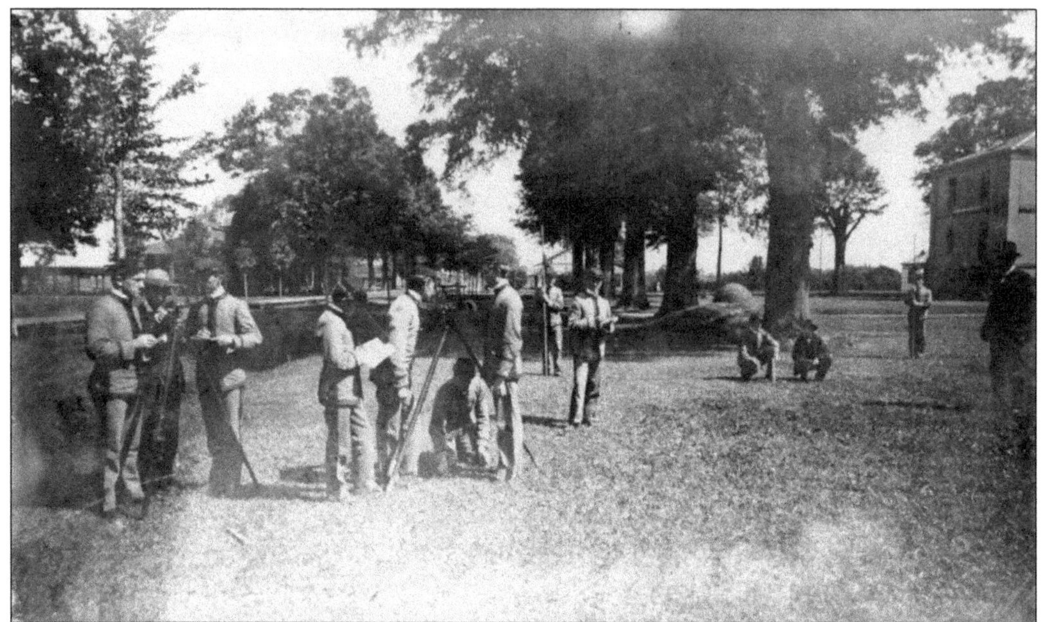

Civil engineering had been a part of the curriculum since the very beginning. Students were taught about road construction, railroad rights-of-way, and drainage for farms. These students are seen on University Avenue (now North Third Street) surveying the campus. LSU took part in the Good Roads Movement to teach building paved roads around campus. (LSUPC.)

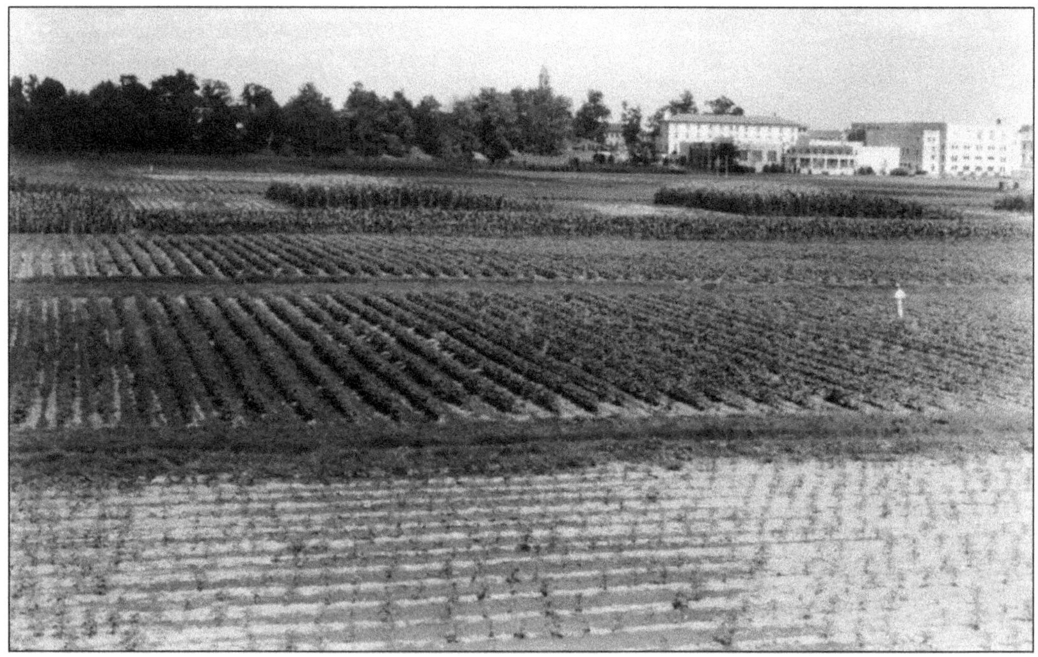

This 1934 photograph shows cotton breeding plots along Nicholson Drive. The wide-open spaces seen here and the alluvial soil were the main reasons Gartness Plantation was chosen as the new university site. In the background are the Huey P. Long Field House and Pool and the Gym-Armory. (Department of Agronomy Photographs, RG #A5000.0505, Louisiana State University Archives, LSU Libraries, Baton Rouge, Lousiana.)

Lillian Louise Garig was one of the first women to enter LSU, in 1906, and was one of the first female faculty members. She received her master's degree in 1911, never married, and taught English at the university for the rest of her life. Her father was Baton Rouge businessman William Garig, who had donated the funds for Garig Hall. (LSUPC.)

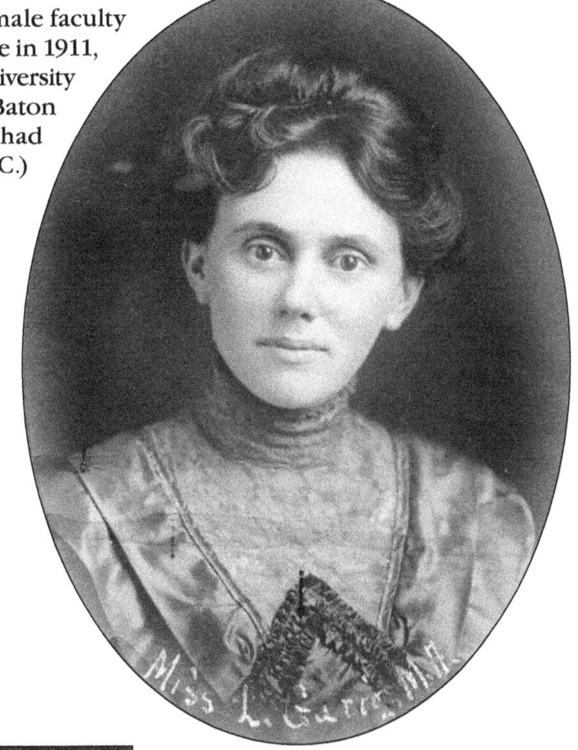

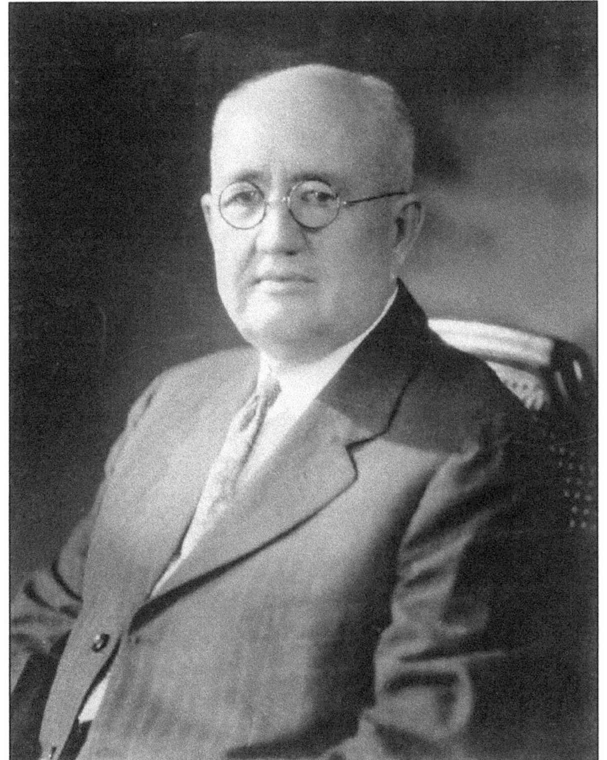

Thomas Atkinson succeeded Thomas Boyd as president from 1927 to 1930. Atkinson graduated from LSU in 1891 as one of its first graduate students. He became a professor of electrical engineering and had risen to dean of the College of Engineering when he was chosen to succeed Boyd as president. Atkinson acquired an option in 1918 to purchase Gartness Plantation for the new campus. He, along with William Dodson and some Baton Rouge businessmen, borrowed the $82,000 purchase price and exercised the option on the property. (OCR.)

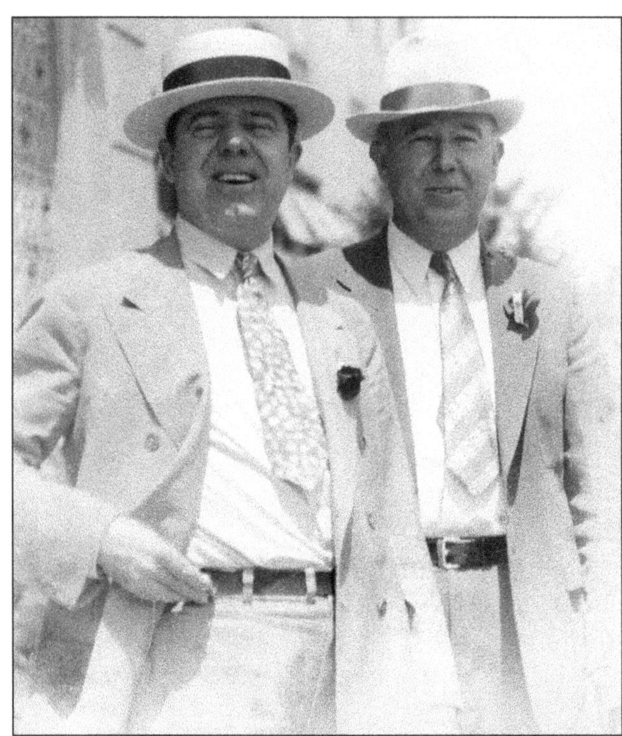

James Monroe Smith (right), LSU's president from 1931 to 1939 and the first to have a PhD, carried out a major building program that was at least partially motivated by Huey Long wanting the university, and everything else with which he could be affiliated, to be the best. Long supported many of the programs encouraged by Smith, such as the *Southern Review* and LSU Press, and found funding for the Huey P. Long Field House, Allen Hall, the French House, and the east and west stadium dormitories. (OCR.)

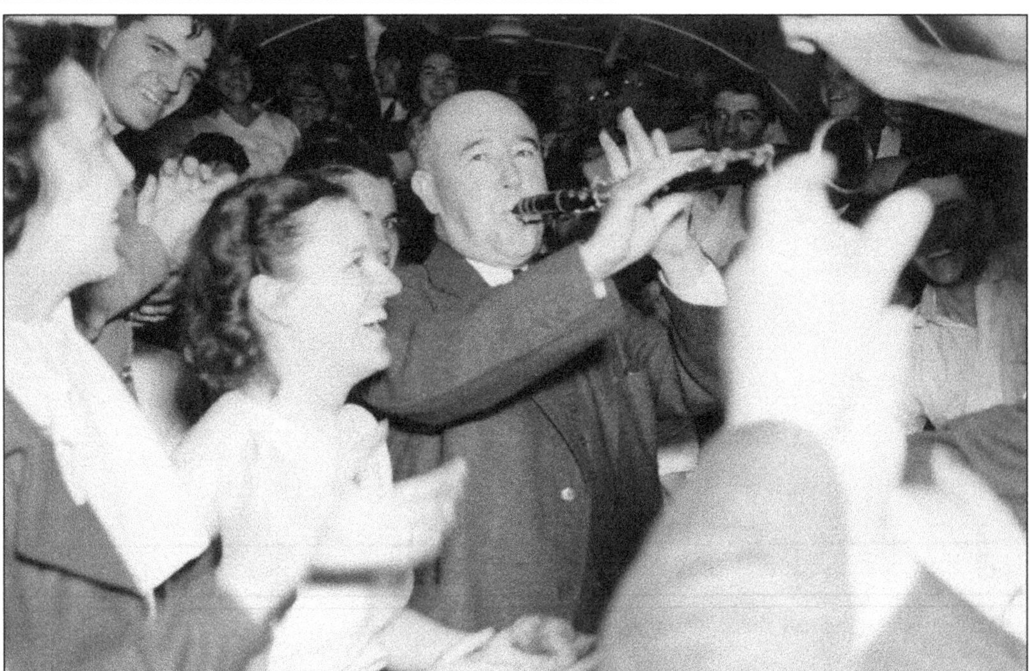

James Monroe Smith was popular with the students and accompanied them on train trips to the away football games. It all came to an end in 1939 when Smith's commodities trading with university funds caught up with him and he was convicted of embezzlement. He held bonds that were supposed to have been cancelled and forged bonds to be used as collateral on loans for trading wheat futures. (OCR.)

Robert Penn Warren (1905–1989) (left) was an English professor at LSU from 1934 to 1942. He, Cleanth Brooks, and Charles Pipkin founded and edited the *Southern Review* literary journal from 1935 until it was discontinued in 1942. Warren is seen here with T.S. Stribling, a best-selling novelist who won the Pulitzer Prize in 1933 for *The Store*. (CEP.)

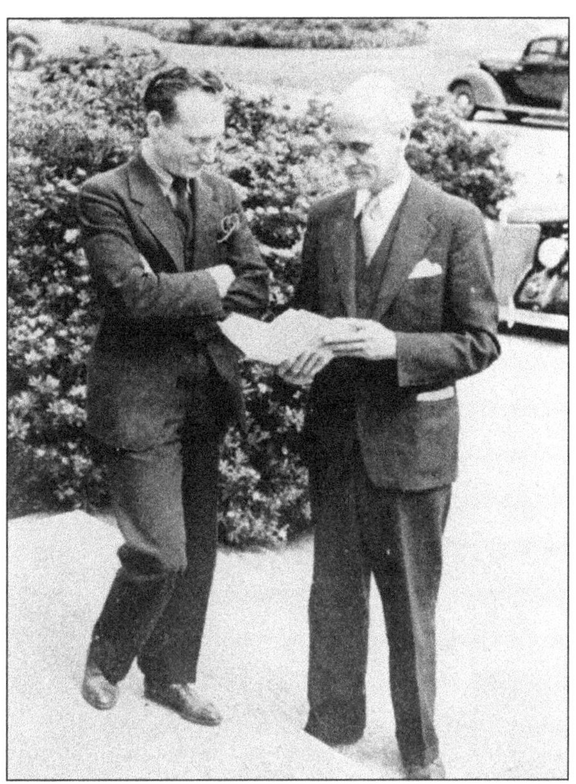

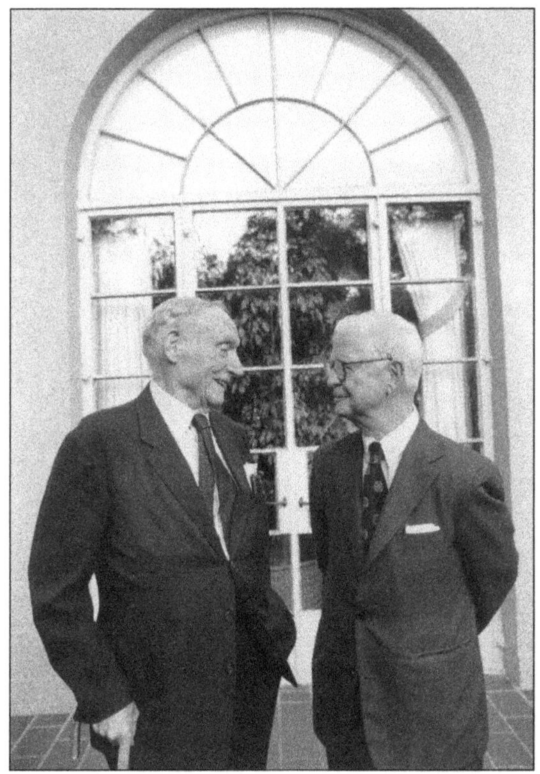

Robert Penn Warren (left) and Cleanth Brooks (1906–1994), cofounders of the *Southern Review,* returned to campus in 1985 for the 50th anniversary of the journal. Brooks was a professor of English at LSU from 1932 to 1947 and, like Warren, was a part of the Fugitives and Agrarian movements in Southern literature. (Southern Review Records, RG #A0040, Louisiana State University Archives, LSU Libraries, Baton Rouge, Louisiana.)

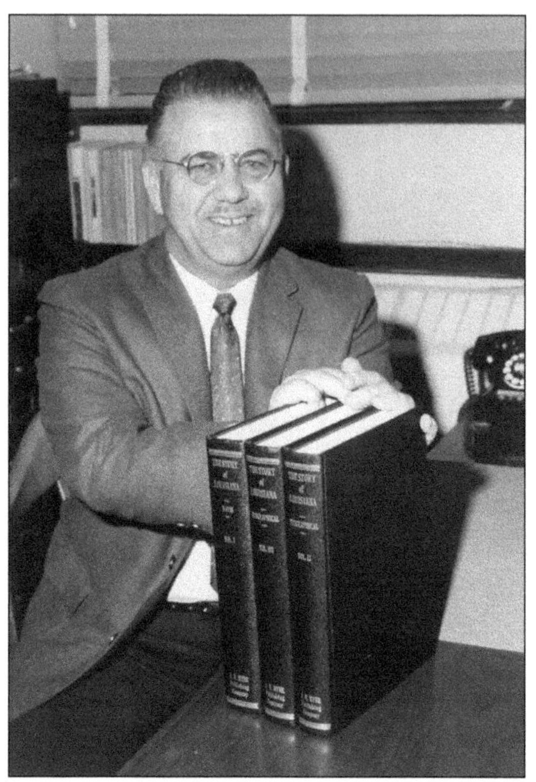

Edwin A. Davis (1904–1994) was a professor in the Department of History from 1932 to 1973 and established the Department of Archives and Manuscripts at LSU in 1935. He wrote several widely used texts on Louisiana history, including *The Story of Louisiana*, seen here. Davis coauthored the State Archives and Records Act, which created the Louisiana State Archives, and was the first state archivist from 1956 to 1984. (OPRR.)

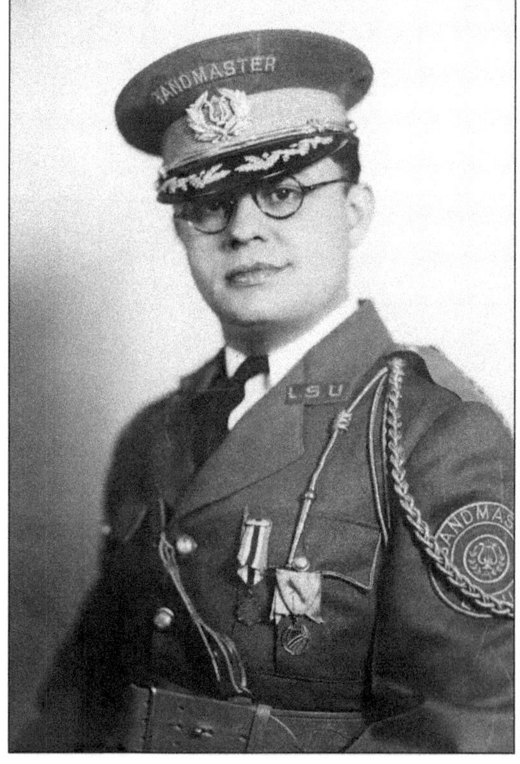

Castro Carazo (1895–1981) was a jazz orchestra leader at the Blue Room in New Orleans's Roosevelt Hotel when he was hired by Huey Long in 1934 to be the bandmaster of the LSU Cadet Band. Carazo's first assignment was to increase the size of the band, which eventually grew to about 250 pieces. Carazo and Long wrote several songs, including *Every Man a King, Darling of LSU,* and the official fight song, *Fight for LSU.* (OPRR.)

Gov. Richard Leche, seen here with cheerleaders in 1937, had as much fun on campus as his predecessor Huey Long. Leche attended away football games and led the bands through the streets of Houston, Nashville, and Knoxville, just as Long did. Leche's success in obtaining funds for new campus buildings such as the Parker Coliseum, Himes Hall, and Nicholson Hall, and enclosing the north end zone of Tiger Stadium, was far greater then Long's. (RWL.)

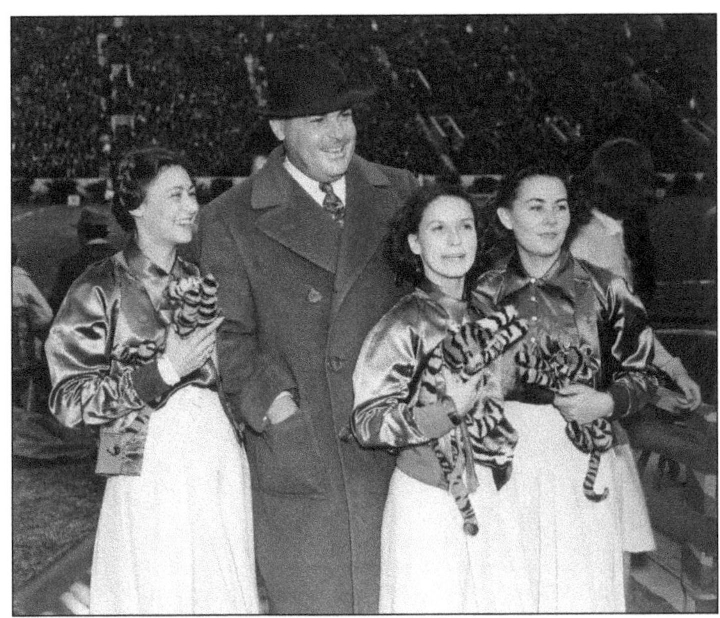

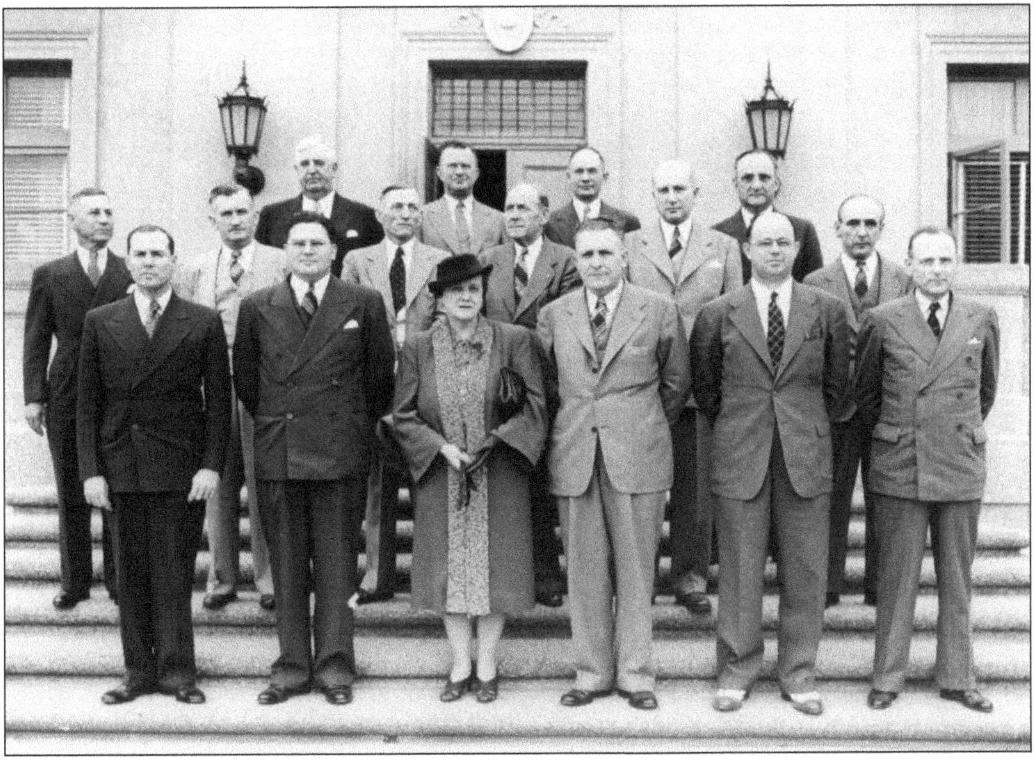

After James Monroe Smith was convicted of embezzlement and other campus officials had been caught up in the "University Scandals," a new university administration and Board of Supervisors was appointed. Paul M. Hebert (front row, second from left), dean of the law school, was appointed acting president. Troy H. Middleton (back row, second from left) became comptroller and was tasked with sorting out the university's financial mess. Fred Frey (back row, third from left) became dean of the university. (THM.)

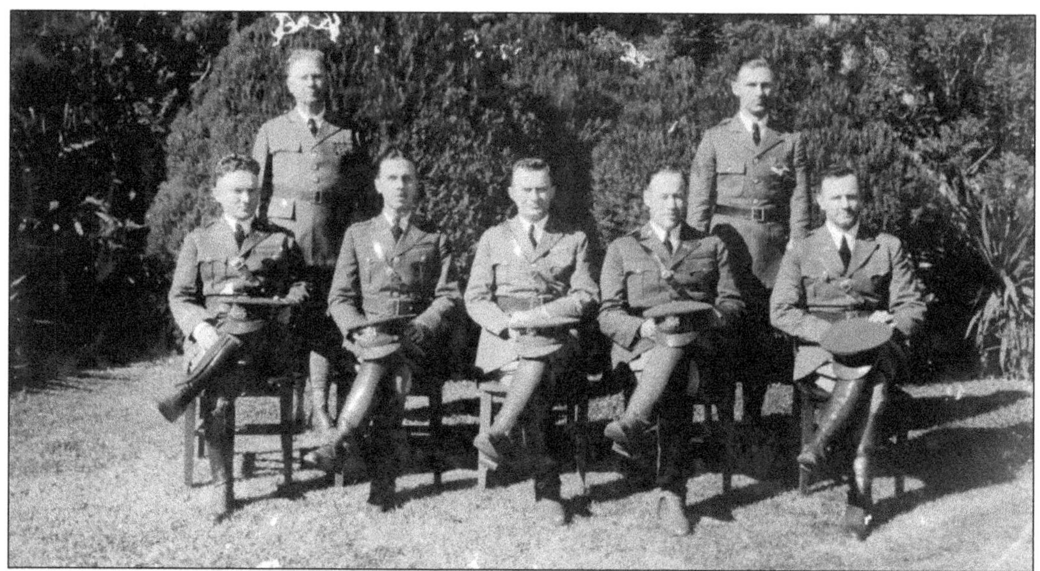

Maj. Troy Middleton (1889–1976) (center) arrived at LSU in 1930 as commandant of cadets. He became dean of men in 1934 and left to resume regular Army duty in 1936. As commandant, Middleton stopped dissent against mandatory ROTC training and worked with Castro Carazo to increase the size of the band. He is pictured here with the other cadet instructors in 1933. To Middleton's left is Capt. Lawrence "Biff" Jones, LSU's football coach from 1932 to 1934. Jones had come from West Point and did not want to resign his Army commission, so he was made an instructor of military science and tactics. (DMS.)

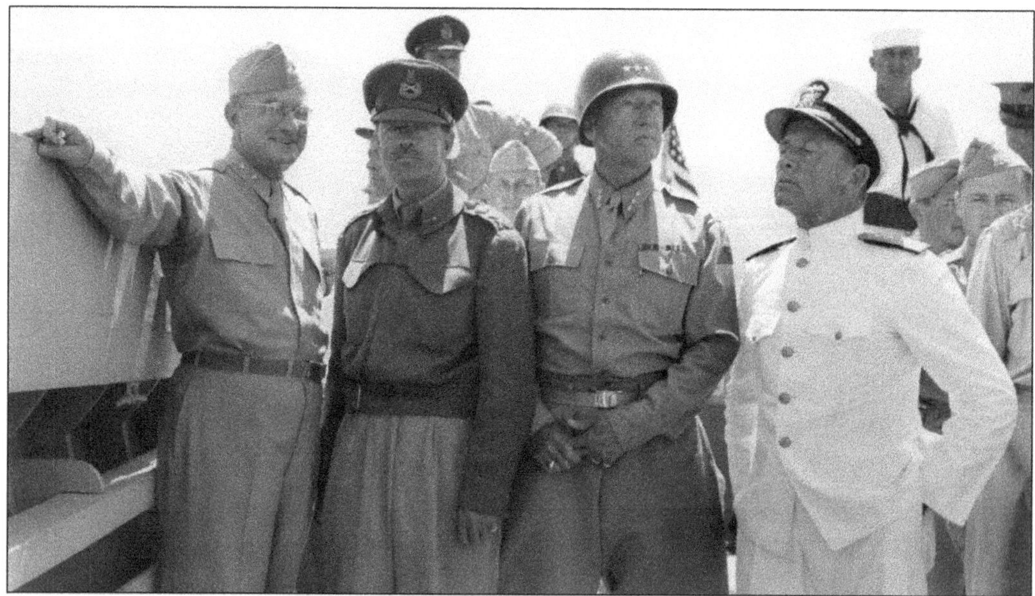

Like many members of faculty, staff, and students, Troy Middleton (left) left LSU to join the military at the outbreak of World War II. He had retired from the Army in 1937 to return to LSU as dean of the administration, but shortly after Pearl Harbor, Middleton offered his services to the Army. He was given command of the 45th Infantry Division in 1942 and is seen here prior to the invasion of Sicily in 1943 with (from left to right) Gen. Sir Harold Alexander, Gen. George S. Patton, and Adm. Alan Kirk. (THM.)

Caroline Durieux (1896–1989) was an artist best known for her satirical lithographs. She taught at LSU from 1943 to 1964 and was named professor emerita. Best known for developing electron printing in the 1950s and creating prints with radioactive ink, Durieux also developed a technique for adding color to cliché verre (printmaking on glass). (OPRR.)

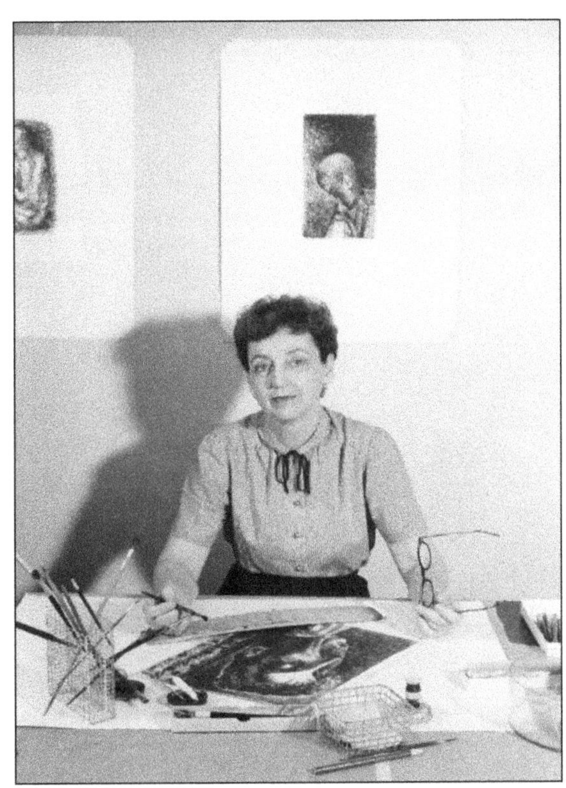

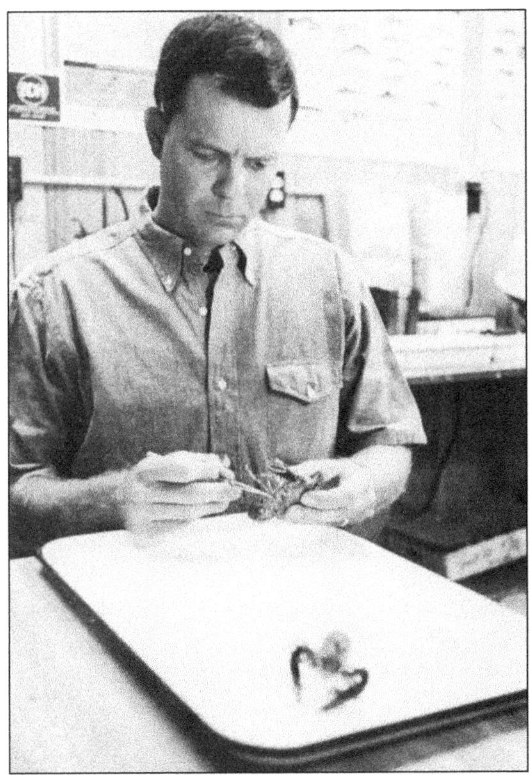

Dr. James W. Avault (1935–) joined the LSU faculty in 1966 and has conducted research in aquaculture, primarily related to the commercial farming of catfish and crawfish. His greatest contributions to Louisiana are studies of diseases, breeding and genetics, and production that have led to major advances in crawfish farming. Avault was also instrumental in developing the Ben Hur Research Farm, where research in aquaculture is performed. (*LSU Alumni News*, 1968.)

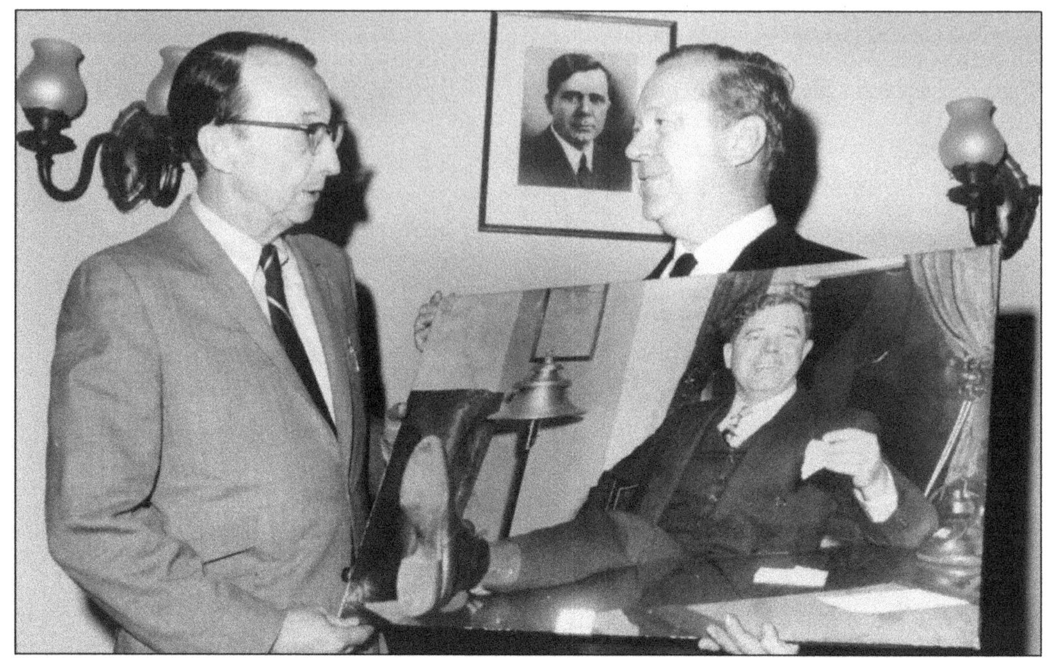

T. Harry Williams (1908–1979) was an award-winning historian who taught at LSU from 1941 until his retirement in 1978. He was named Boyd Professor, the highest honor LSU bestows upon its faculty, in 1953. In 1970, his *Huey Long: A Biography* won the Pulitzer Prize and the National Book Award. Williams was a proponent of oral history and he used the technique extensively in *Huey Long.* The T. Harry Williams Center for Oral History on campus is named in his honor. Williams (left) is seen here with Sen. Russell Long, holding a portrait of his father, Huey P. Long. (RBL.)

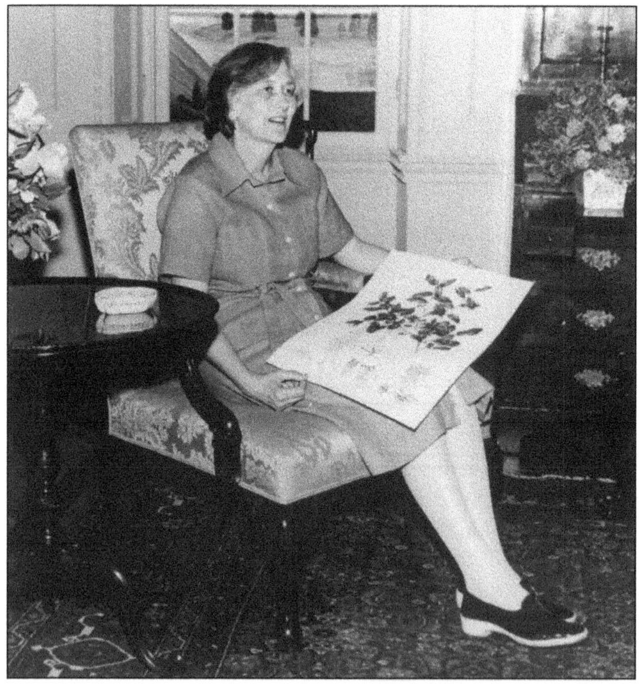

Renowned botanical artist Margaret Stones (1920–) was commissioned by LSU in 1976 to produce six watercolor drawings of Louisiana flora to celebrate the American bicentennial and the 50th anniversary of LSU's Baton Rouge campus. The Native Flora of Louisiana Collection was expanded to 200 drawings, many of which Stones created in her room at the Faculty Club. The original drawings are housed at Hill Memorial Library. The entire collection was finished in 1987. (OPRR.)

Three

STUDENTS AND STUDENT LIFE

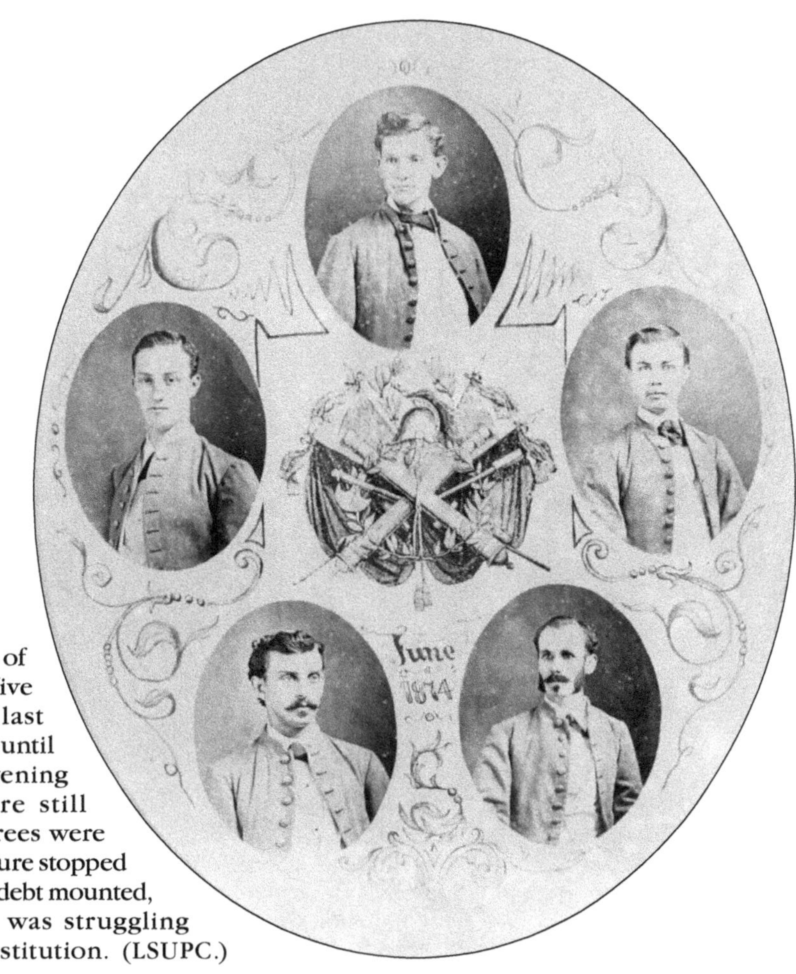

The graduating class of 1874 consisted of five and would be the last to receive diplomas until 1882. In the intervening years, courses were still offered, but no degrees were awarded. The legislature stopped appropriating funds, debt mounted, and the university was struggling to survive as an institution. (LSUPC.)

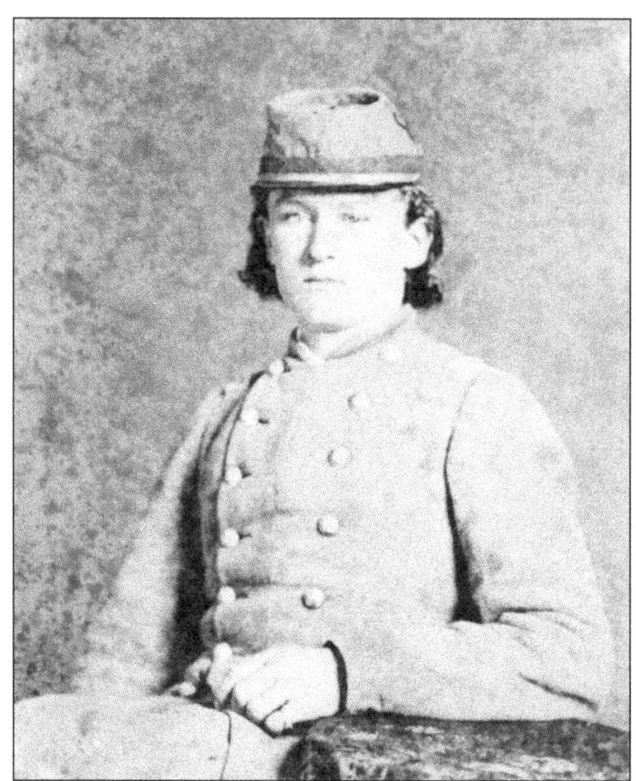

George Waters Stafford (1844–1890) was one of the first cadets to enter the seminary in 1860 and was one of the first cadets to leave at the outbreak of the Civil War. He joined the 8th Louisiana Infantry and is seen in this image from 1862 wearing the uniform of a first lieutenant. (LSUPC.)

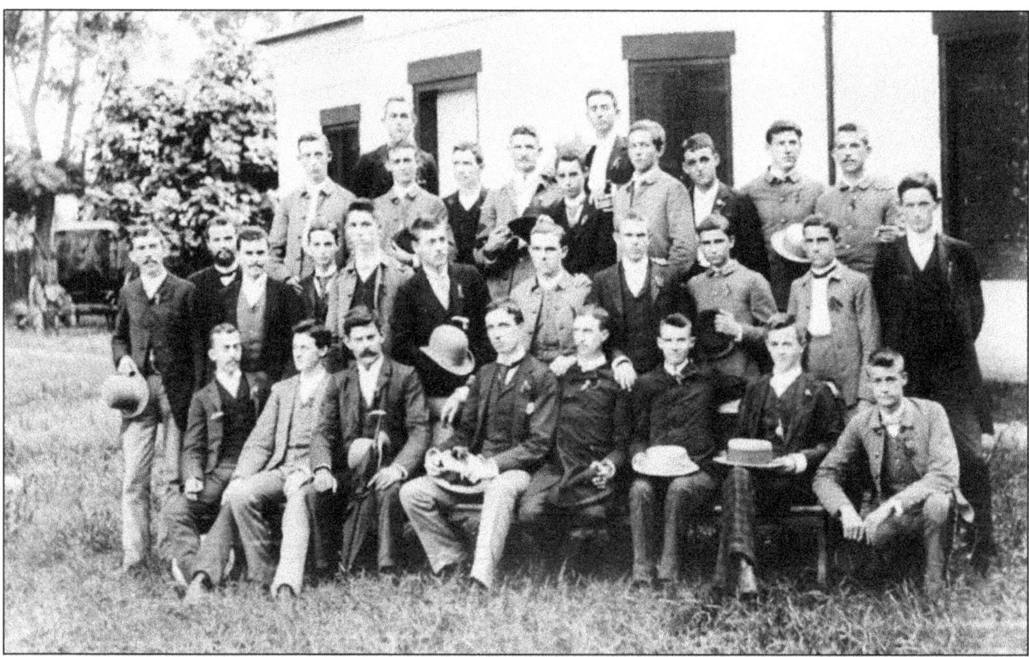

Kappa Alpha fraternity was established at LSU in 1885. The members are seen here next to the fraternity hall on the downtown campus. Arthur Prescott, a member of the class of 1884 who became a professor of natural history and librarian in 1887, is the man with a beard standing second from left. (LSUPC.)

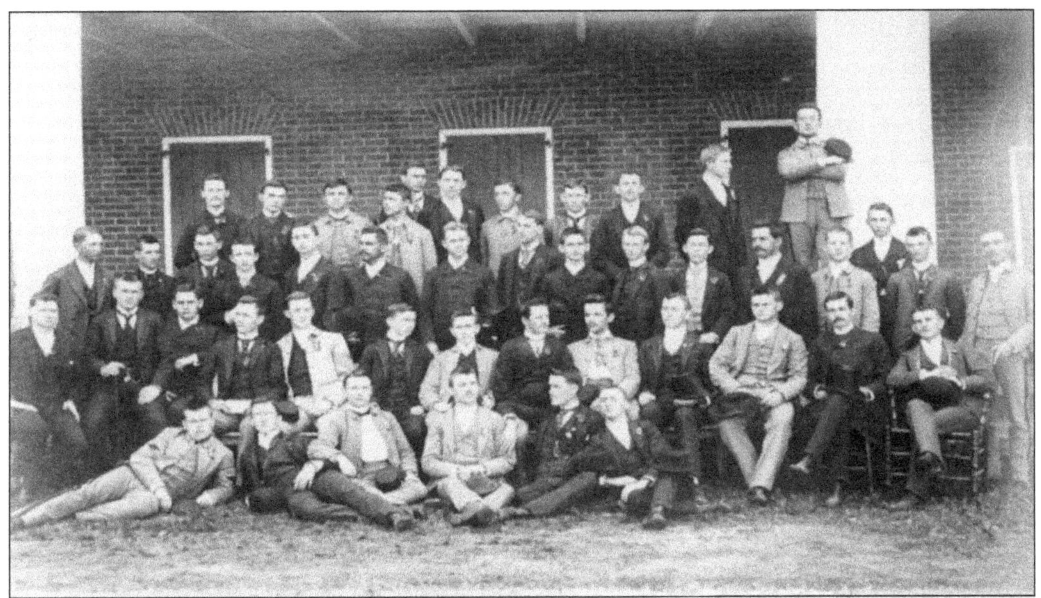

Kappa Sigma fraternity began at LSU in 1887. They and Kappa Alpha, established in 1885, are the oldest fraternities on campus. After the move to the downtown campus, the organizations met in a shared hall, but later rented houses in town. On-campus fraternity houses came in the 1930s. (LSUPC.)

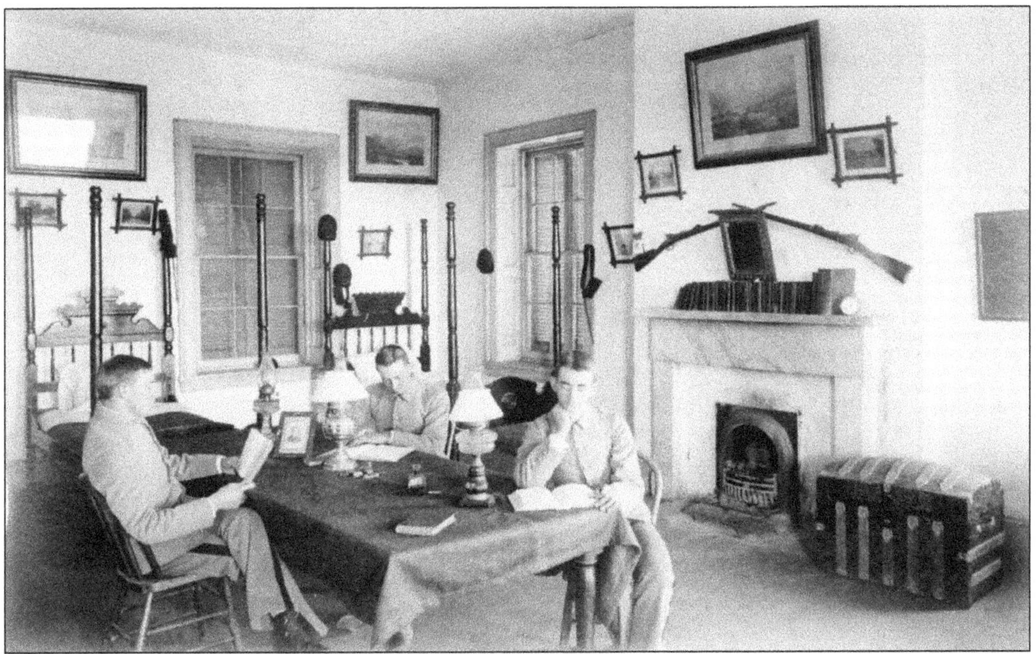

These three cadets studying in the Pentagon Barracks, around 1890, are members of Infantry Company A. Cadets were responsible for maintaining a rifle and its accoutrements, such as the cartridge box and bayonet hanging near the window frame. Rooms were inspected daily and a major inspection was held weekly. Demerits were issued for failing inspection and for other infractions of the rules. Any cadet receiving 100 demerits or more in a 90-day period was expelled. (LSUPC.)

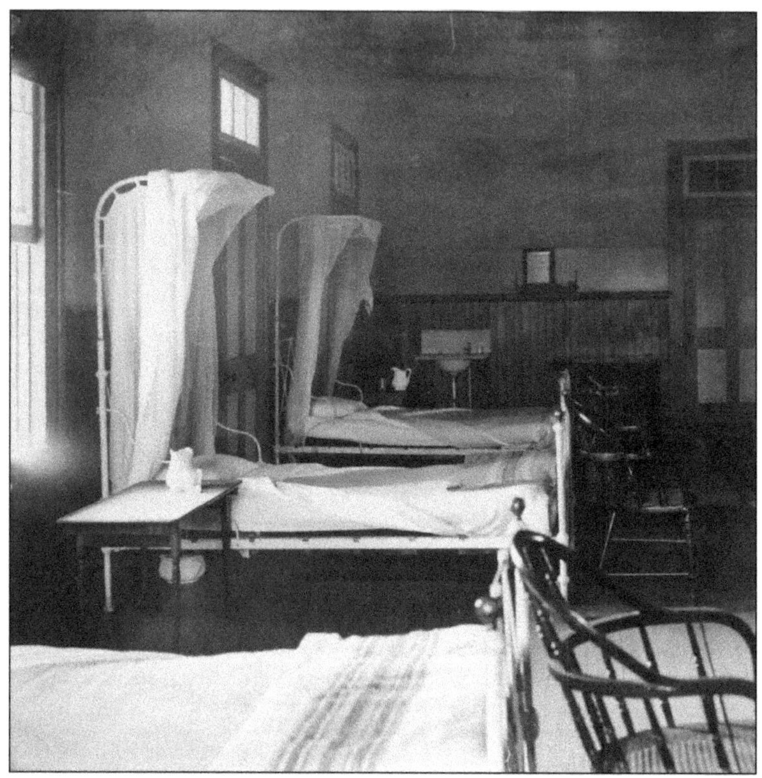

The hospital ward of the infirmary had indoor plumbing, but had a wood stove for warmth and heating water. The downtown campus used cistern water, but after an outbreak of cerebritis from bacteria or fungus found in the cisterns in 1894, LSU made arrangements to connect to the Baton Rouge water supply. Sickness was taken very seriously and late summer outbreaks of yellow fever were not uncommon. Note the curtains over the beds and the chamber pot underneath. (LSUPC.)

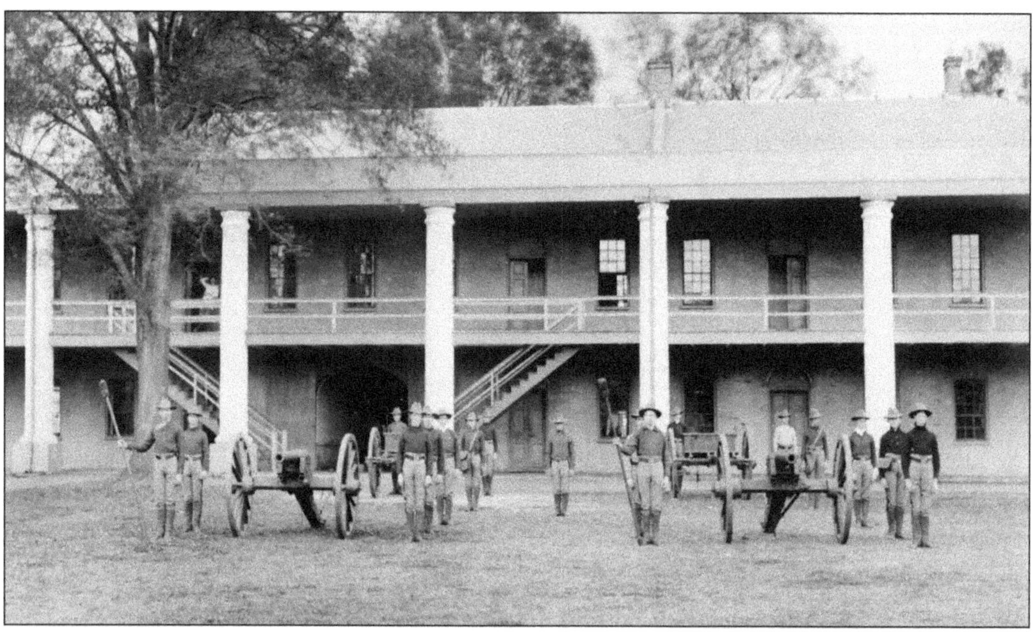

The artillery battery is standing at attention in the "hollow square" in the center of the Pentagon Barracks. These cast iron cannons were surplus ordnance from the Civil War period and remained university property until they were sacrificed in a World War II scrap metal drive. Cadets in the artillery company were among the best mathematicians on campus because they were required to compute range and trajectory. (LSUPC.)

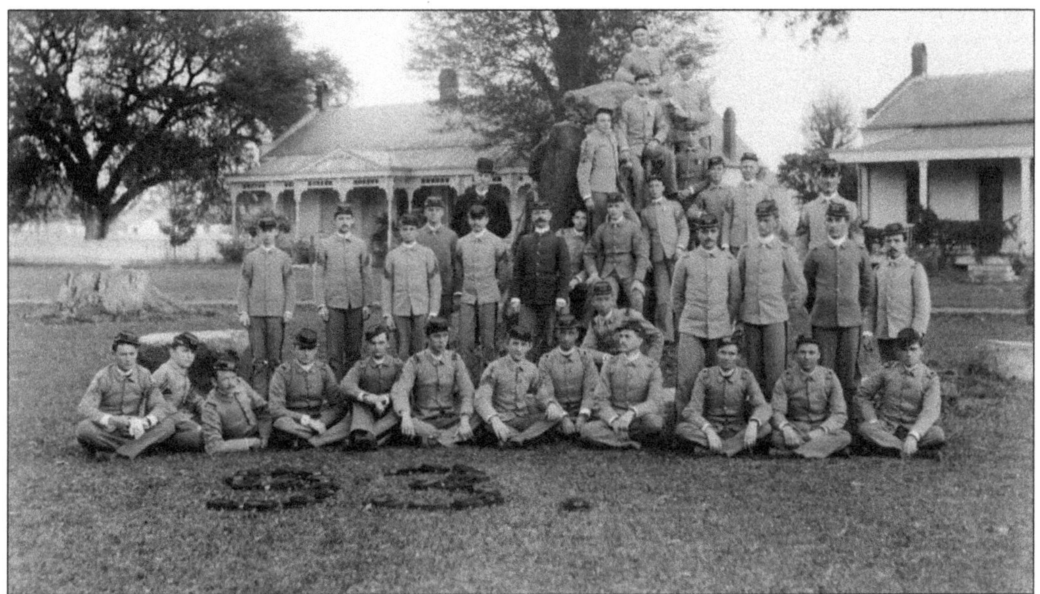

The class of 1893 is shown here in front of the treasurer's and the commandant's houses. Wearing the bowler hat in the back row is Pres. James W. Nicholson. Seated in the front row, sixth from left, is Ruffin G. Pleasant. Pleasant played on the first football team, helped organize the first band, and wrote some of the first cheers. (LSUPC.)

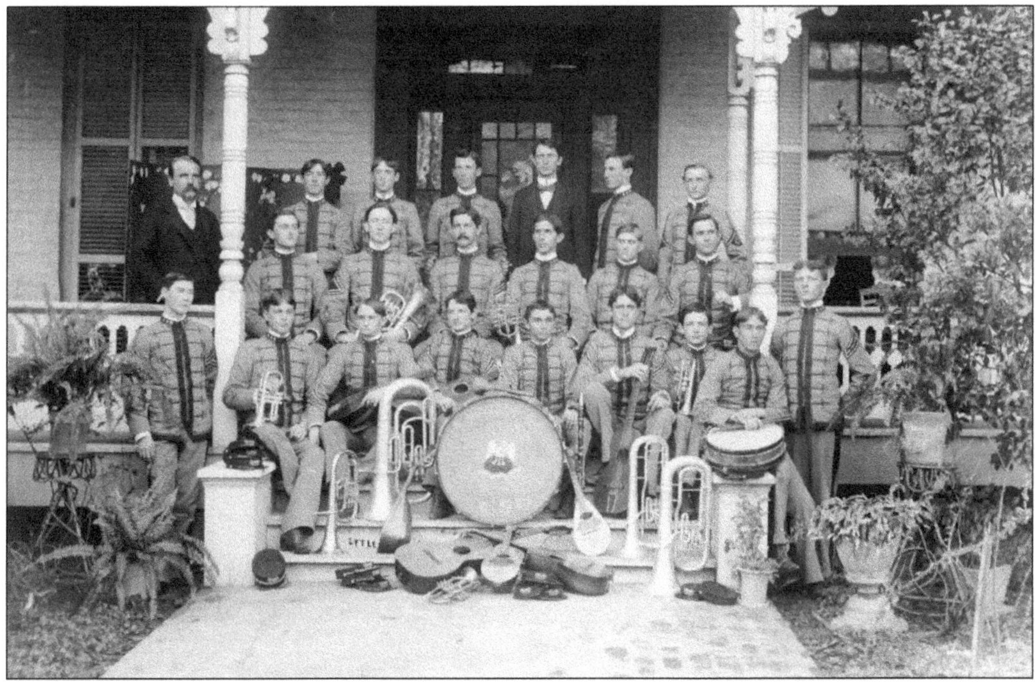

The LSU Cadet Parade Band is seen here on the front porch of the treasurer's house. The band started out as a music club in 1893. Wearing a suit in the rear center is Ruffin G. Pleasant. He was a member of the class of 1893 and served as Louisiana's governor from 1916 to 1920. The "Lytle" on the step refers to Baton Rouge photographer Andrew Lytle, who took many of LSU's early photographs. (LSUPC.)

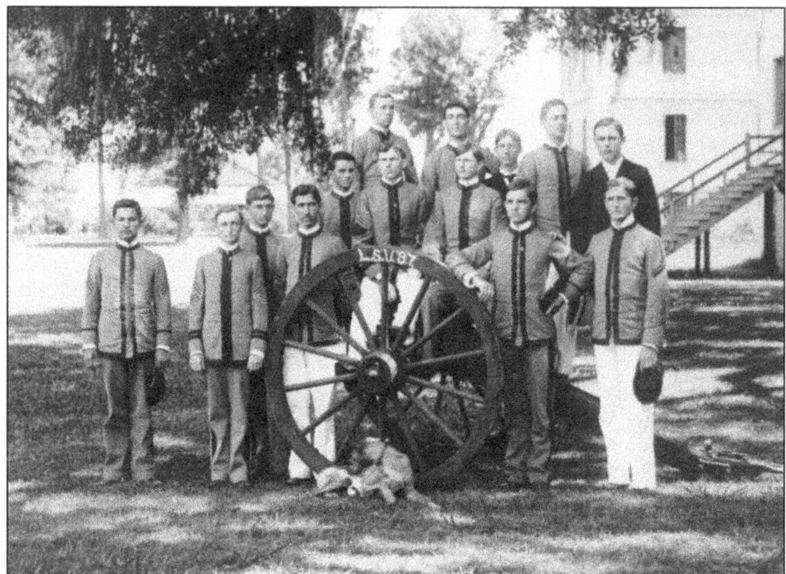

These 12 cadets and two town students (not in uniform) made up the class of 1897. They are seen in the front yard of the president's residence next to the chemistry building. (LSUPC.)

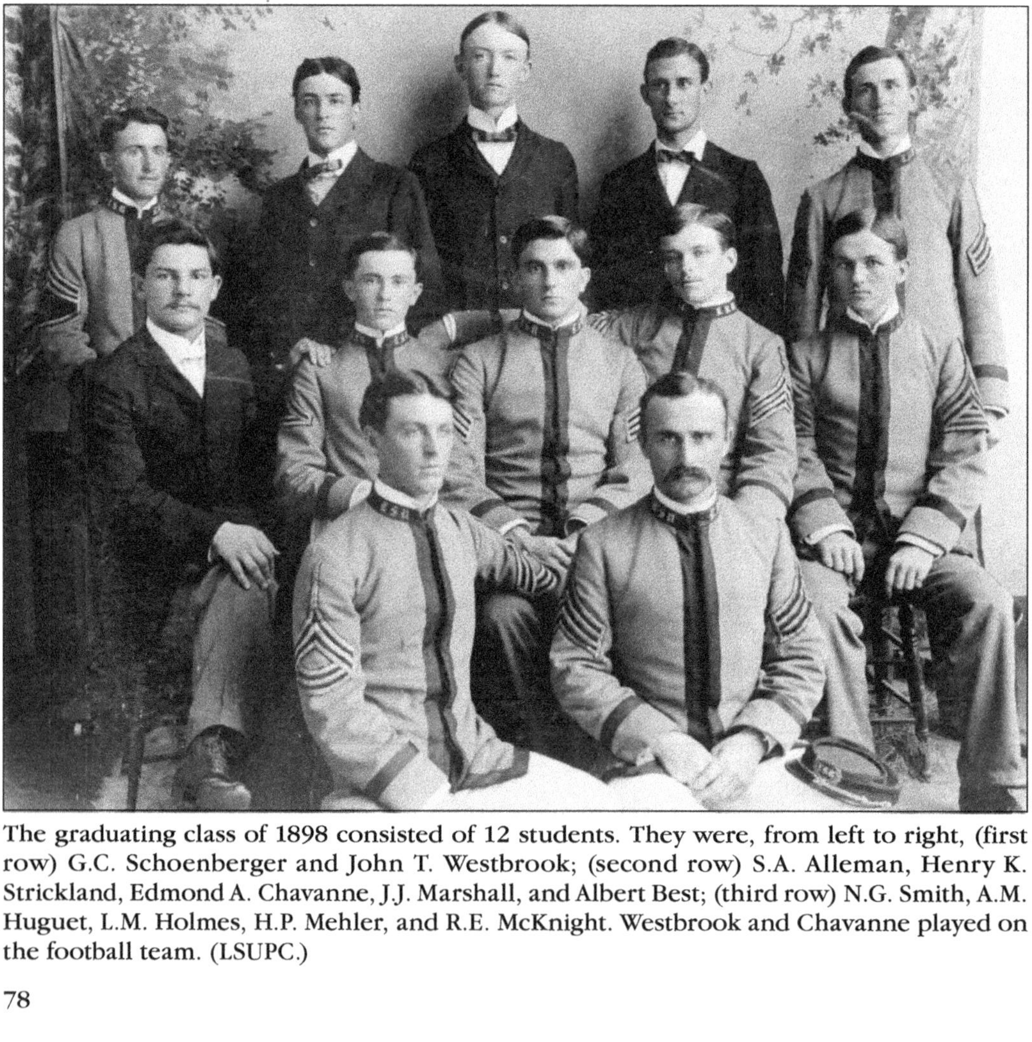

The graduating class of 1898 consisted of 12 students. They were, from left to right, (first row) G.C. Schoenberger and John T. Westbrook; (second row) S.A. Alleman, Henry K. Strickland, Edmond A. Chavanne, J.J. Marshall, and Albert Best; (third row) N.G. Smith, A.M. Huguet, L.M. Holmes, H.P. Mehler, and R.E. McKnight. Westbrook and Chavanne played on the football team. (LSUPC.)

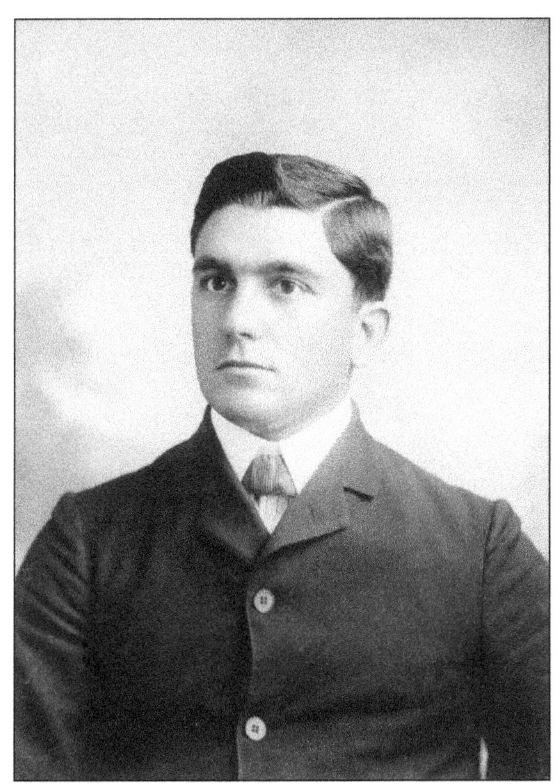

Edmond Chavanne was a member of the 1898 graduating class and played football from 1896 to 1898. He was captain of the team and coach for the Tulane game in 1898, leading the Tigers to a 37–0 victory. He became commandant of cadets in 1899 and coached a full season of football in 1900. (LSUPC.)

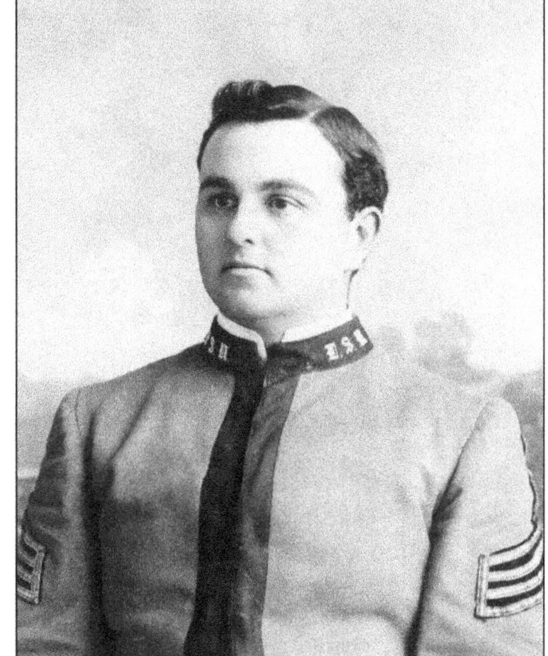

Cadet sergeant Leopold Kaffie was a member of the class of 1899 and played center on the 1897 and 1898 football teams. The uniforms were "cadet gray" with black trim and closely resembled those worn by cadets at West Point. (LSUPC.)

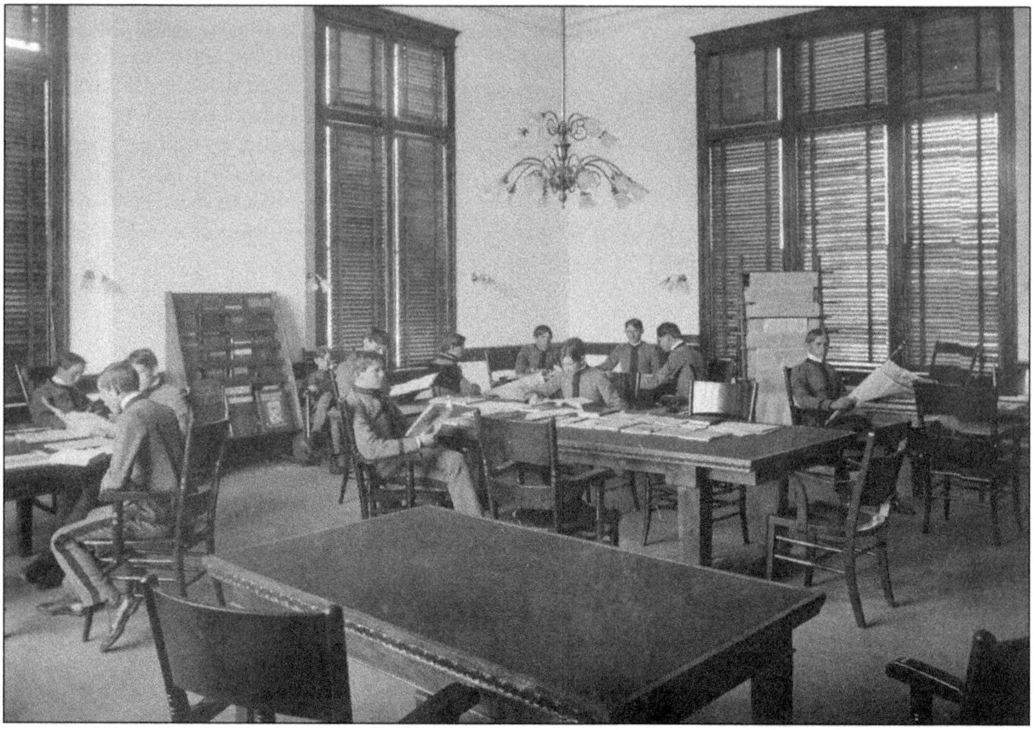

These cadets in the reading room of Hill Memorial Library enjoyed periodicals such as *Harper's Weekly* and *The Saturday Evening Post*, as well as various newspapers. This photograph was taken shortly after the library opened in 1903. (LSUPC.)

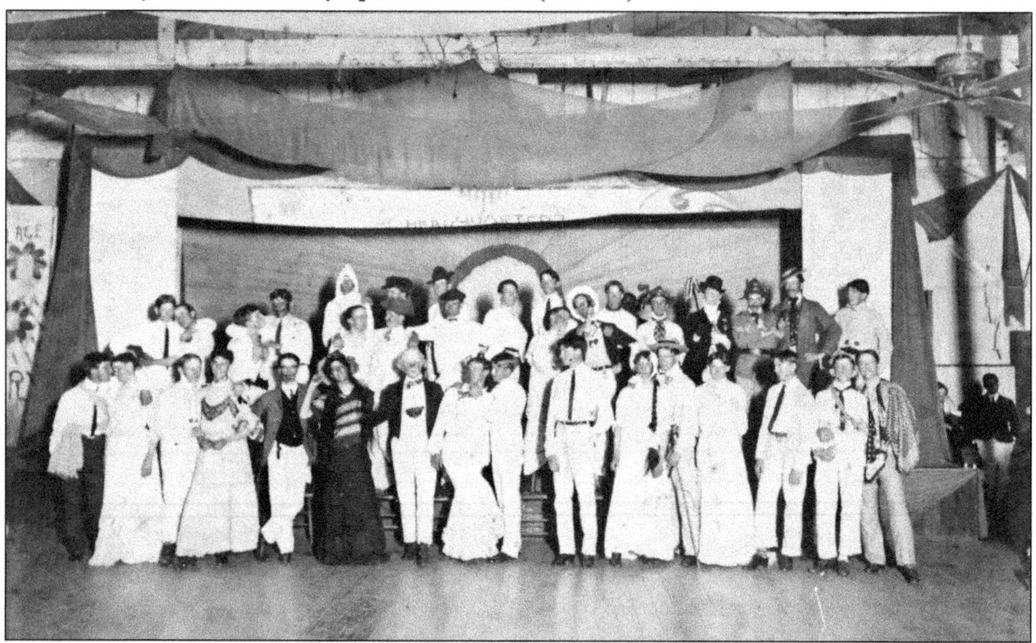

The Fancy Dress Stag Ball of 1904 was a burlesque show put on for fun by the cadets. The people wearing dresses in the photograph are male students, there being but one female student on campus at the time. (LSUPC.)

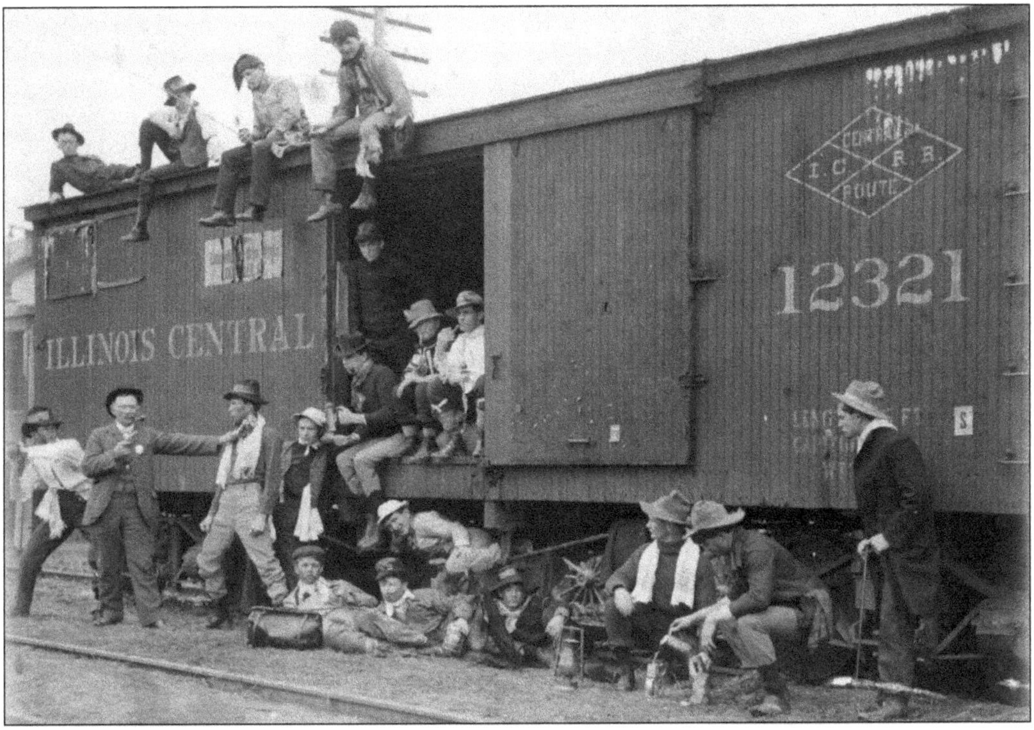

The Hobo Gang, seen here in 1905, was one of many informal student organizations on campus. Their colors were red, yellow, and goose green and their motto was "Wherever I hang my hat is home sweet home to me." Other groups were the New Orleans and Mississippi Clubs, and the Camera Club. (LSUPC.)

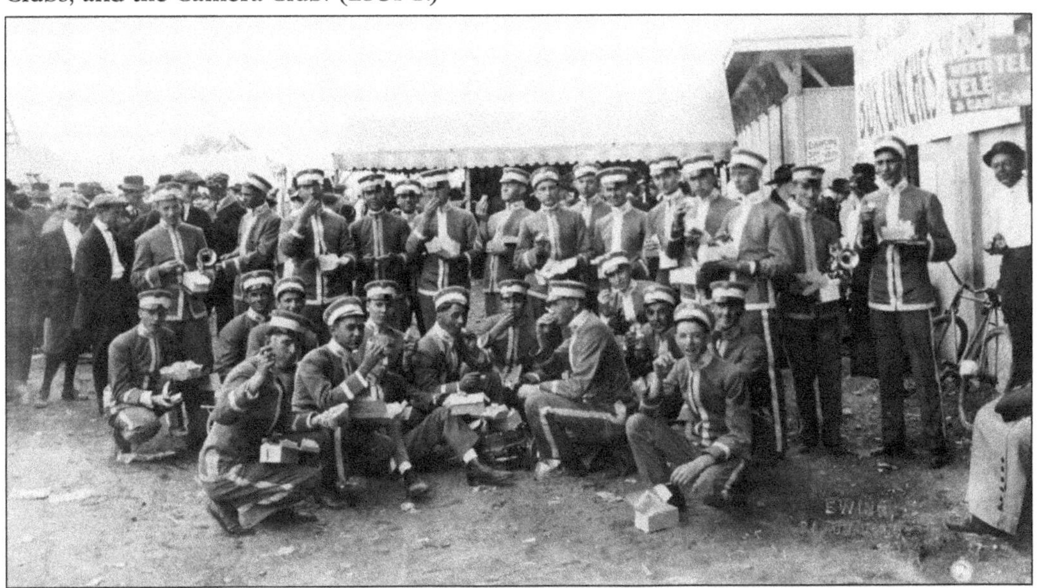

The Cadet Band is seen here eating box lunches at the Louisiana State Fair in Shreveport around 1914. The band played a public relations role as a recruitment tool for prospective students and for many years performed at the state fairs in Shreveport and Donaldsonville. The band was also asked to perform in parades and in gubernatorial inauguration ceremonies. (LSUPC.)

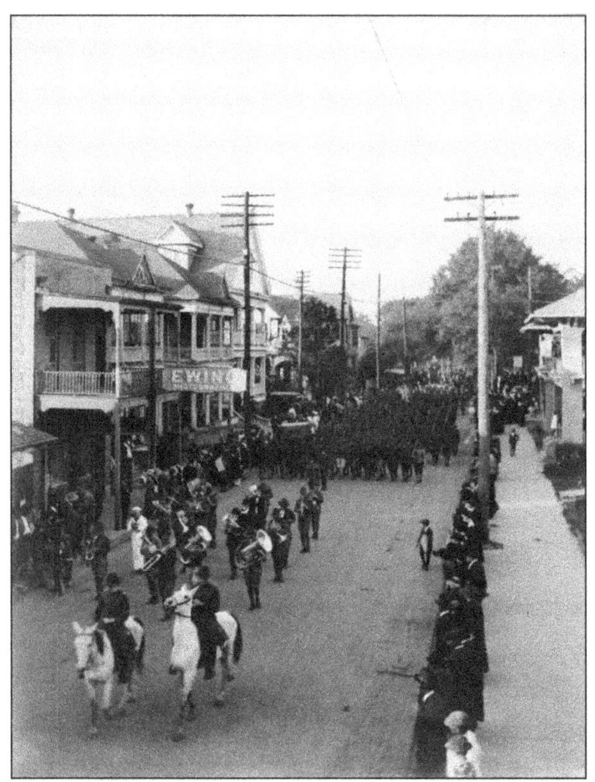

On November 11, 1918, the cadets of the Student Army Training Corps (SATC) paraded down Third Street in celebration of the end of World War I. SATC briefly replaced the Reserve Officers Training Corps on college campuses in order to involve higher education in preparing soldiers for war. LSU's SATC unit was disbanded shortly after the armistice. (LSUPC.)

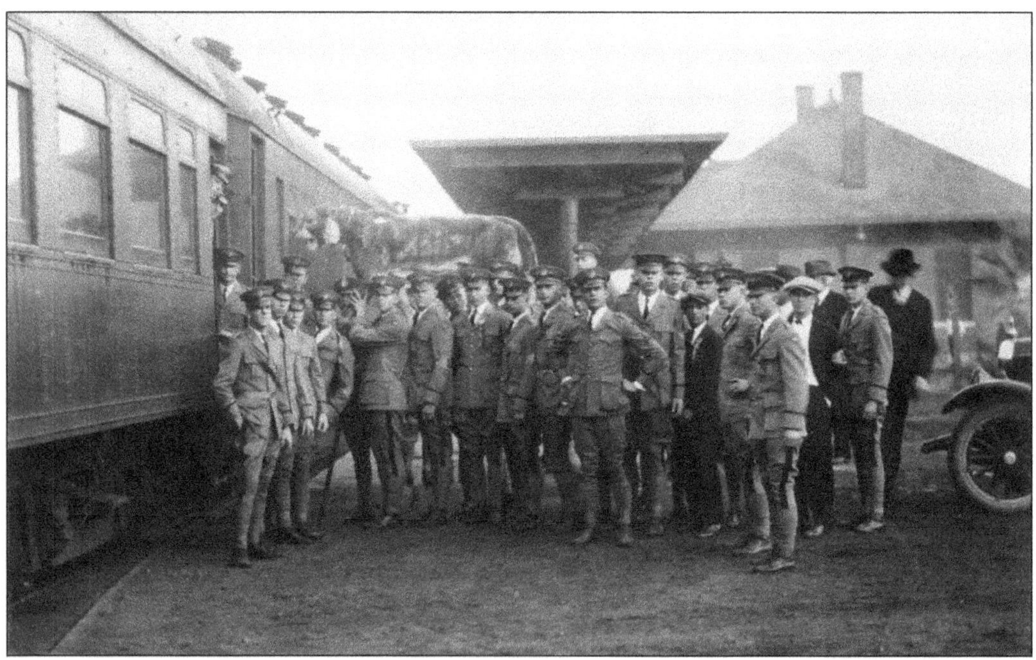

Before the first live tiger mascot arrived, students made papier-mâché tigers, like this one being loaded onto a train in 1923. These cadets are preparing to depart Baton Rouge for an away football game. The papier-mâché tigers were usually placed on the sidelines and did not survive the games. (DMS.)

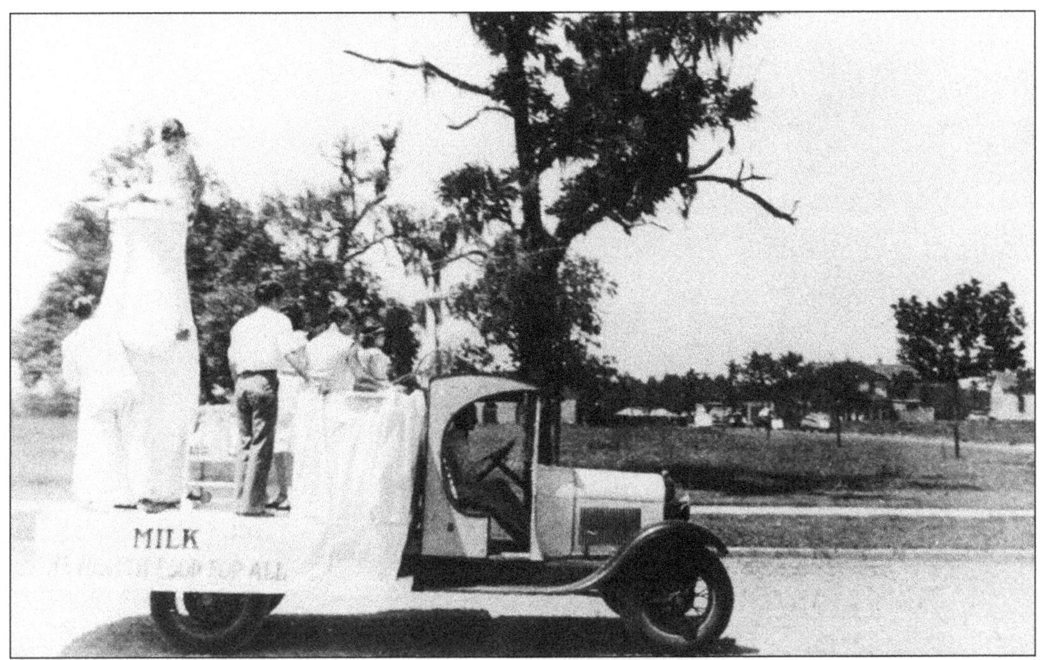

The College of Agriculture held a parade on May 7, 1929, featuring each department in the college and ran from the campus to downtown Baton Rouge. The dairy department's entry won third place. It is not known if the coed sitting atop the milk bottle remained there for the entire route. (Marcelite Segura Mestayer Photograph Collection, Mss. 4365, Louisiana and Lower Mississippi Valley Collections, LSU Libraries, Baton Rouge, Louisiana.)

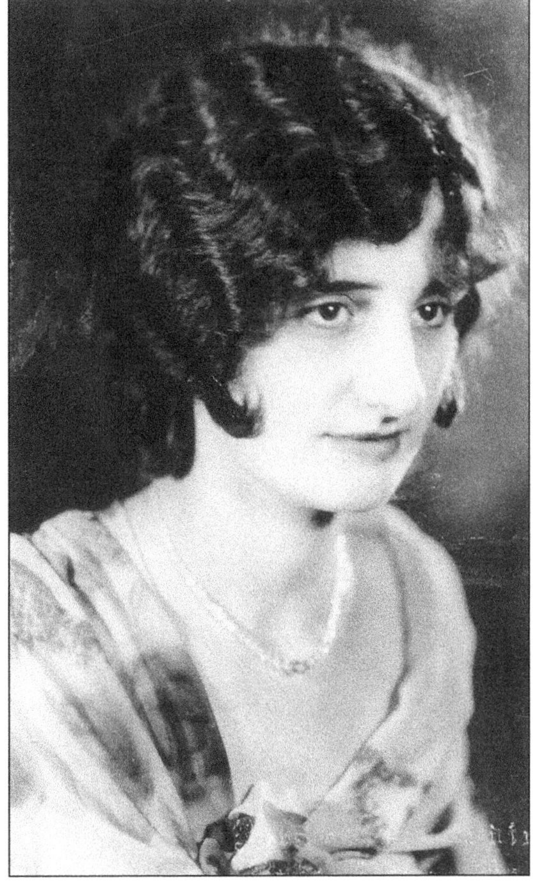

Marcelite Segura, a junior in home economics, was named Goddess of Agriculture and reigned over the parade held by the College of Agriculture on May 7, 1929. She rode in a special float with a throne along with her court. (Marcelite Segura Mestayer Photograph Collection, Mss. 4365, Louisiana and Lower Mississippi Valley Collections, LSU Libraries, Baton Rouge, Louisiana.)

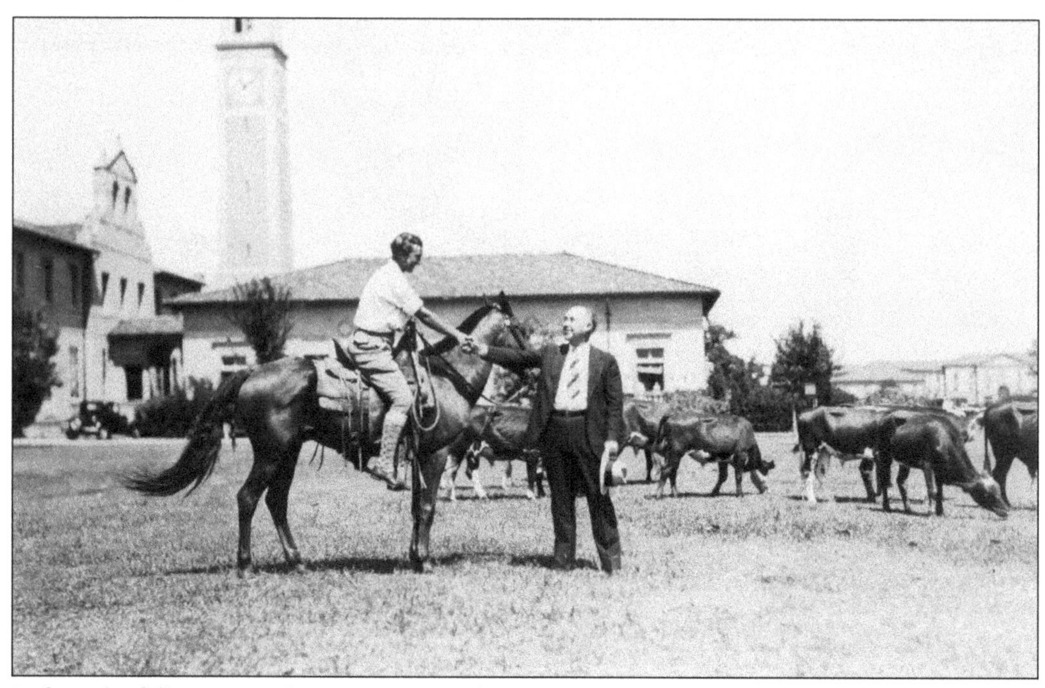

Before the fall semester began in 1932, Elena Carter Percy (on horseback) drove nine head of cattle from her home near St. Francisville to campus to exchange them for her room and board. Pres. James Monroe Smith accepted them with a handshake. (LSUPC.)

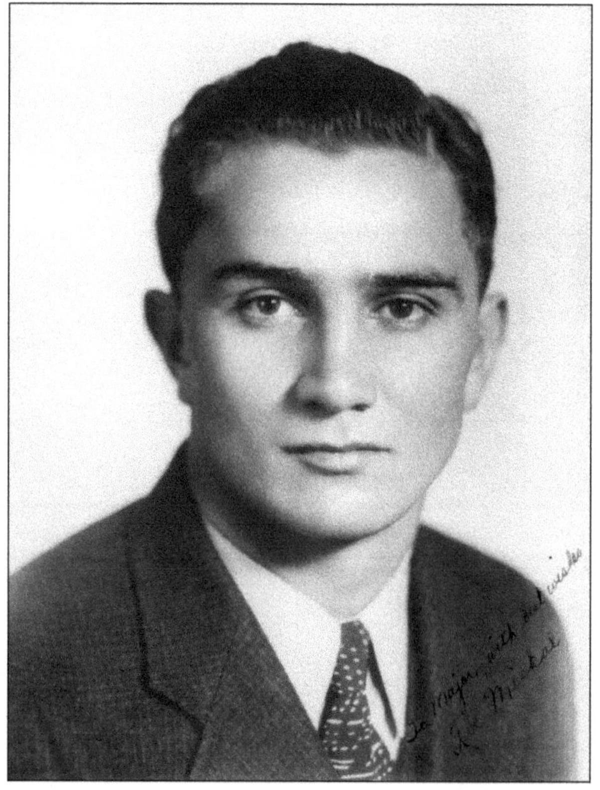

Abe Mickal (1913–2001) was elected president of student government in 1935. Born in Lebanon and raised in McComb, Mississippi, Mickal played football and in 1934 was embroiled in controversy when Huey Long tried to make him a state senator because of his prowess in the field. Long relented after it was pointed out that the per diem given to senators would jeopardize Mickal's amateur status. Mickal received an MD degree in 1940 from the LSU School of Medicine and became its head of obstetrics. (LSUPC.)

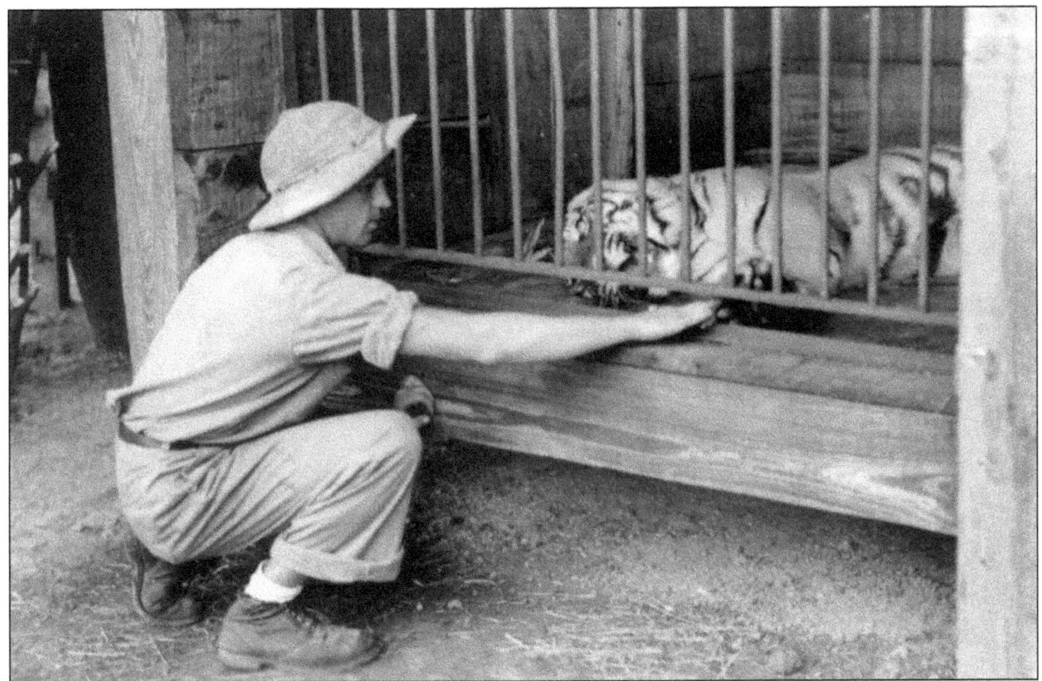

LSU's first live tiger mascot arrived in October 1936. Students ended classes and turned away faculty coming into campus. Named Mike, the tiger was kept at the small zoo in Baton Rouge's City Park until a permanent home could be built for him. Mike was named after athletic trainer Mike Chambers, who helped procure the tiger from the Little Rock, Arkansas, zoo. Mike I lived until 1956. (OPRR.)

Castro Carazo was bandleader for the LSU Cadet Band during its expansion in the 1930s. Formed in 1935, the Dancing Tigerettes integrated precision dance routines with traditional cheerleading. Two of the Tigerettes are seen here with Carazo and a drum major. (OPRR.)

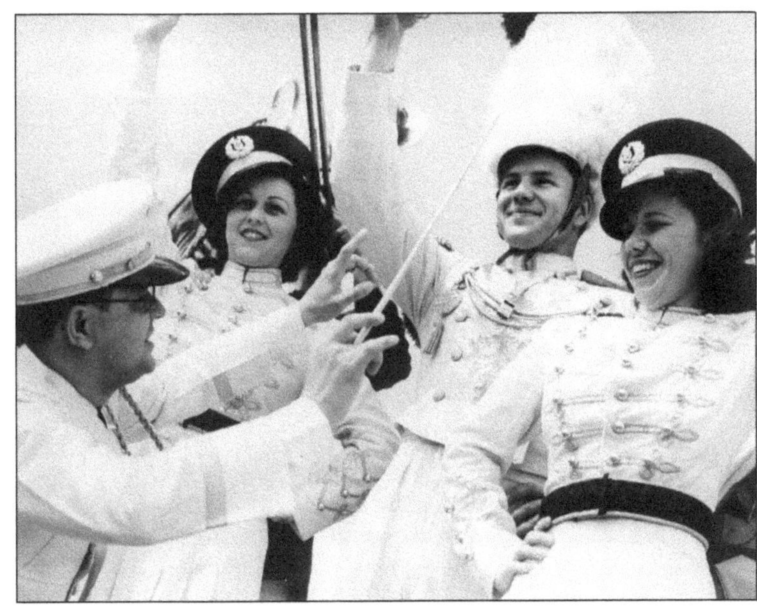

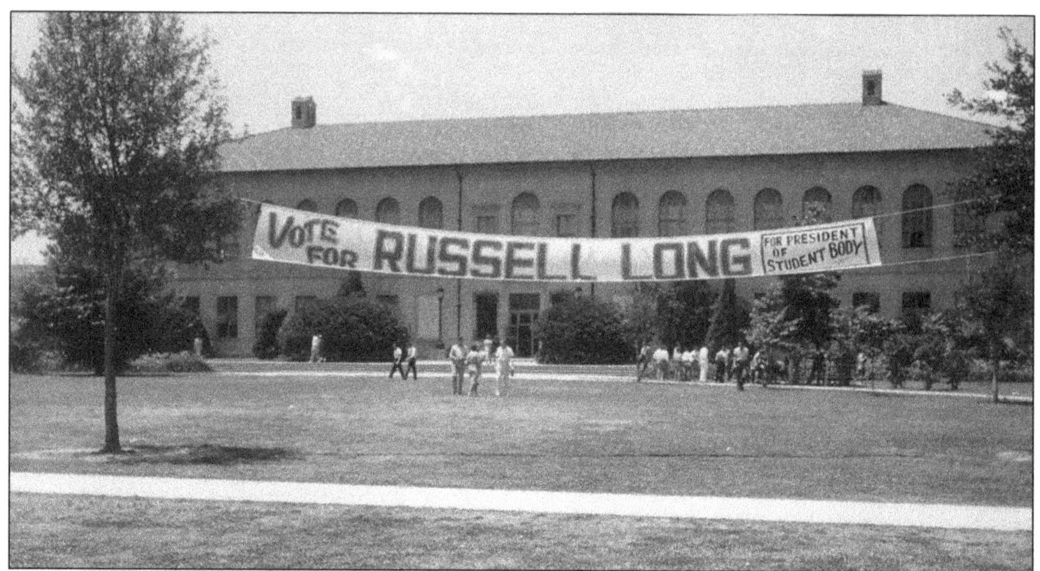

Russell Long's campaign for Student Government president in 1938 was one of the more elaborate, featuring large banners, parades, and bands. Seen here are students voting in front of Hill Memorial Library on election day. (RBL.)

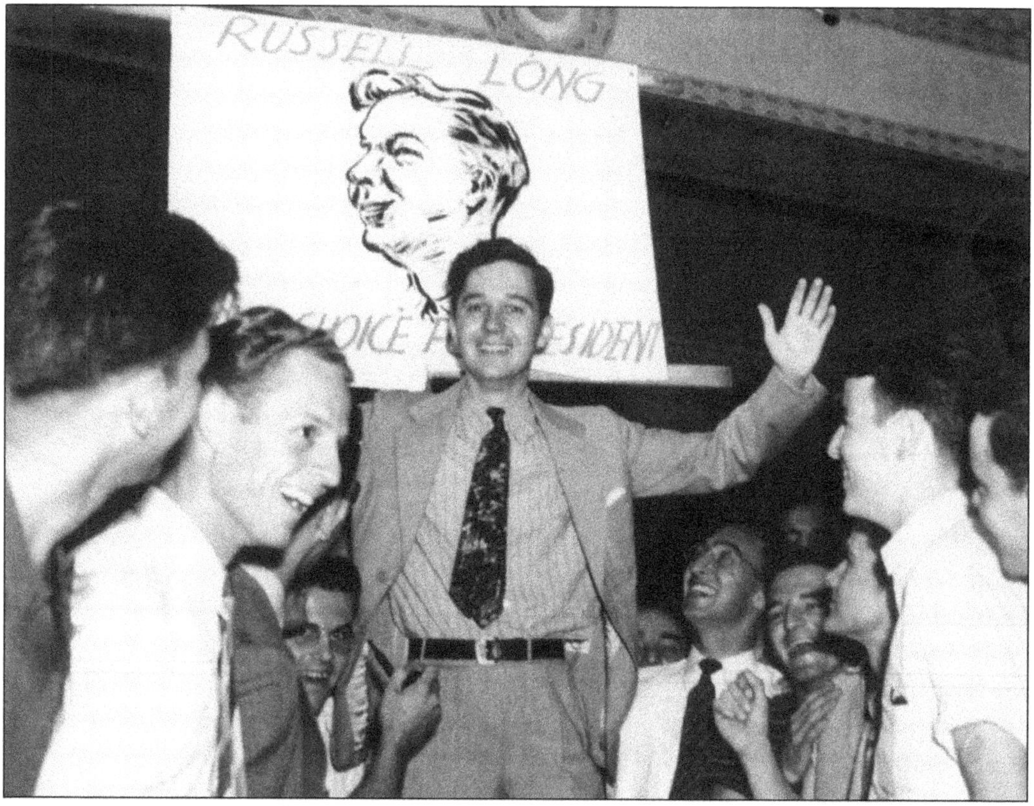

Long (1918–2003), son of Huey Long, was a member of Delta Kappa Epsilon and graduated from the LSU Law School in 1942. During World War II, he served in the Naval Reserve. He was elected to the US Senate in 1948 and served until 1987. (RBL.)

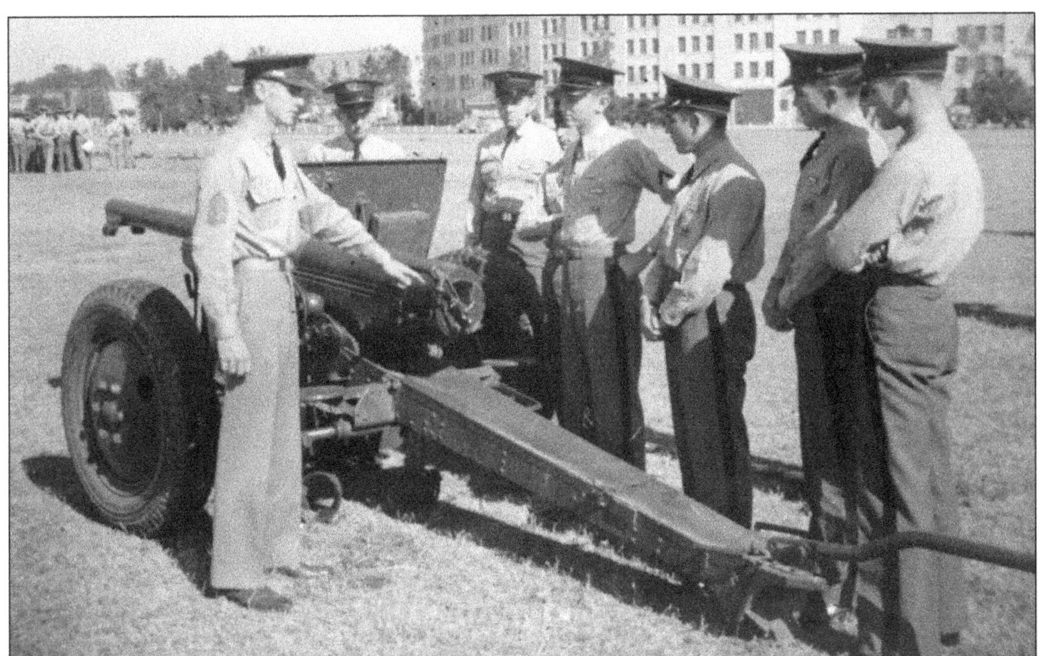

ROTC cadets are seen here, around 1938, learning about the M1897 75mm cannon. These "French 75s" replaced the Civil War–era cast iron muzzleloaders that cadets had drilled with since the 1880s. Cadets also learned to use .30 caliber machine guns and were responsible for maintaining all the equipment. (LSUPC.)

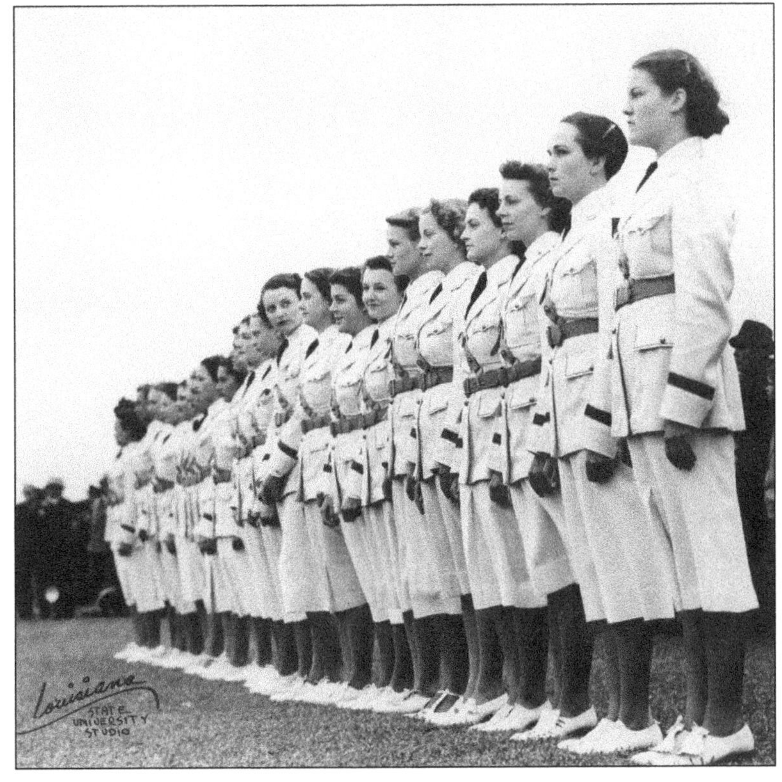

Each company of cadets chose a sponsor who served as a mascot for the company. These were the sponsors for 1937–1938. Company sponsors ended in the early 1960s in favor of Scotch Guard (Army) and Angel Flight (Air Force), both of which are women's auxiliaries for their respective branches of the service. (DMS.)

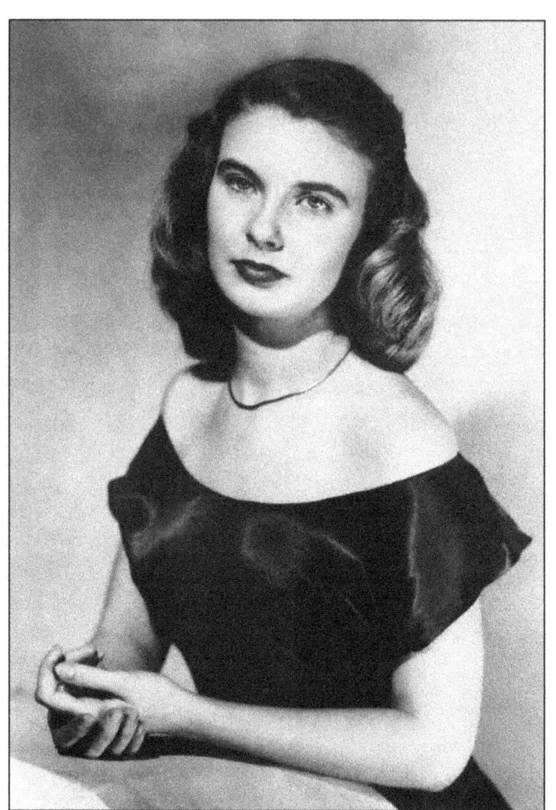

Oscar-winning actress Joanne Woodward studied drama at LSU from 1947 to 1949 and was elected Darling of LSU in 1949. The contest for Darling of LSU was held from 1936 to 1973 and was essentially a beauty contest sponsored by the *Gumbo* editorial staff. The runners-up were named Gumbo Beauties. (*Gumbo* 1949.)

Until 1969, LSU students had to adhere to a strict dress code. Women had to wear skirts or dresses, men had to wear slacks or jeans. Neither men nor women were allowed to wear shorts unless they were playing a sport. This photograph from the early 1960s shows a lower-level class in Dodson Auditorium. The student in front wearing the LSU cap is a freshman; all freshmen males were required to wear the "beanie." (OPRR.)

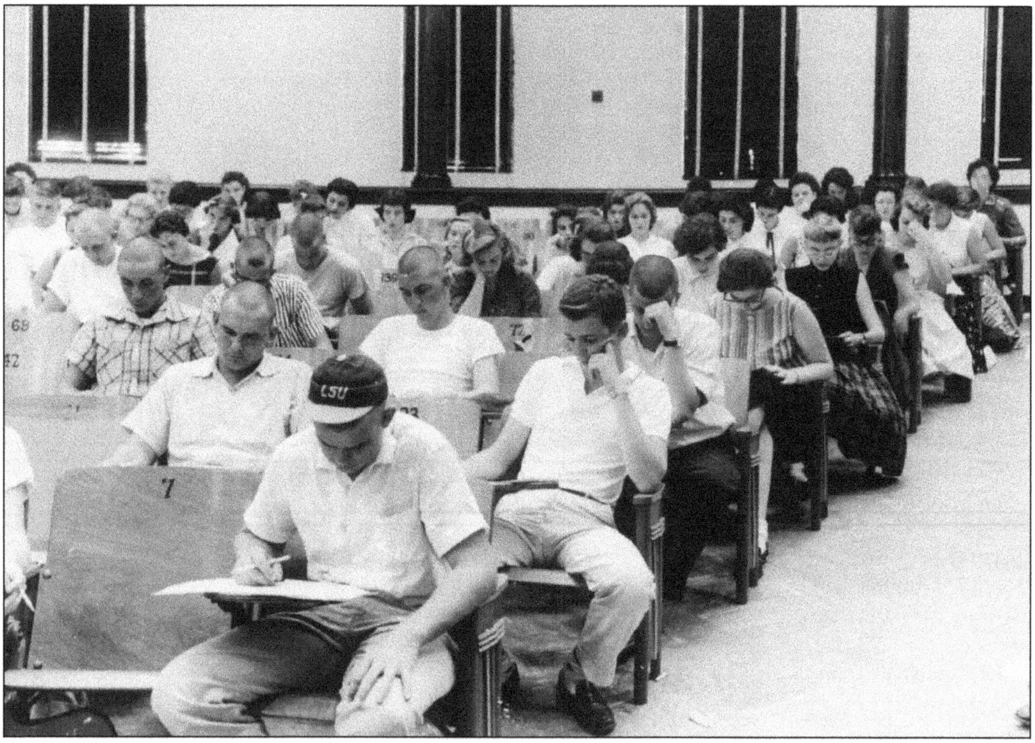

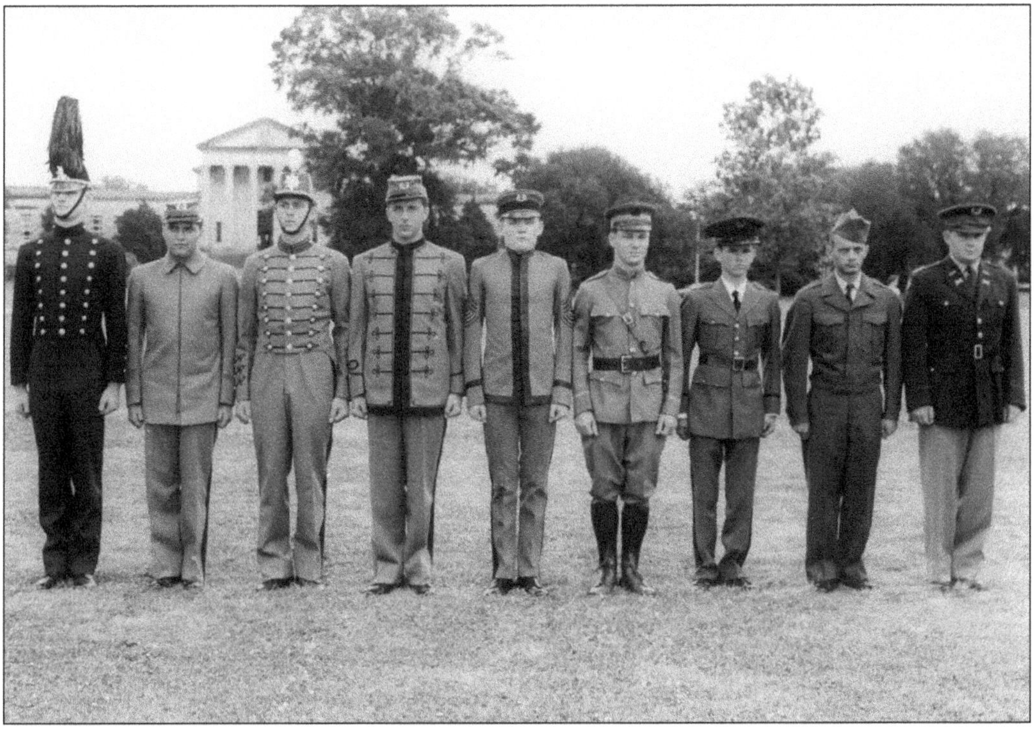

During LSU's centennial year from September 1959 to April 1960, one of the events was a military review featuring cadet uniforms from 1860 to 1953. Seen here on the Parade Ground, these cadets are modeling, from left to right, the uniforms for 1860–1863, 1869–1894, prize company uniform for 1886–1887, 1894–1919 (fourth and fifth from left), 1919–1929, 1929–1941, 1946–1947, and 1948–1953. (LSUCR.)

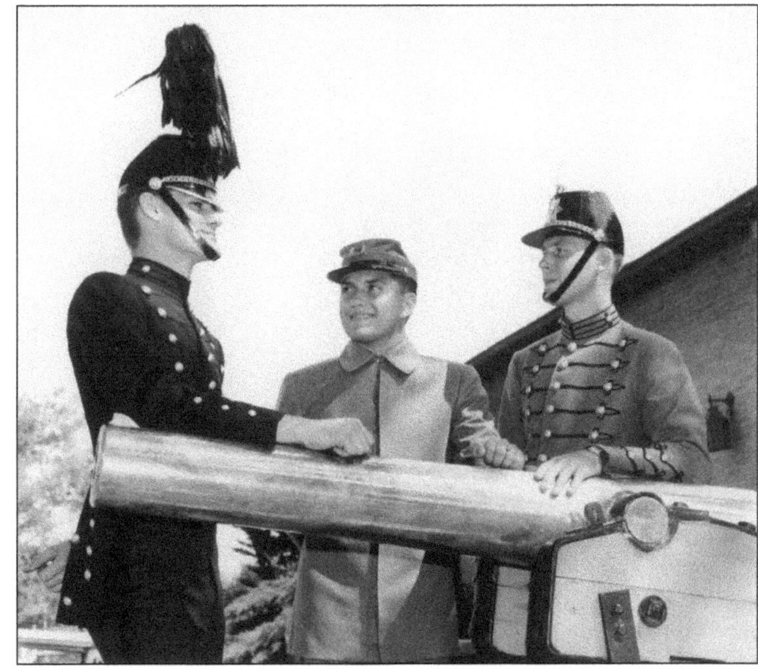

Another photograph from the military review shows cadets wearing uniforms for the 1860–1863 and 1869–1894 periods, and the prize company uniform. Also seen is one of the bronze James rifles in front of the military science building. Legend says that these field artillery pieces from the Civil War period were captured at Fort Sumter, but they were actually surplus that had fallen out of favor with the Army midway through the war. (LSUCR.)

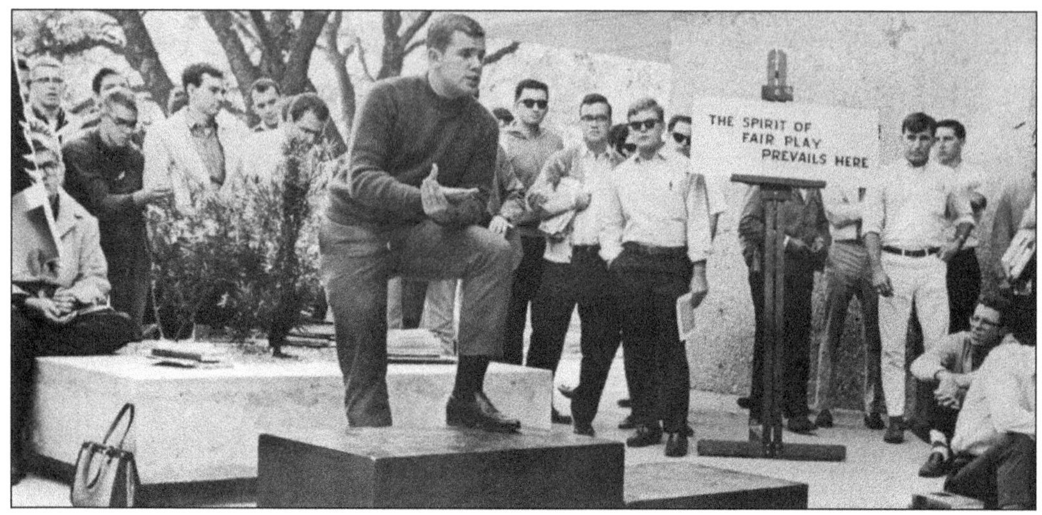

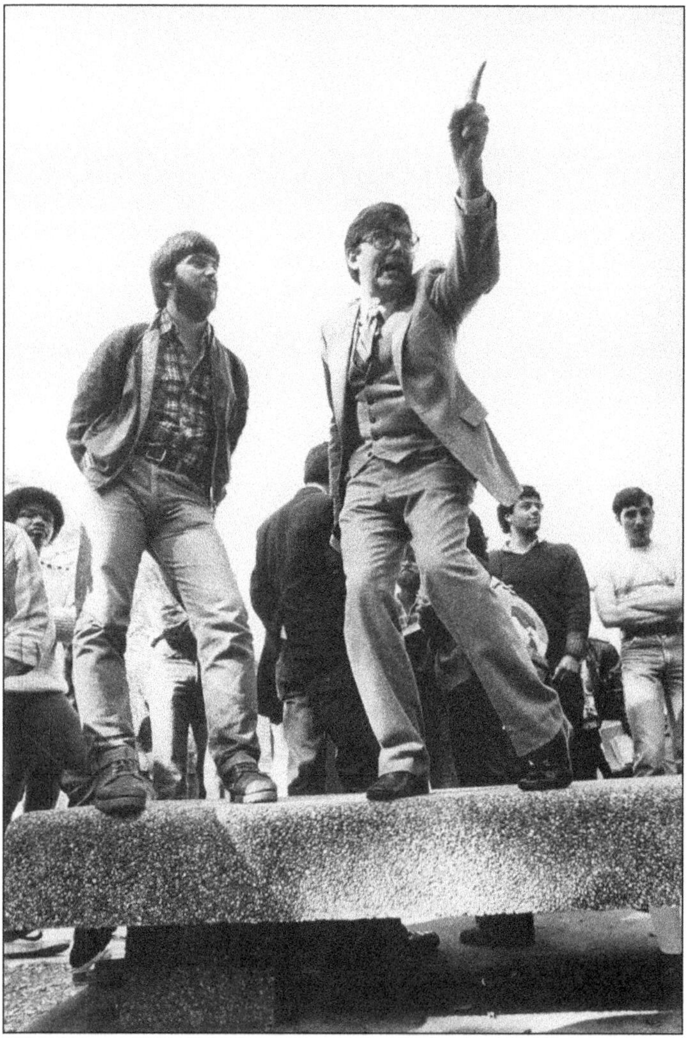

Free Speech Alley began in 1964 as a student forum to discuss topics of interest. It was first held in the Memorial Oak Grove behind the LSU Union, then moved to the area between the LSU Union and Union Theater where this 1966 photograph was taken, then to the front steps of the Union. It is now held on the walkway in front of the Union. (*Gumbo* 1966.)

Brother Jed Smock, seen here in 1983, proselytizes at Free Speech Alley. Smock traditionally arrived on campus in time for Spring Break to warn students about drinking, fornication, and the wages of sin in general. By the mid-1970s, religion became one of the more popular topics of discussion. (*Gumbo* 1983.)

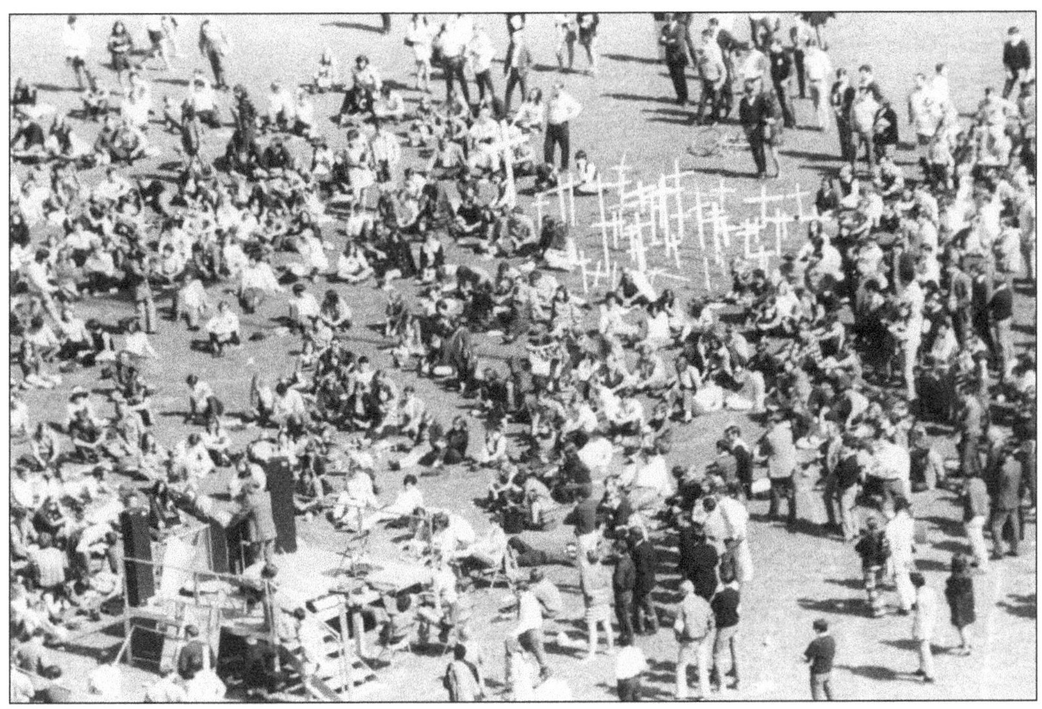

The largest anti–Vietnam War rally and march ever held on campus took place on May 8, 1970. The catalysts for the rally were the shootings at Kent State University and the bombing of Cambodia. Beginning on the Parade Ground, hundreds of students marched from campus to the state capitol, where another rally took place while the legislature was in session. Included were vehicles carrying water and medical supplies. (JFP.)

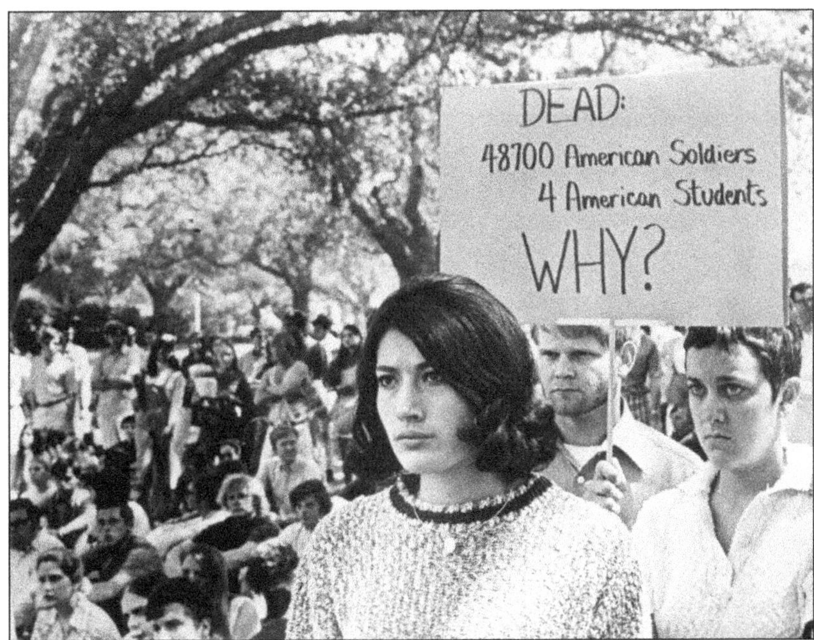

Luana Perea is seen here at the rally on the Parade Ground. Before the Kent State shootings and the bombing of Cambodia, students at LSU were generally in favor of the war in Vietnam. After 1969, as the war escalated, more students began to speak out against it. (JFP.)

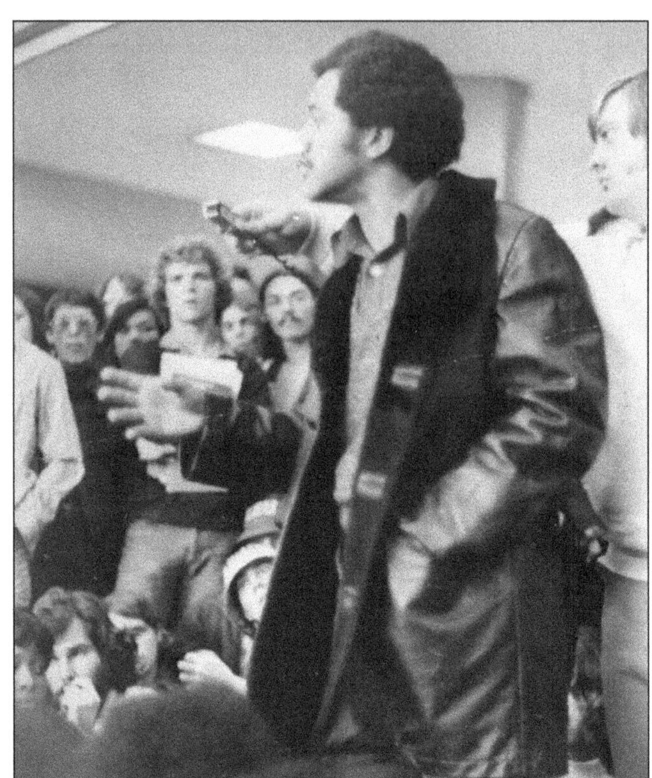

Kerry Pourciau (1951–1994) was elected LSU's first African American student government president in 1972. LSU's student body and administration had always been fairly conservative and that was one of the issues Pourciau tried to remedy during his term as president. He was also involved with Harambé, an African American student group that asked for increased efforts in recruiting black students and faculty, and advocated for a Black Studies Program. (*Gumbo* 1973.)

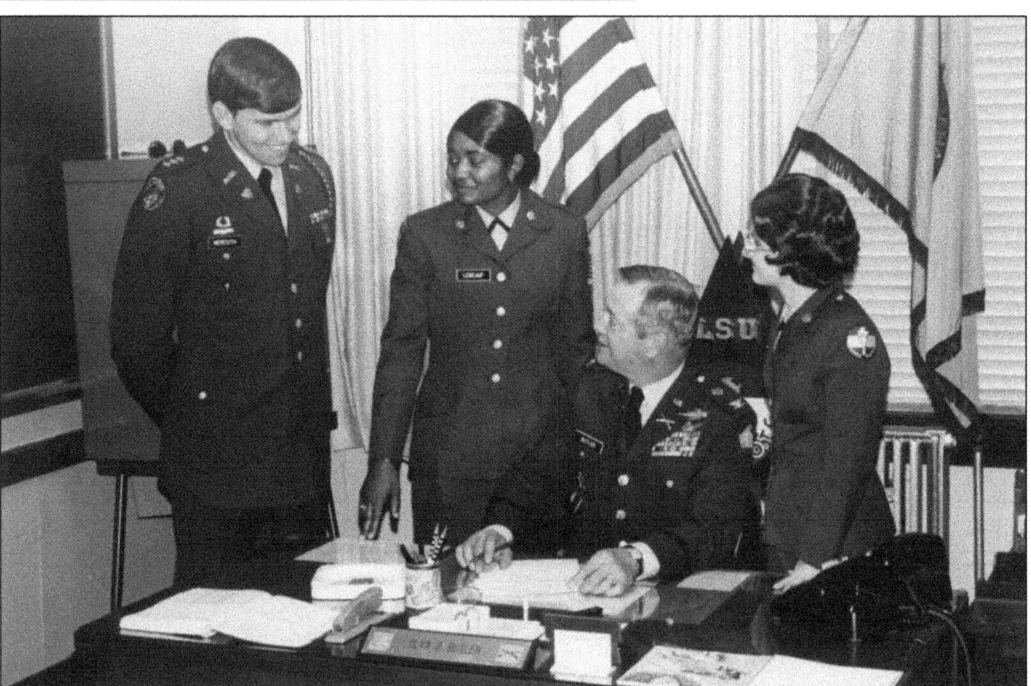

Women were first allowed to take military science classes in 1969, but could not become ROTC cadets until 1972. Mandatory ROTC ended for male freshmen and sophomores in 1969 and the Corps of Cadets became an all-volunteer unit. (OPRR.)

Four

Athletics

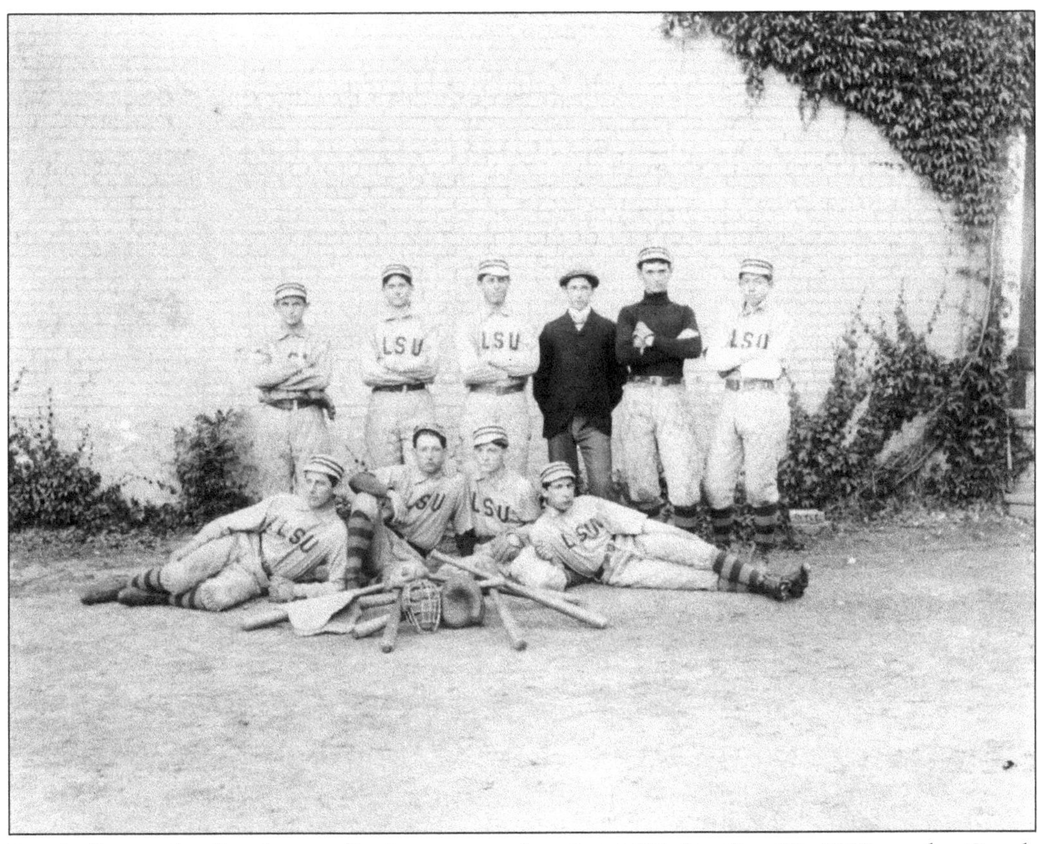

Baseball was the first intercollegiate sport played at LSU. On May 13, 1893, under Coach E.B. Young, the team defeated Tulane in the only game played that year. The baseball team was the first to wear the purple and gold that would become LSU's official colors. The 1900 team seen here had a 2–3 record under Coach L.P. Piper. (LSUPC.)

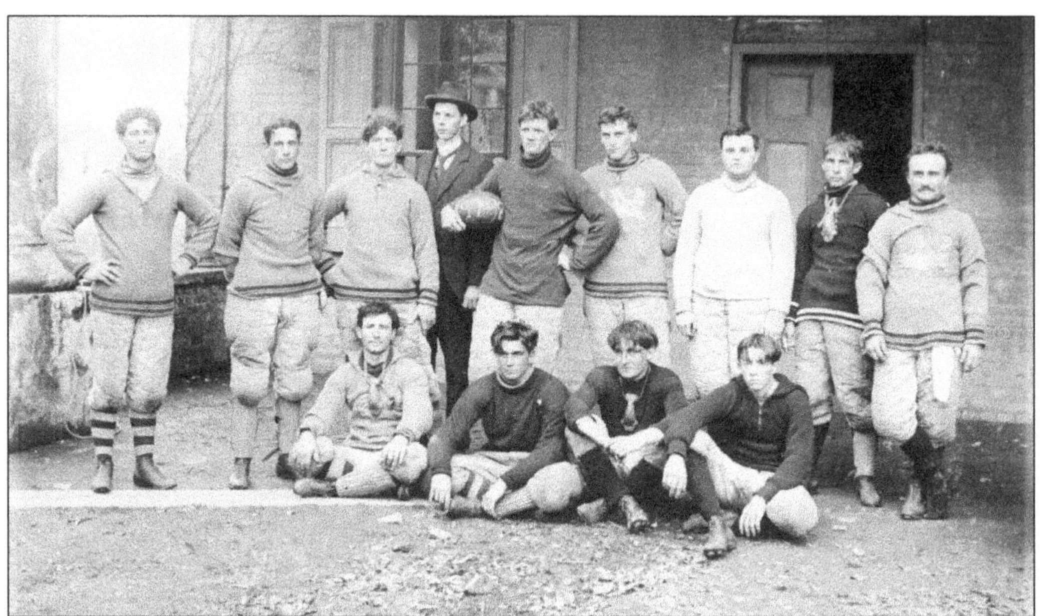

LSU's first football game was against Tulane on November 25, 1893. Chemistry professor Charles Coates was the first coach and had played football as a student at Johns Hopkins. LSU lost 34–0 against the more experienced Tulane team. The 1897–1898 Tigers, seen here, played only a two-game season due to a major yellow fever outbreak throughout the South. They played one game each in 1897 and 1898 and ended with a 1–1 record. Coach Allen Jeardeau is in the back wearing a suit. Standing third from right is center Leopold Kaffie and at far right is end John T. Westbrook. (LSUPC.)

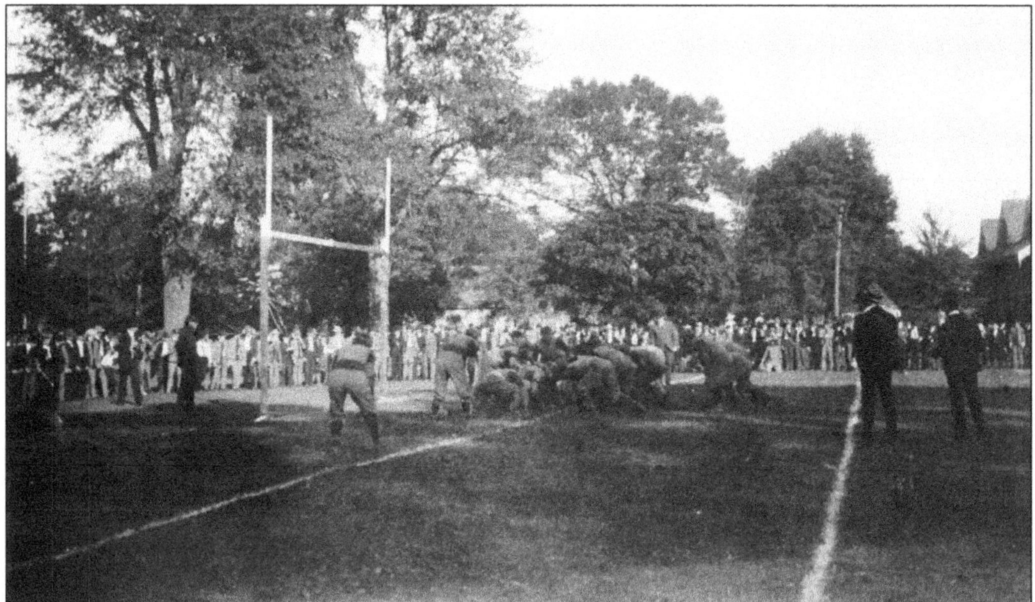

LSU defeated Auburn 5–0 in their 1902 meeting and finished the season with a 6–1 record. The game was played on the athletic field in Baton Rouge, south of the Pentagon Barracks. The goal posts appear to be homemade, and there seems to have been no crowd control. (LSUPC.)

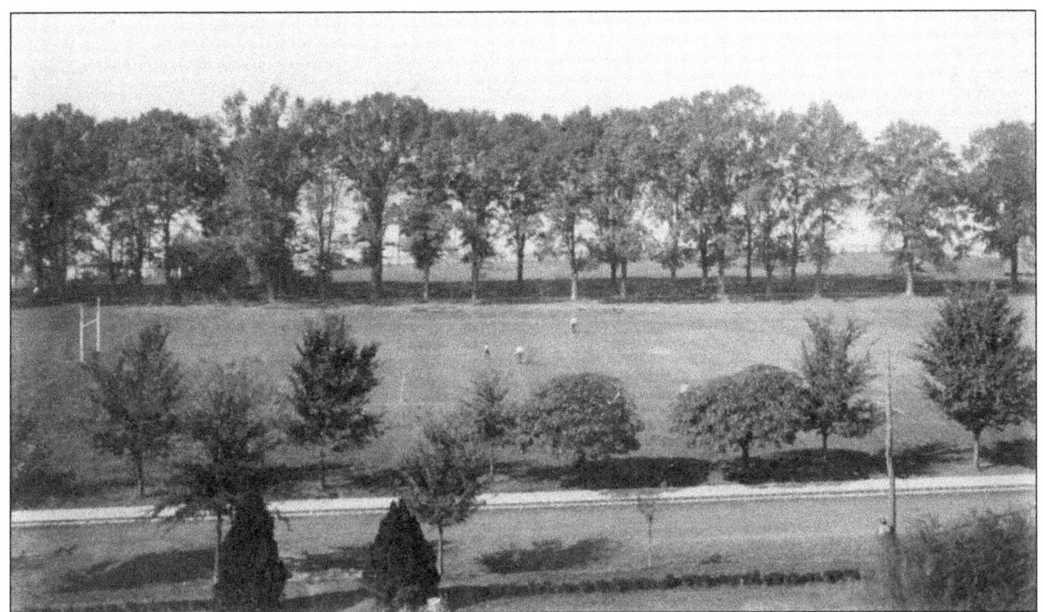

The athletic field on the downtown campus was located immediately south of the Pentagon Barracks. Lafayette Street can be seen at the bottom. Football games were later played on a field with bleachers located north of the experimental garden. (LSUPC.)

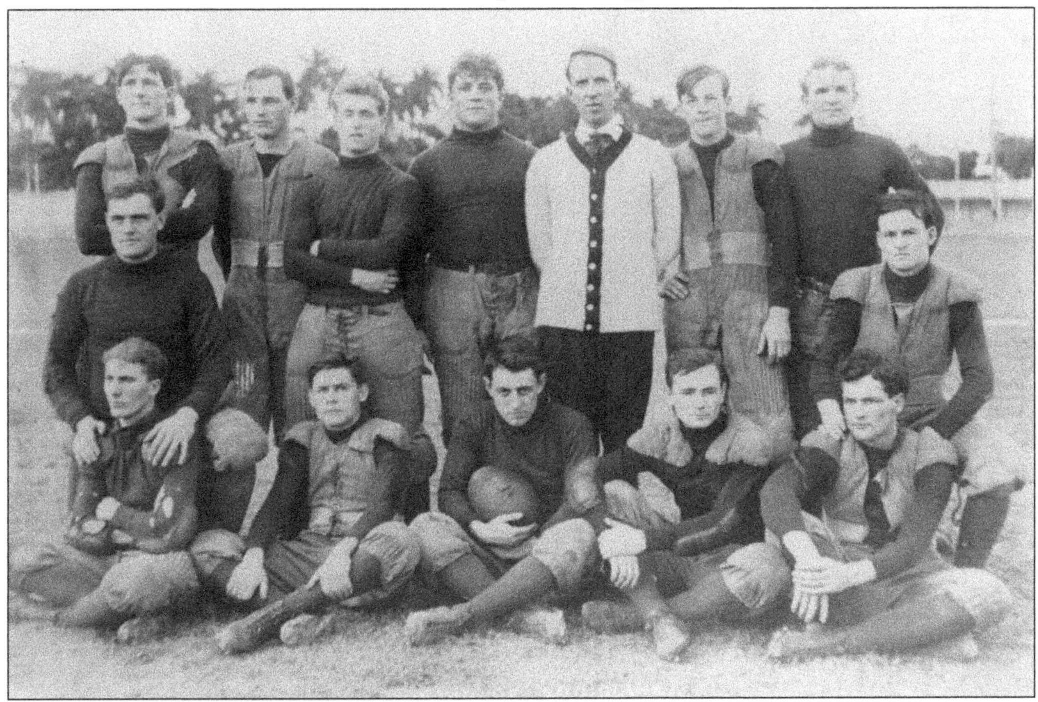

The 1907 Tigers played the first football game on foreign soil against the University of Havana on Christmas Day. The smaller but faster LSU team won 56–0. It was reported that the largest men in Cuba were recruited to play for the University of Havana and that they were fortified with wine (or rum) on the sideline. Coach Edgar Wingard (wearing cardigan) had bet on the Tigers to win and stayed in Havana for a few days to enjoy his winnings. (LSUPC.)

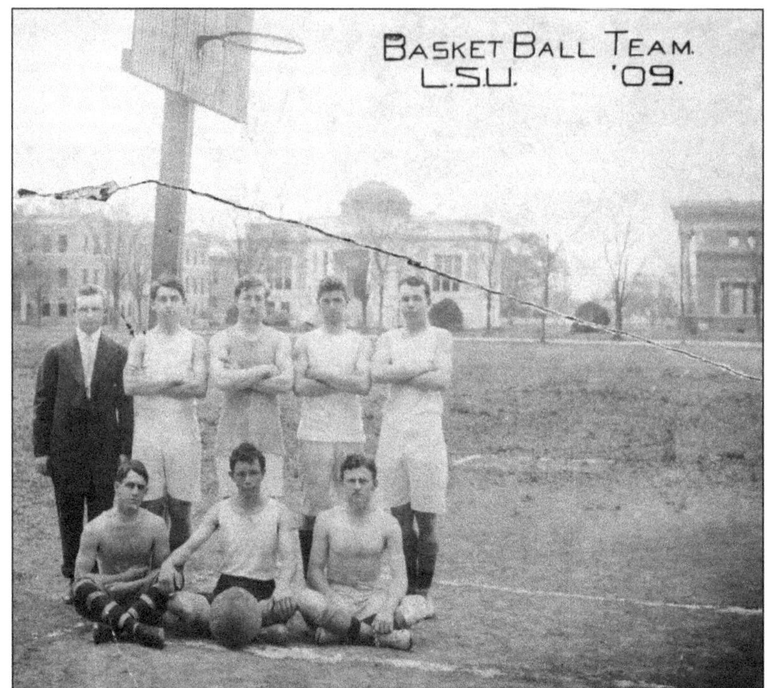

LSU played its first basketball game in 1909 against Dixon Academy, a prep school in Covington, Louisiana. The Tigers won 35–20 led by Edgar Wingard, who also coached the football and baseball teams, and ended the season with a 5–2 record. (LSUPC.)

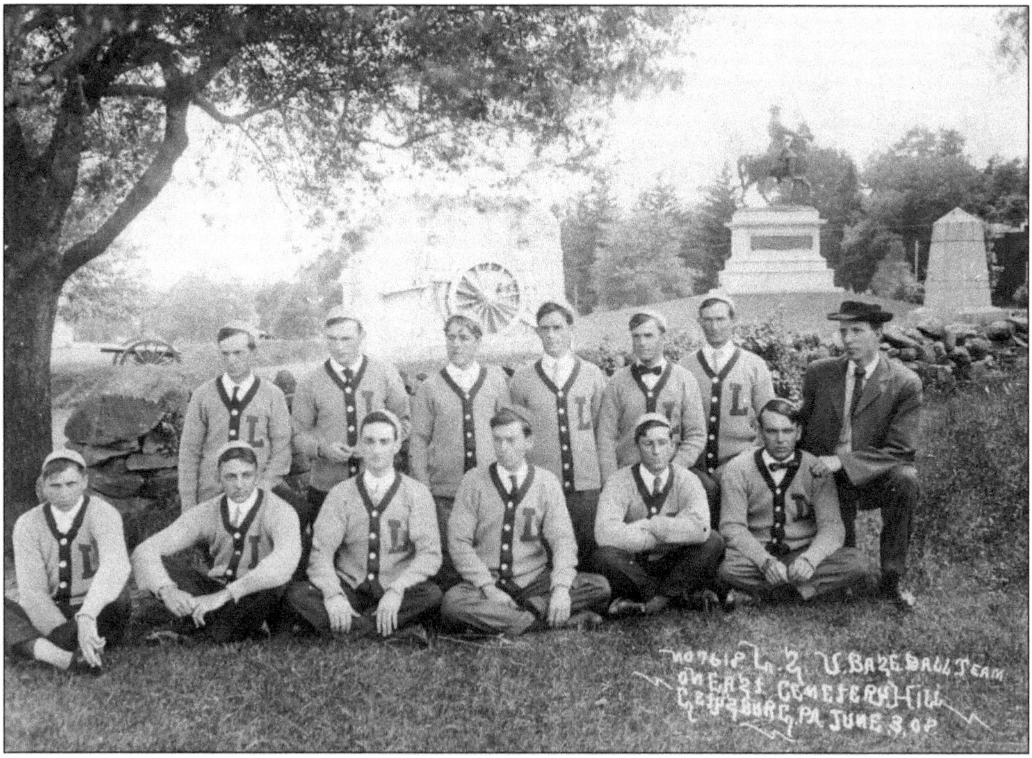

Under Coach Edgar Wingard (right, wearing suit), the Tiger baseball team had a 9–12 record during the 1908 season. It is not known why the baseball team is at the Gettysburg battlefield. (LSUPC.)

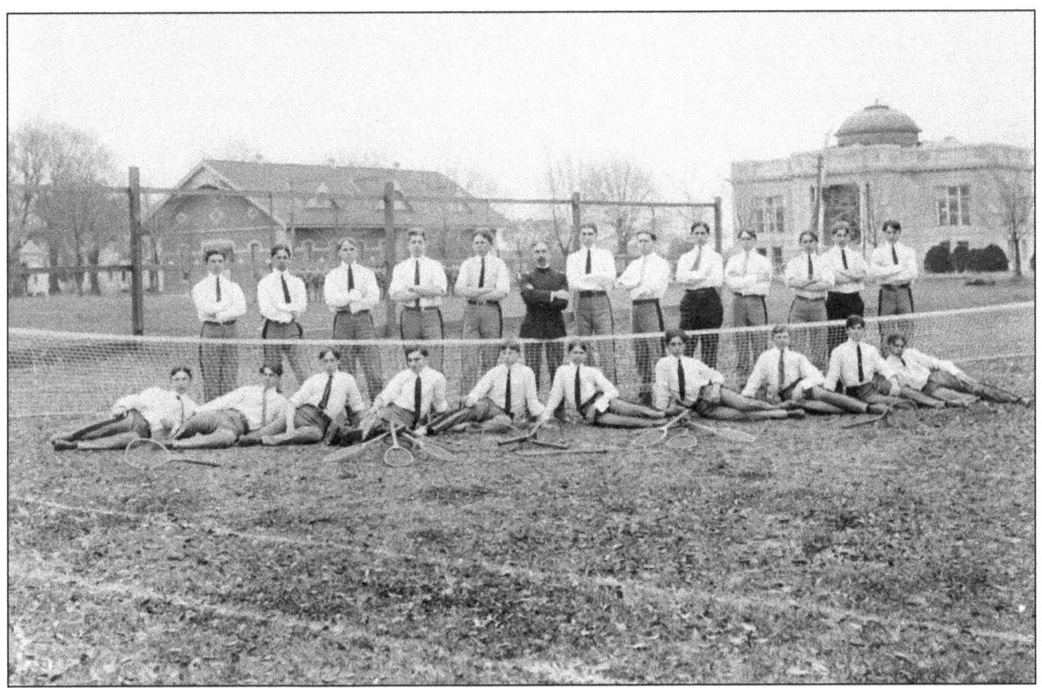

The tennis club is seen here around 1903 on the athletic field south of the Pentagon Barracks. At this time, tennis was an intramural sport; LSU would not play its first intercollegiate game until 1925. Garig Hall and Hill Memorial Library are in the background. (LSUPC.)

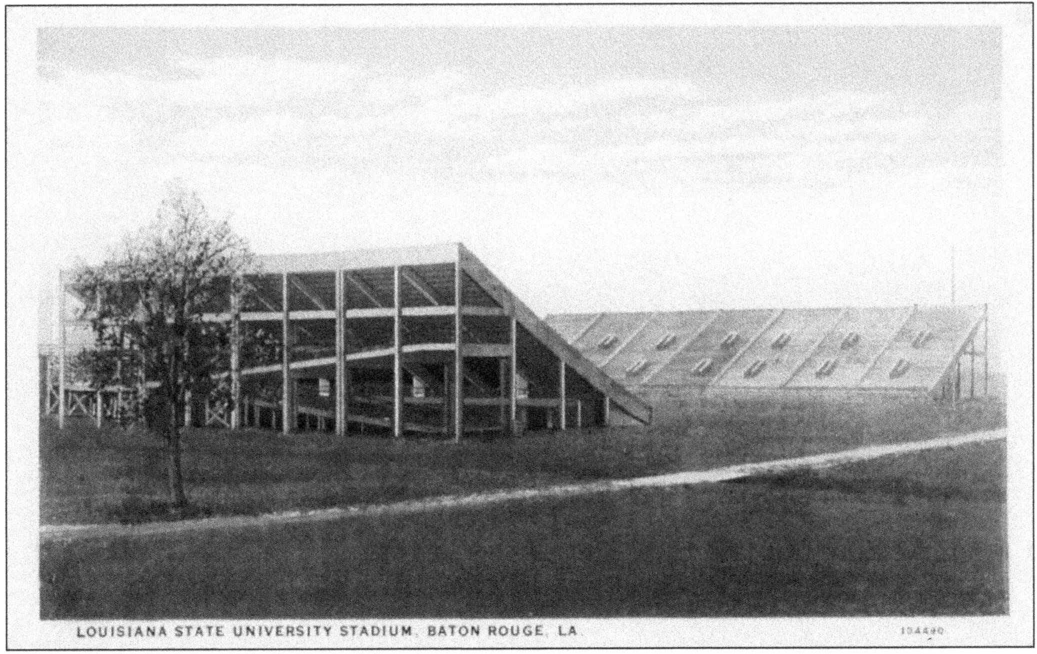

This postcard from around 1925 shows the newly constructed Tiger Stadium. The first game, played on Thanksgiving Day 1924 against long-time rival Tulane, resulted in a 13–0 loss for the Tigers. A crowd of 18,000, the largest in Louisiana football history at that time, saw the game, even though the stadium was still under construction. (LSUPC.)

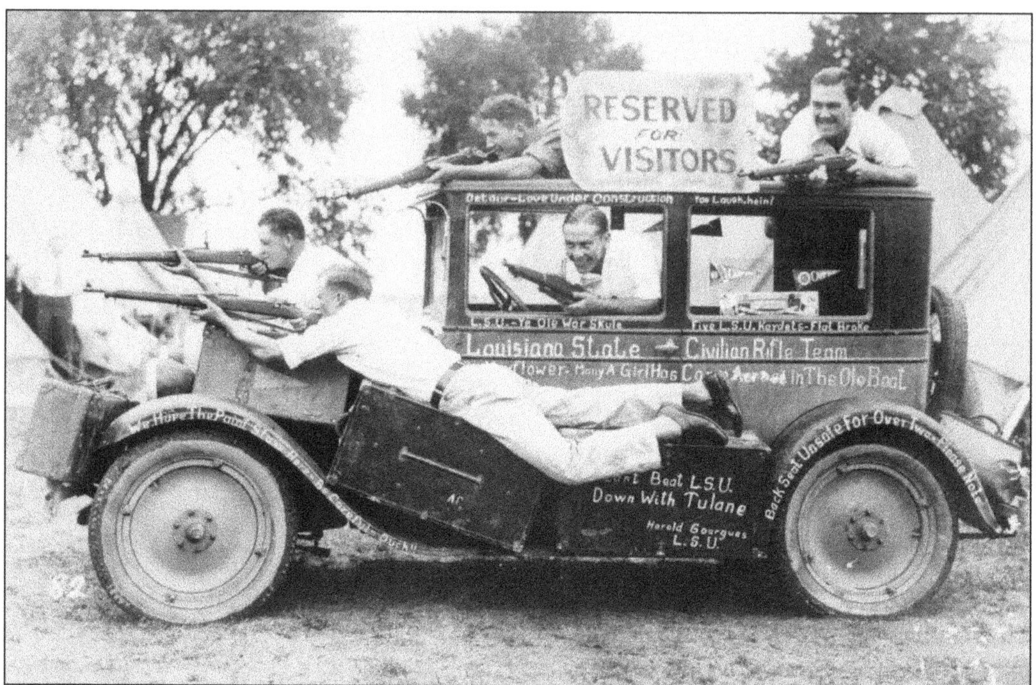

In 1930, LSU's civilian rifle team helped win the Soldier of Marathon Trophy for the 4th Corps Area ROTC at the national match in Camp Perry, Ohio. The team shot from sitting and standing positions at targets from 200 to 1,000 yards. (LSUPC.)

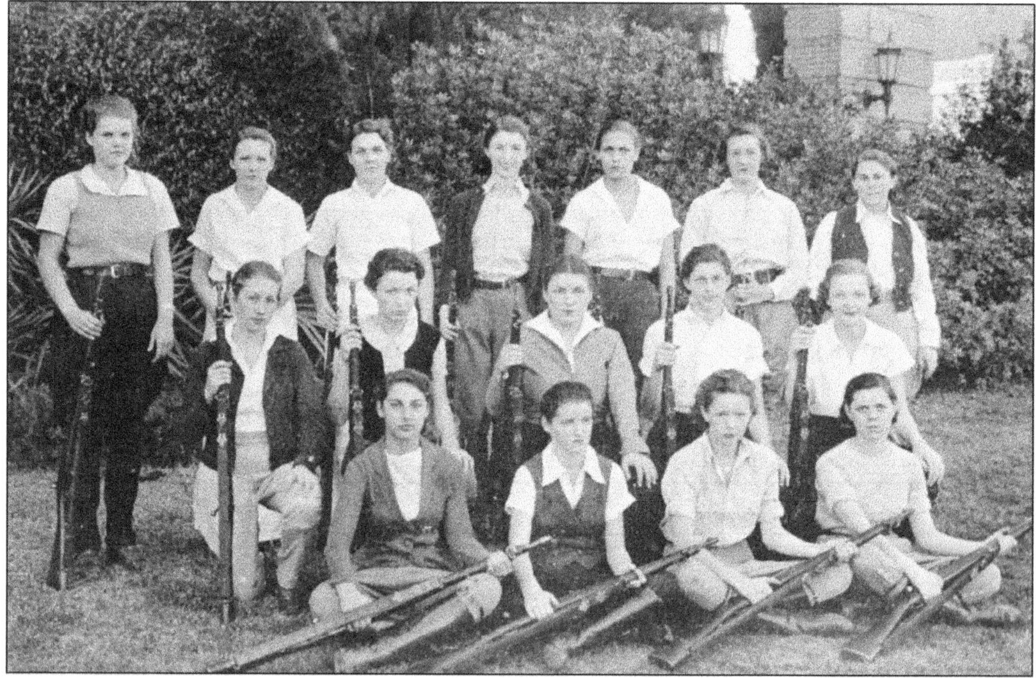

Although considered an intramural team, the 1935 women's rifle team shot in matches against other schools. Both the men's and women's teams were coached by ROTC instructors. (LSUPC.)

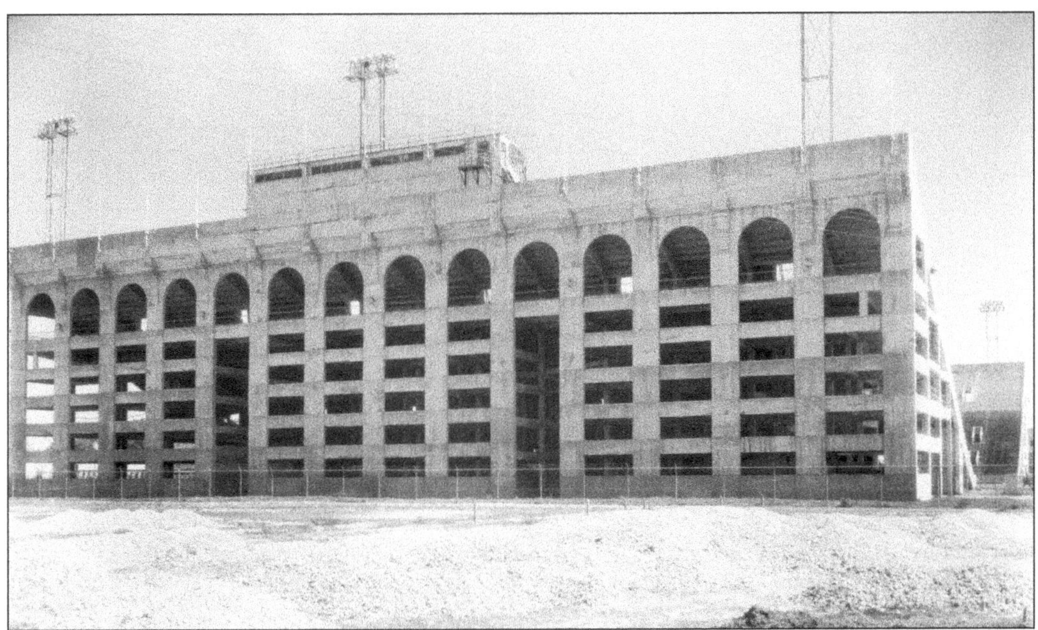

This 1934 photograph of Tiger Stadium, taken by Jasper Ewing, shows the west stadium dormitory rooms and the press box under construction. The east stadium had 75 rooms while the west had 157. Lights were added in 1931. (JES.)

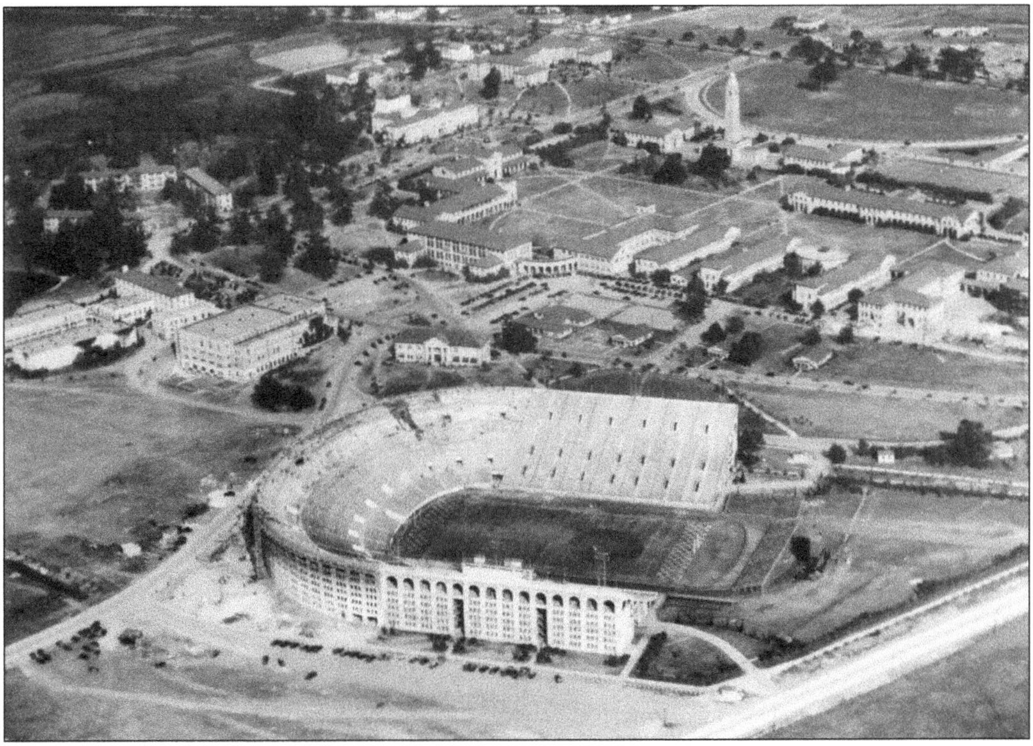

Tiger Stadium's north end zone was enclosed in 1936, bringing the seating capacity to 46,000. The first game played in the expanded stadium was the annual Thanksgiving Day contest with Tulane. LSU won 33–0. (LSUPC.)

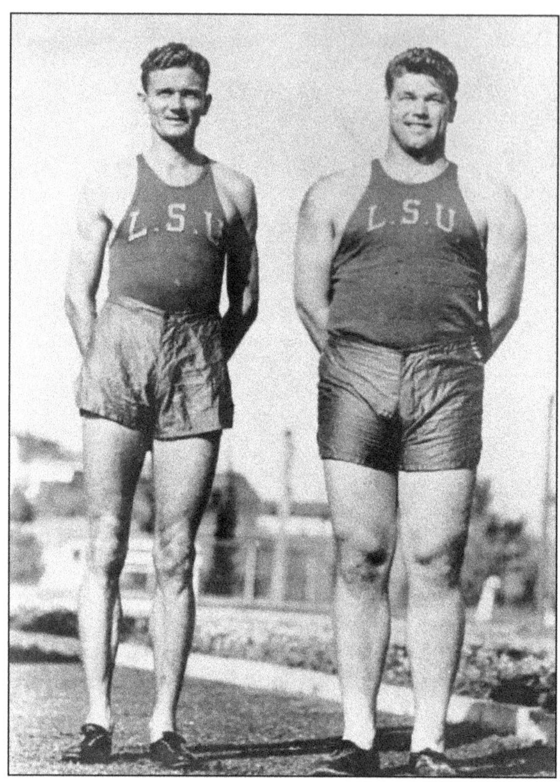

Glenn "Slats" Hardin (1910–1975), left, and "Baby" Jack Torrance (1912–1969), right, were two of the stars of the 1933 NCAA champion track and field team. Hardin won the 400-meter hurdles and was dominant in that event throughout the 1930s. He set a world record that stood from 1934 to 1953. Torrance won the shot put and held the NCAA record in that event from 1934 to 1948. Both competed in the 1932 and 1936 Olympics; Hardin won the gold medal in 1936. Torrance also played guard, tackle, and center on the football team. (*Gumbo* 1935.)

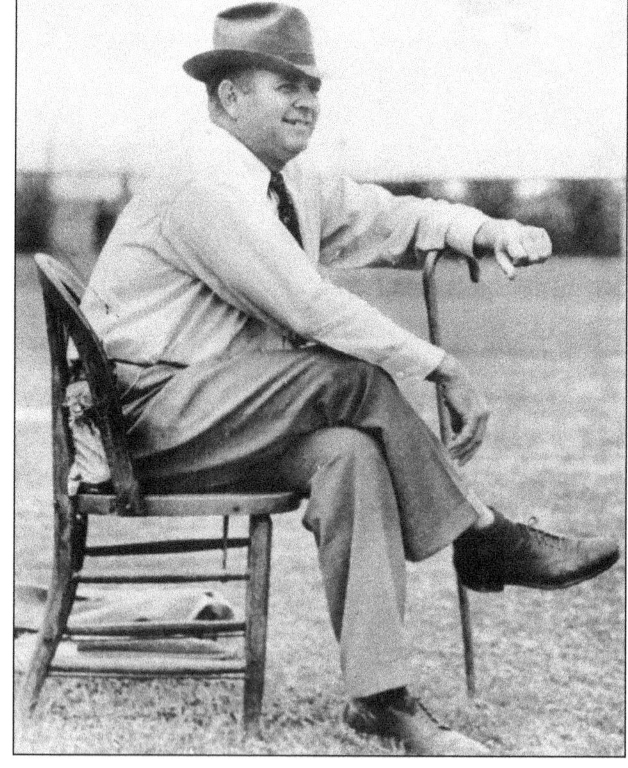

Bernie Moore (1895–1967) was the track and field coach from 1930 to 1947 and head football coach from 1935–1947. His track and field teams won 12 Southeastern Conference championships and the national championship in 1933. As football coach, he compiled an 83–39–6 record and won the Southeastern Conference Championship in 1935 and 1936. (LSUPC.)

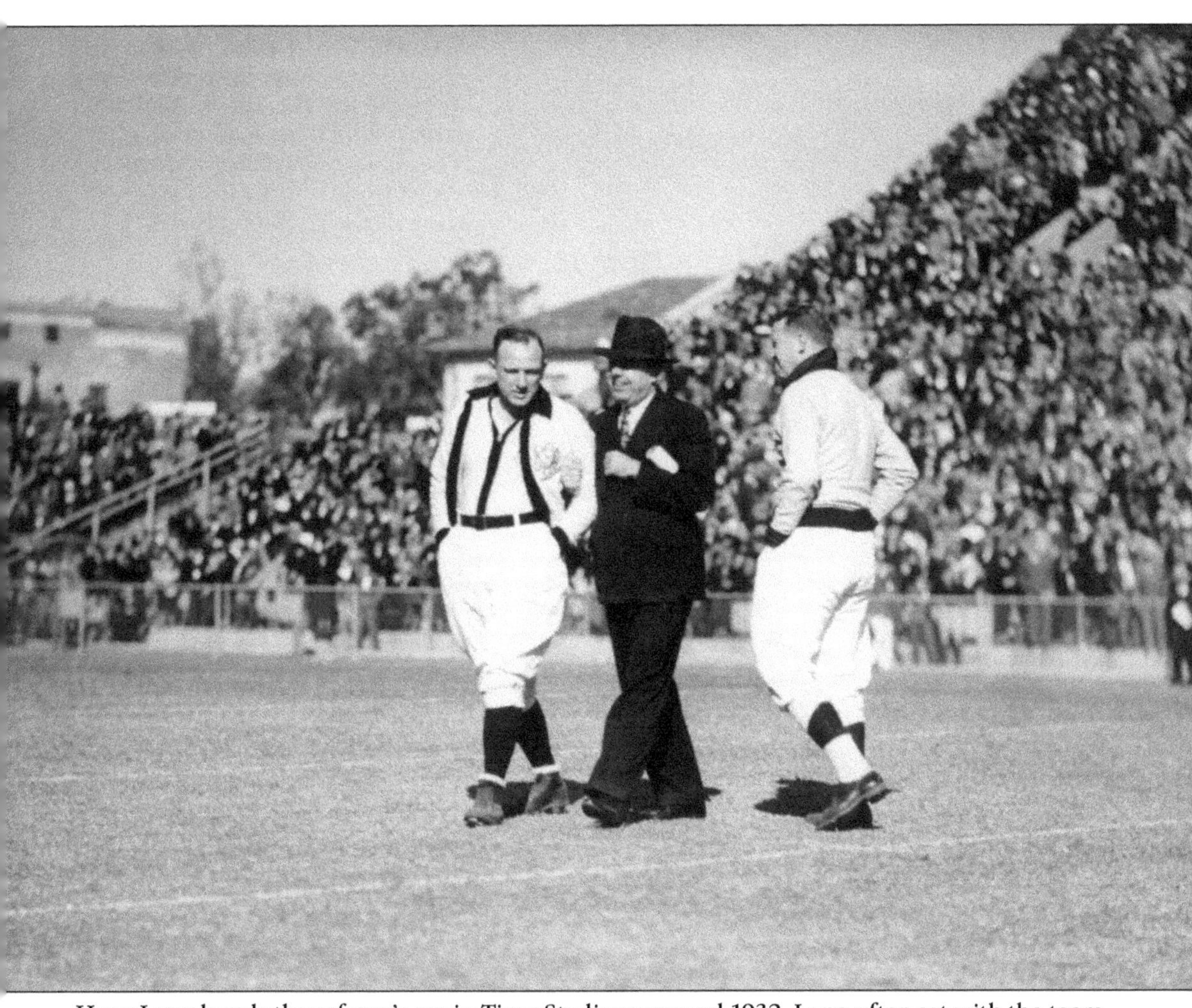

Huey Long bends the referee's ear in Tiger Stadium around 1932. Long often sat with the team on the sidelines, gave pep talks, and disputed the referees' calls. (Huey P. Long Photograph Album, LOUISiana Digital Library, Baton Rouge, Louisiana.)

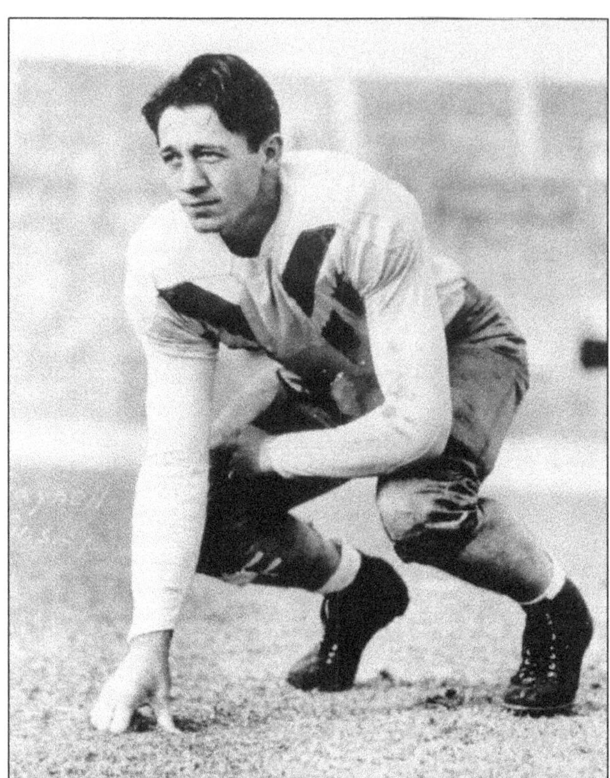

Gaynell "Gus" Tinsley became LSU's first All-American athlete in 1935. He was the Tigers' leading scorer in 1936 with 48 points. Tinsley served as head football coach from 1948 to 1954 and compiled a 35–34–6 record. (LSUPC.)

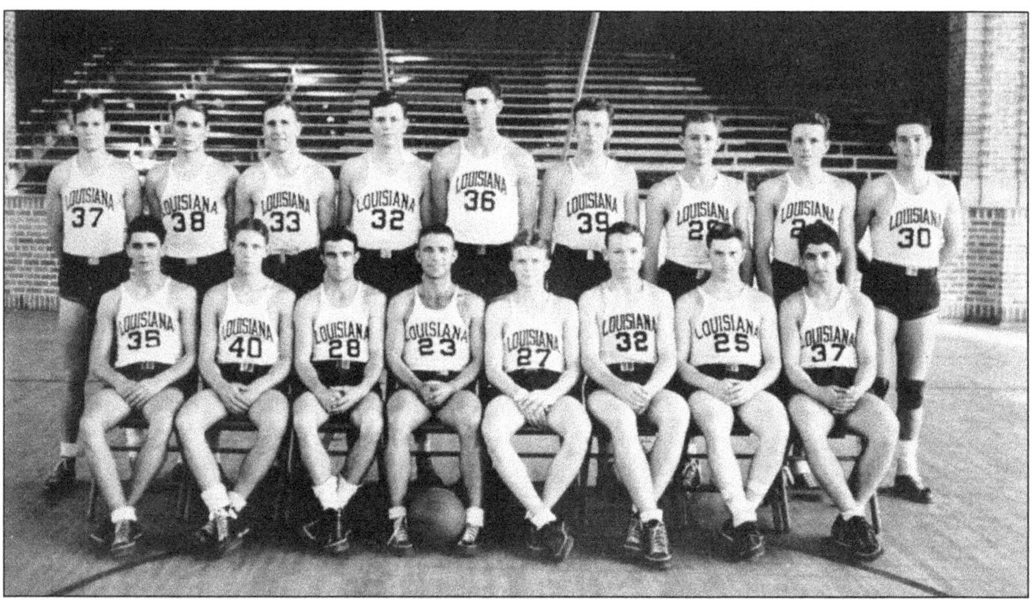

The 1935 basketball team won the SEC championship and the American Legion Bowl against the Pittsburgh Panthers. Coached by Harry Rabenhorst, the Tigers went 14–1 that season; their only defeat was against Rice. From left to right are (front row) Blackie Banker, Wally Wells, Henry Young, Sparky Wade, Nolan Miller, Guy Ottwell, Milford McDonald, and Mac Michael; (second row) Judge Bryan, Bill Leathers, Shongaloo Lindsey, Sid Adger, Bo Bohannon, Red Beeson, Jack Harris, Ben Journeay, and Buddy Blair. (*Gumbo* 1935.)

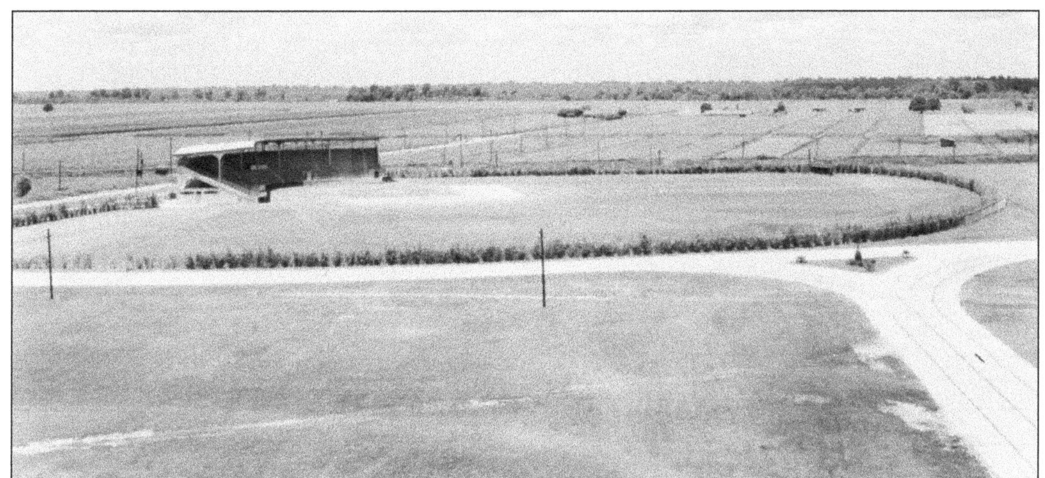

Called the LSU Varsity Baseball Field when it opened in 1938, the baseball field was named for Simeon Alex Box after he was killed in combat in North Africa in 1942. In 1938 and 1939, the stadium played host to the New York Giants during spring training. The facility closed in 2008, replaced by a larger and more modern Alex Box Stadium. (JES.)

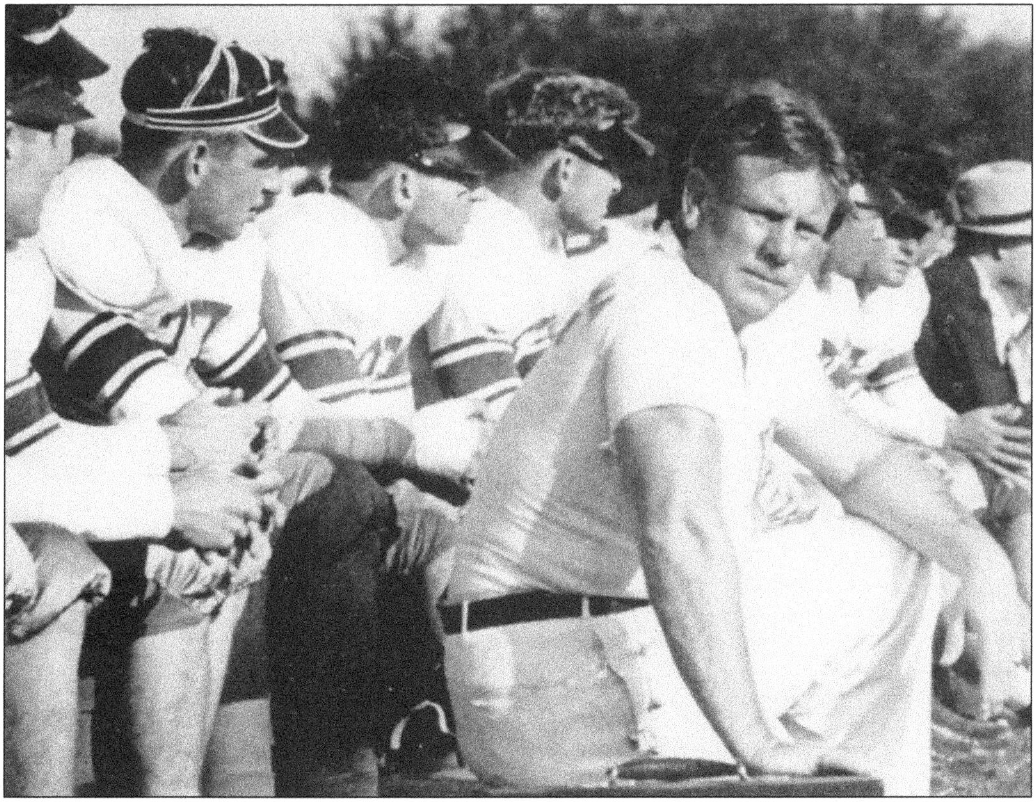

Mike Chambers (facing the camera) was an athletic trainer for the Tiger football team, but also played a large in role in obtaining LSU's first live tiger mascot. Chambers had a friend at the Little Rock, Arkansas, zoo. The zoo had an extra tiger named Sheik, and Chambers arranged for its purchase. The price was $750. When Sheik arrived, his name was changed to Mike in honor of Chambers. (*Gumbo* 1938.)

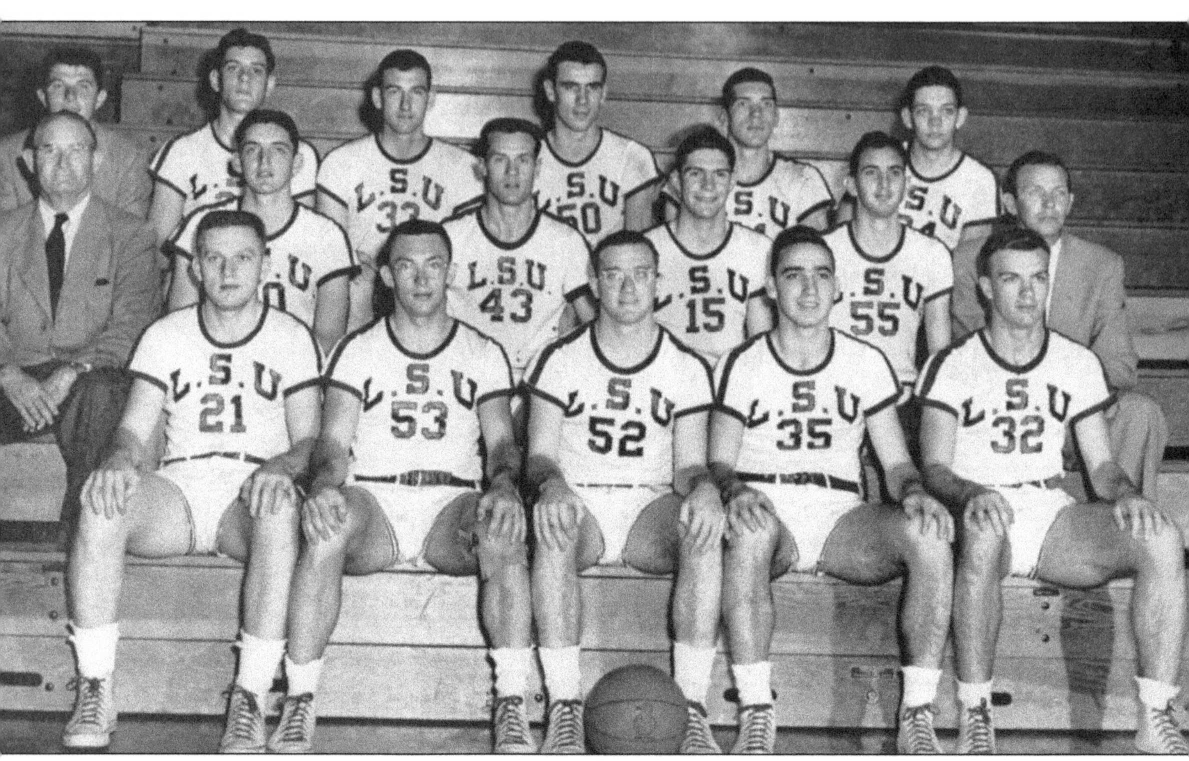

The 1953 Tiger basketball team won the SEC championship and made its first NCAA Final Four appearance. Their record was 22–3 overall and they went undefeated (13–0) in conference play. From left to right are (first row) Don Loughmiller, Darrell Schultz, Bennie McArdle, Norman Magee, and Charley Robert; (second row) Coach Harry Rabenhorst, Bill Lee, Leslie Jones, Don Belcher, Kenny Bridges, and Assistant Coach John Chaney; (third row) Manager Fred Poerschke, James McNeilly, Bob Freshley, Bob Pettit, Ned Clark, and Paul Braymen. Pettit, an All-American in 1953 and 1954, was the first player to have his number (50) retired. (*Gumbo* 1953.)

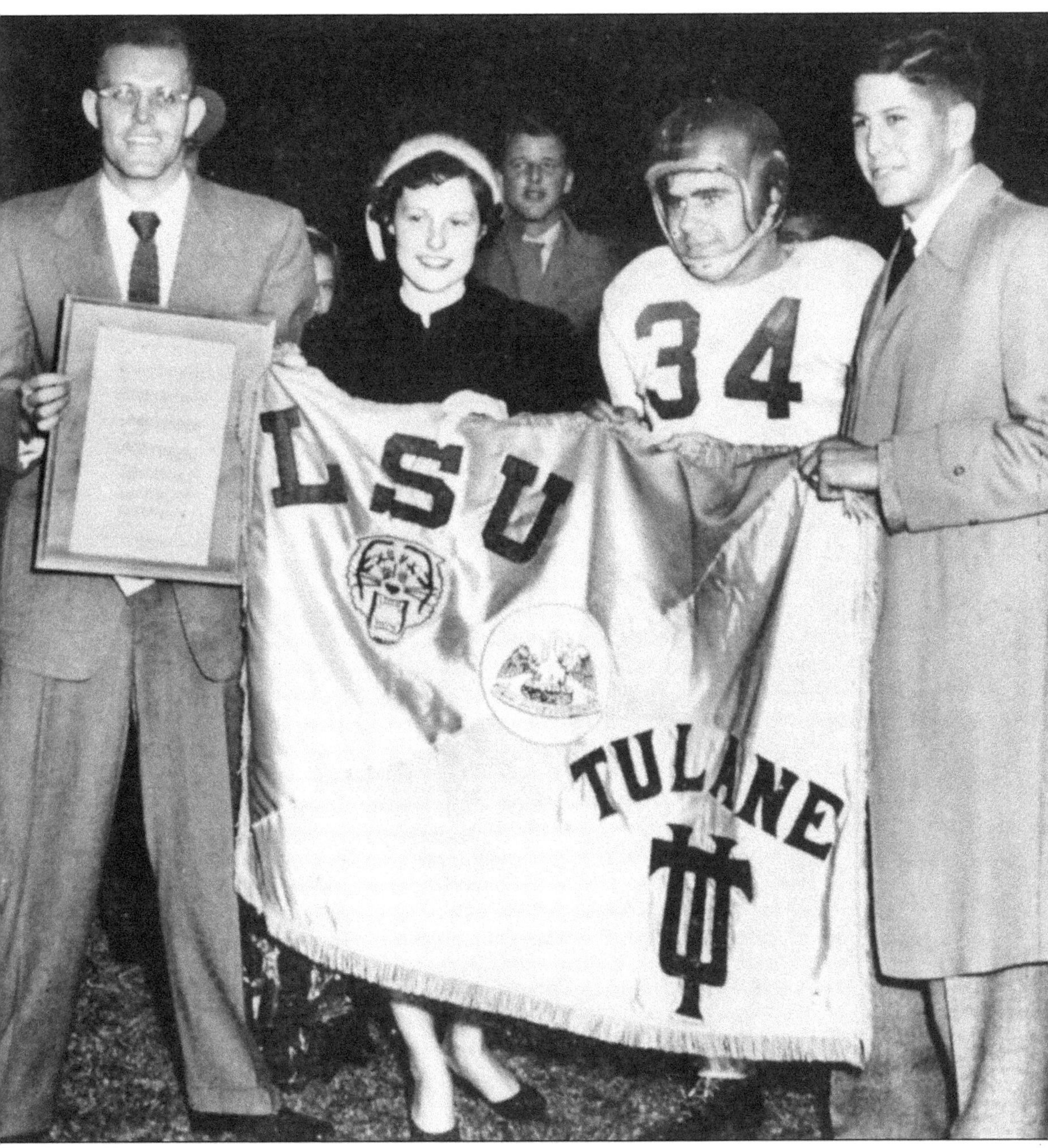

The tradition of the LSU-Tulane "Rag" began in response to a riot that broke out following the Tigers' loss to the Green Wave in 1938. The "Rag" was created in 1940 as a gesture to foster good sportsmanship between the teams and the fans. The winner of the annual game was awarded the flag at a dinner. In this photograph from 1953, Tiger halfback Jerry Marchand is receiving the "Rag." The flag burned in a fire that broke out in Tulane's University Center in 1982. (*Gumbo* 1954.)

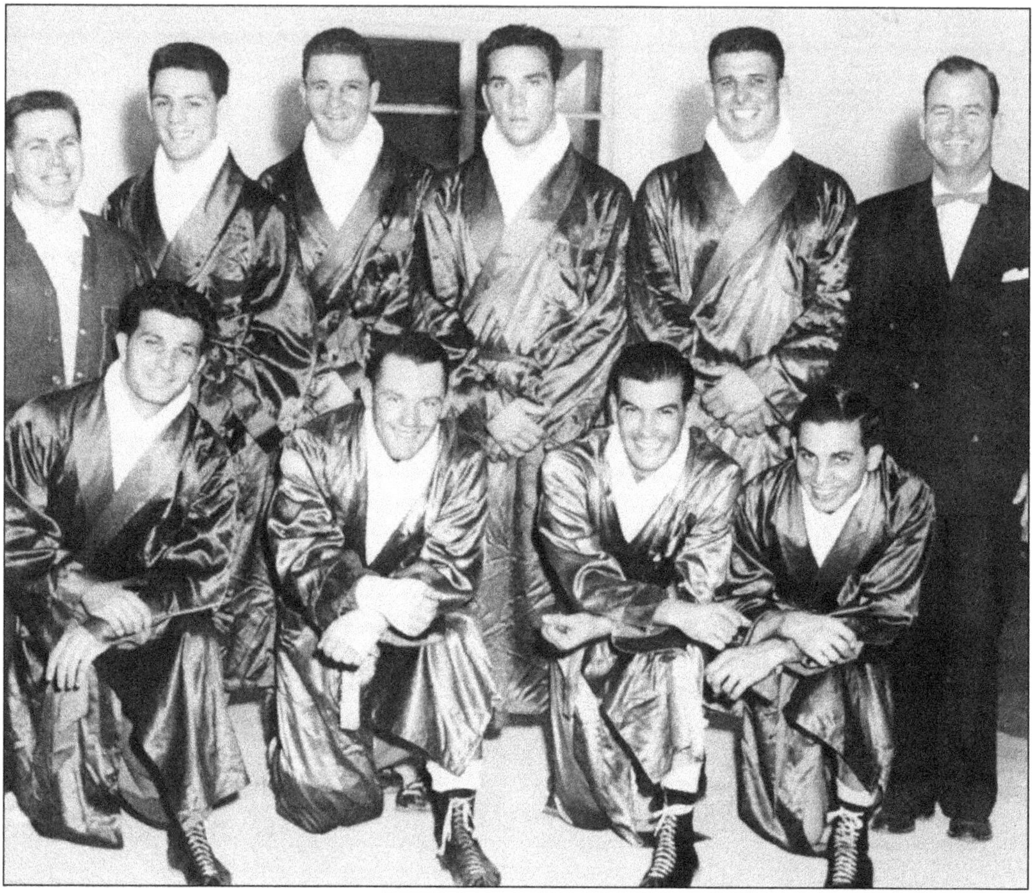

From 1930 to 1956, boxing was a varsity sport. LSU was the last school in the Southeastern Conference to field a boxing team and won the SEC championship in 1949. The 1955 team shown here features Crowe Peele, kneeling second from right, and Bobby Freeman, right. Peele won the NCAA heavyweight title in 1955. (*Gumbo* 1955.)

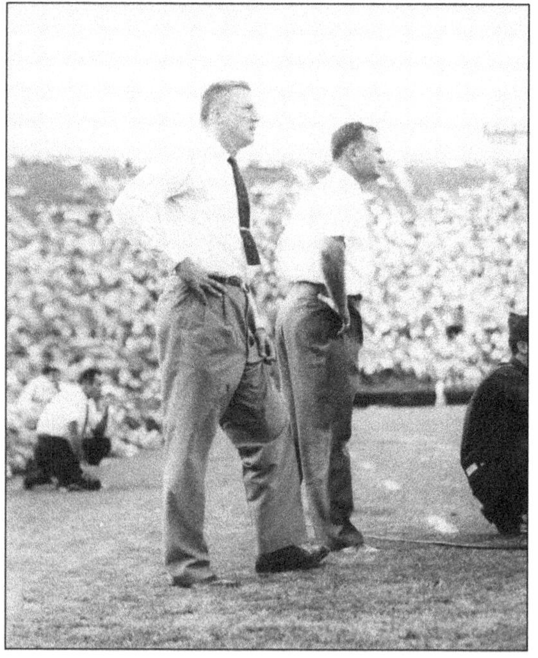

Paul Dietzel (left) served as head football coach from 1955 to 1961 and steered the Tigers to their first national championship in 1958. The Tigers also won the SEC championship in 1958 and 1961. Dietzel compiled a 46–24–3 record. Charles McClendon (right), an assistant coach since 1952, succeeded Dietzel from 1962 to 1979. He was LSU's longest-serving and winningest head coach, with a 137–59–7 record. (CEP.)

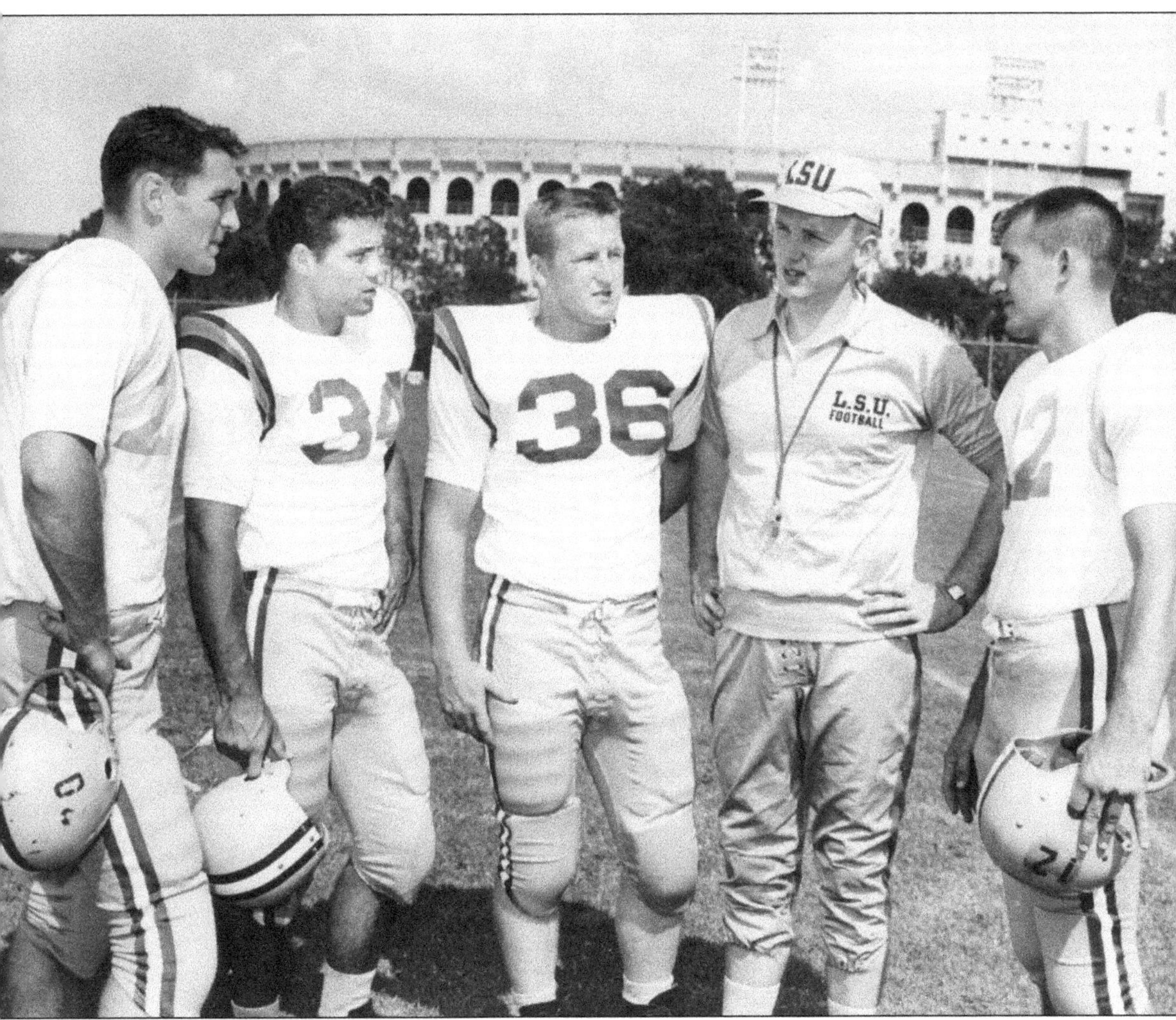

The 1958 White Team stands on the practice field with Tiger Stadium in the background. From left to right, they are Billy Cannon (20), Johnny Robinson (34), J.W. "Red" Brodnax (36), Paul Dietzel, and Warren Rabb (12). Dietzel had devised a three-squad team in 1958. The White Team played offense and defense equally well, the Go Team was a smaller and faster group of offensive specialists, and the Chinese Bandits were the biggest and slowest (relatively speaking) players and were defensive specialists. The three-squad system allowed fresh players to rotate depending on the situation. (CEP.)

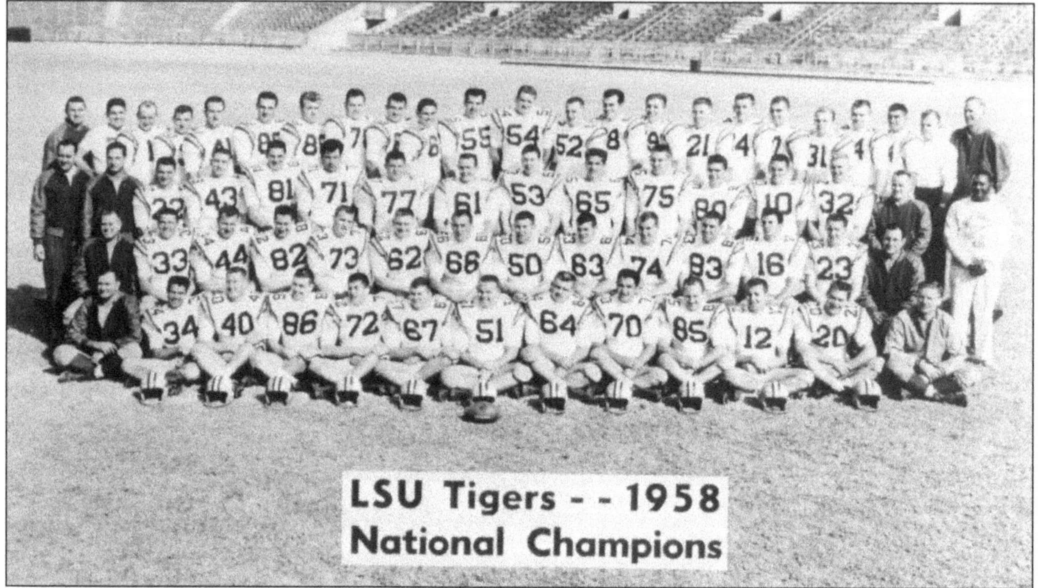

The Tigers had a perfect 11–0 season (the first since 1908) and celebrated their first national championship in 1958. LSU also won the SEC championship for the first time since 1936. The Tigers began the season ranked 35th nationally, handed Tulane its worst loss since the series began (62–0), and defeated Clemson in the Sugar Bowl. The Sugar Bowl victory was LSU's first in four previous tries. (LSUPC.)

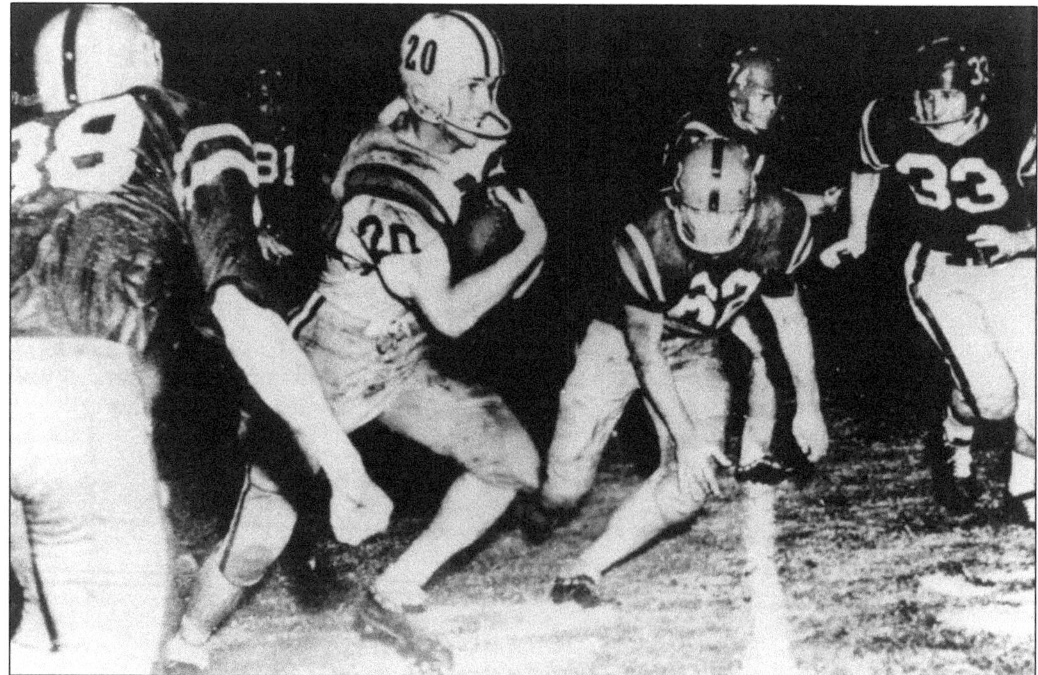

On Halloween Night 1959, in Tiger Stadium, with 10 minutes remaining in the fourth quarter, Billy Cannon returned an Ole Miss punt from the LSU 11-yard line 89 yards for a touchdown and a Heisman Trophy. The Tigers won 7–3 and handed the Rebels their first loss of the season. (LSUPC.)

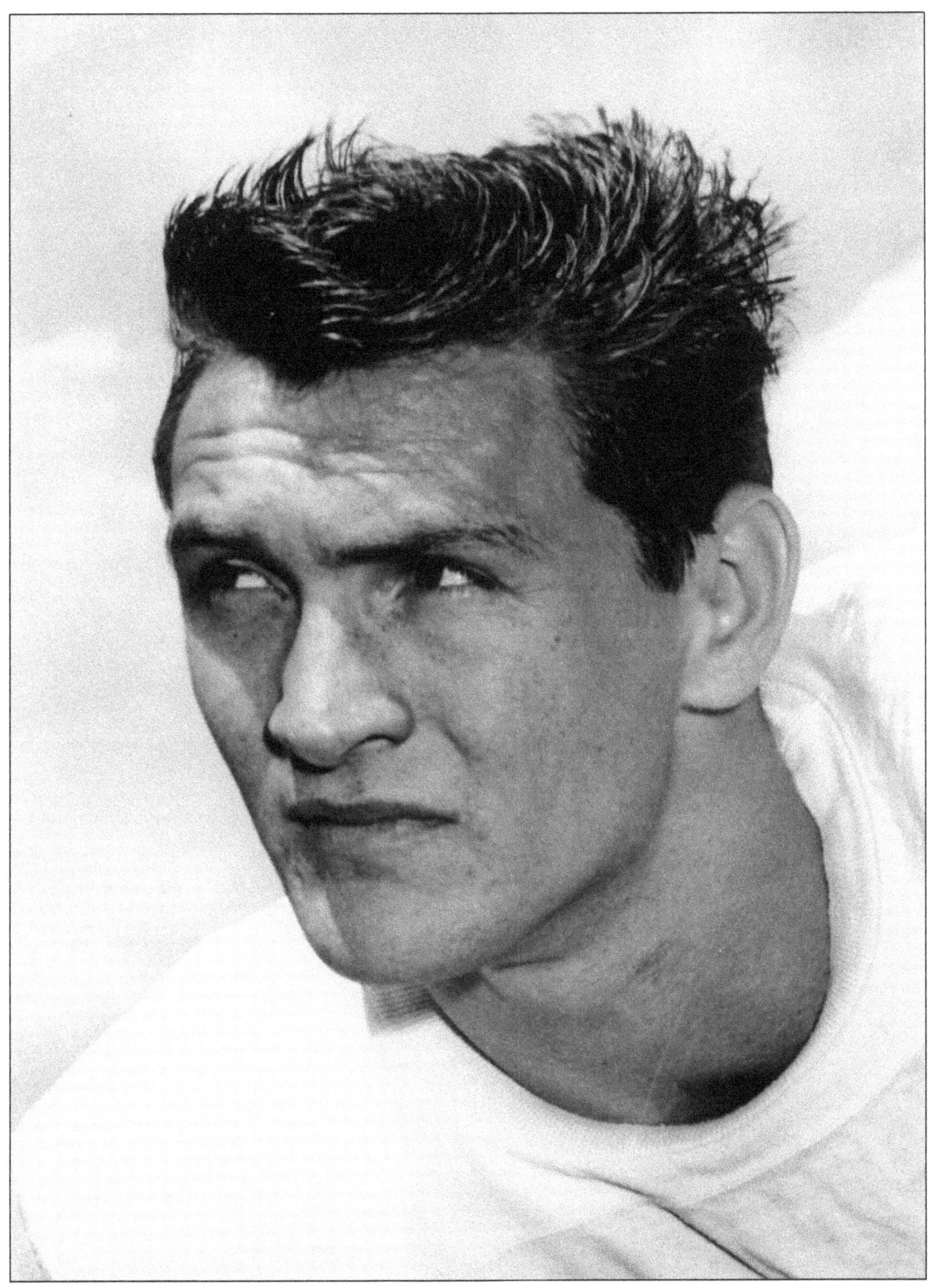

Halfback Billy Cannon, a Baton Rouge native and graduate from Istrouma High School, became the Tigers' rushing and scoring leader. He was named All-American in 1958 and 1959 and is LSU's first, and so far only, Heisman Trophy winner. (LSUPC.)

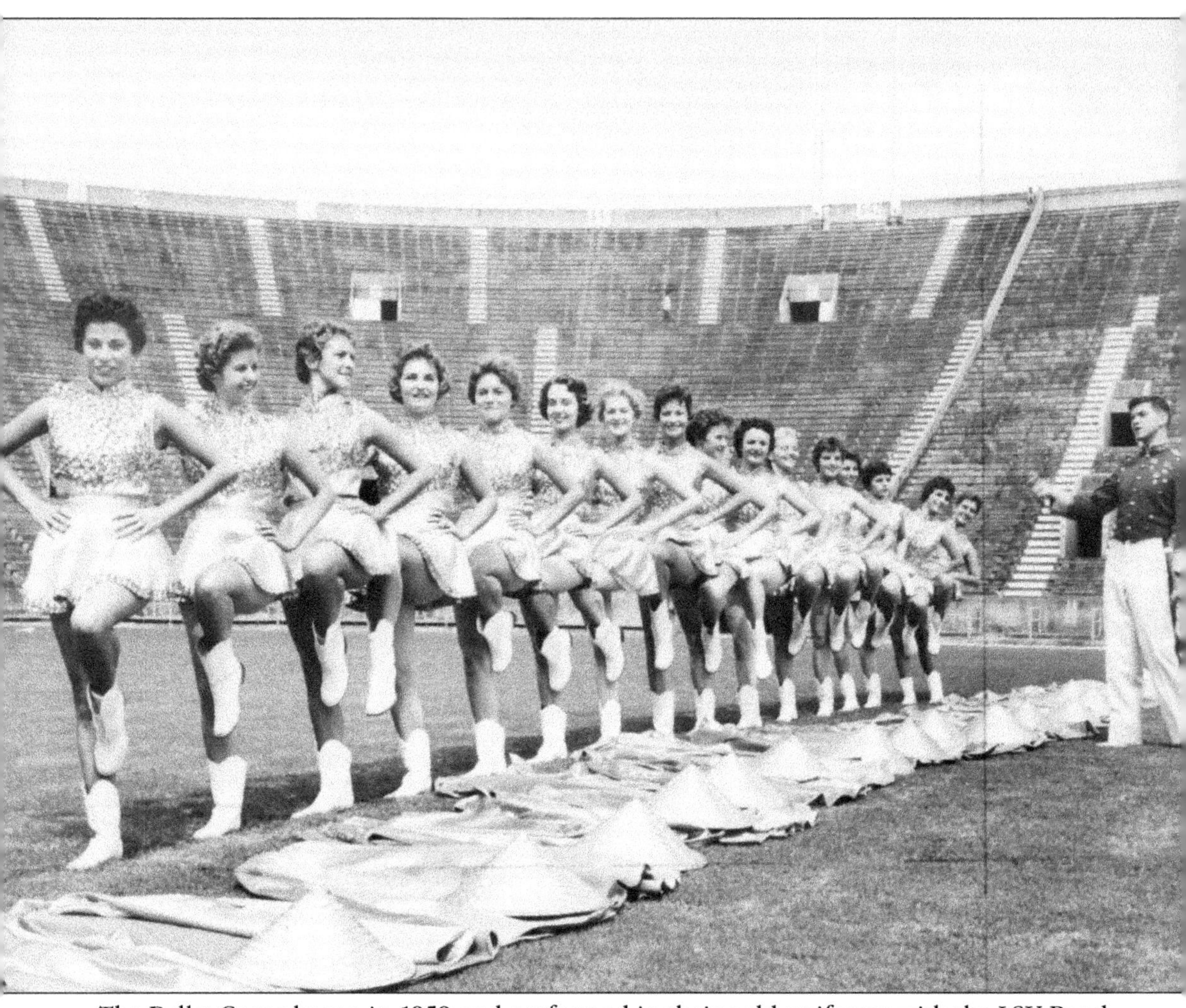

The Ballet Corps began in 1959 and performed in their gold uniforms with the LSU Band. Lying on the ground are capes and coolie hats worn when the Chinese Bandits stopped an opposing team's drive. (OPRR.)

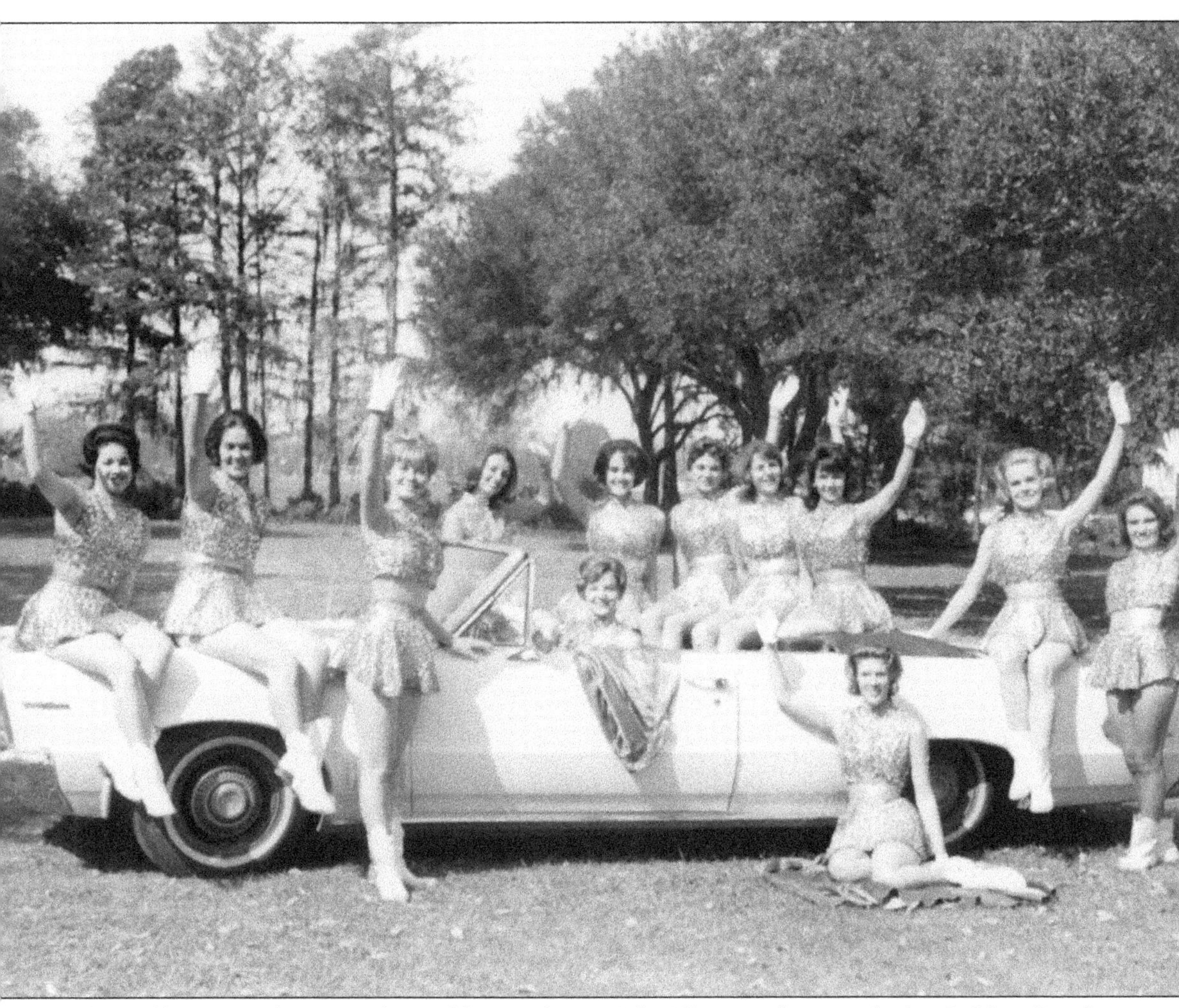

The Ballet Corps became the Golden Girls in 1965. They perform with the Golden Band from Tigerland for home and away games, and for selected campus and community outreach events. (OPRR.)

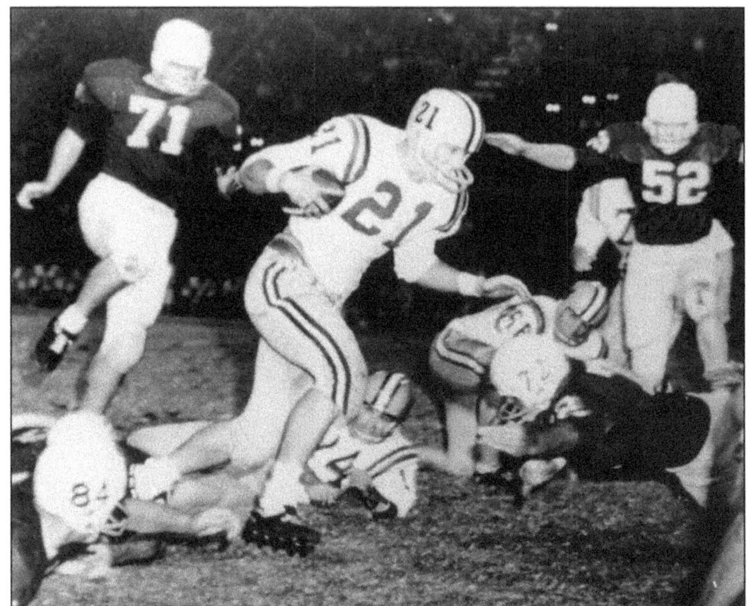

Halfback Jerry Stovall (21) outruns the Texas Christian University defense in 1962. The Tigers beat the Horned Frogs 5–0 that year. Stovall was an All-American and finished second in the Heisman Trophy voting in 1962. Stovall would become LSU's head coach from 1980 to 1983. (LSUPC.)

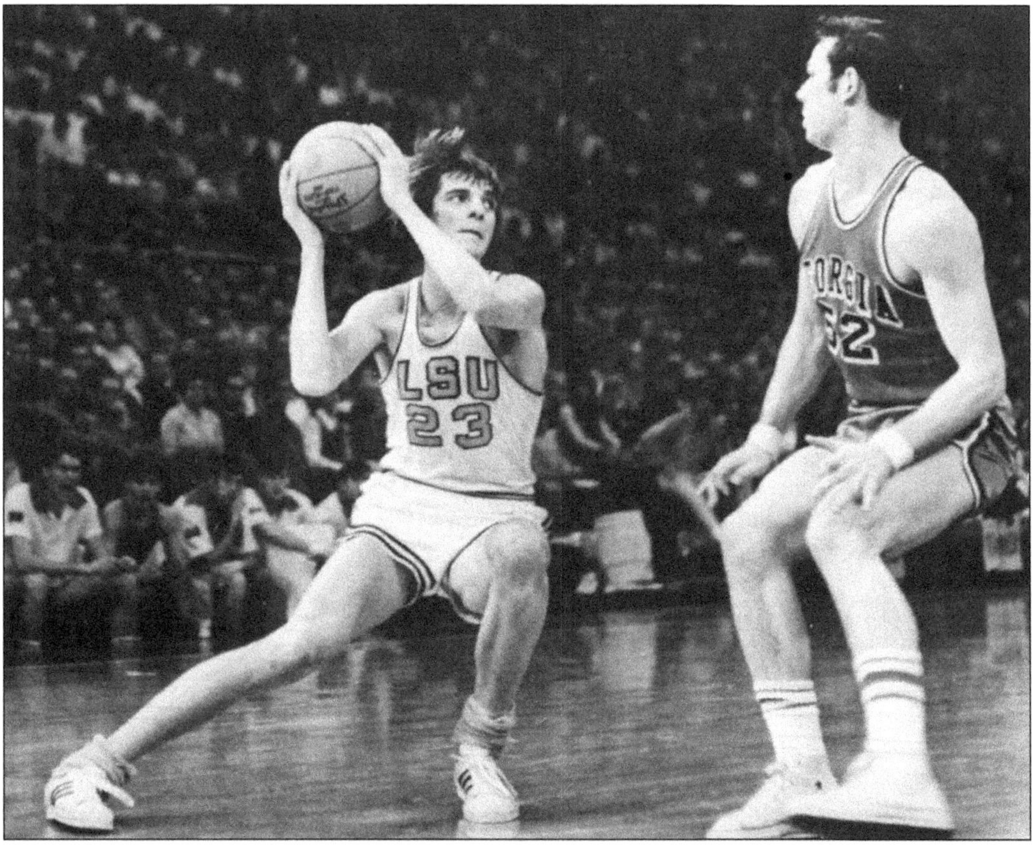

"Pistol" Pete Maravich (1947–1988) played from 1967 to 1970 and still holds the all-time NCAA records for points scored (3,667) and average points per game (44.2). He led the NCAA in scoring in 1968, 1969, and 1970, and was an All-American in those years. (*Gumbo* 1970.)

Lora Hinton was the first African American player awarded a football scholarship at LSU, in 1971. He was forced to sit out the 1972 season due to a knee injury, but started from 1973 to 1975. (LSUPC.)

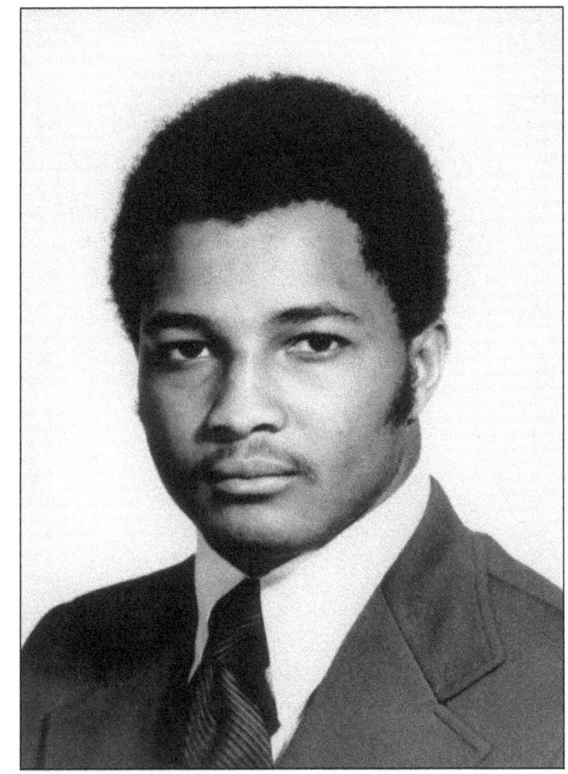

Running back Lora Hinton (24, carrying the ball), a three-year letterman, runs through the Ole Miss defense in 1973. Hinton was the first African American player to letter in football. The Tigers defeated the Rebels 51–14 in the 1973 game. (LSUPC.)

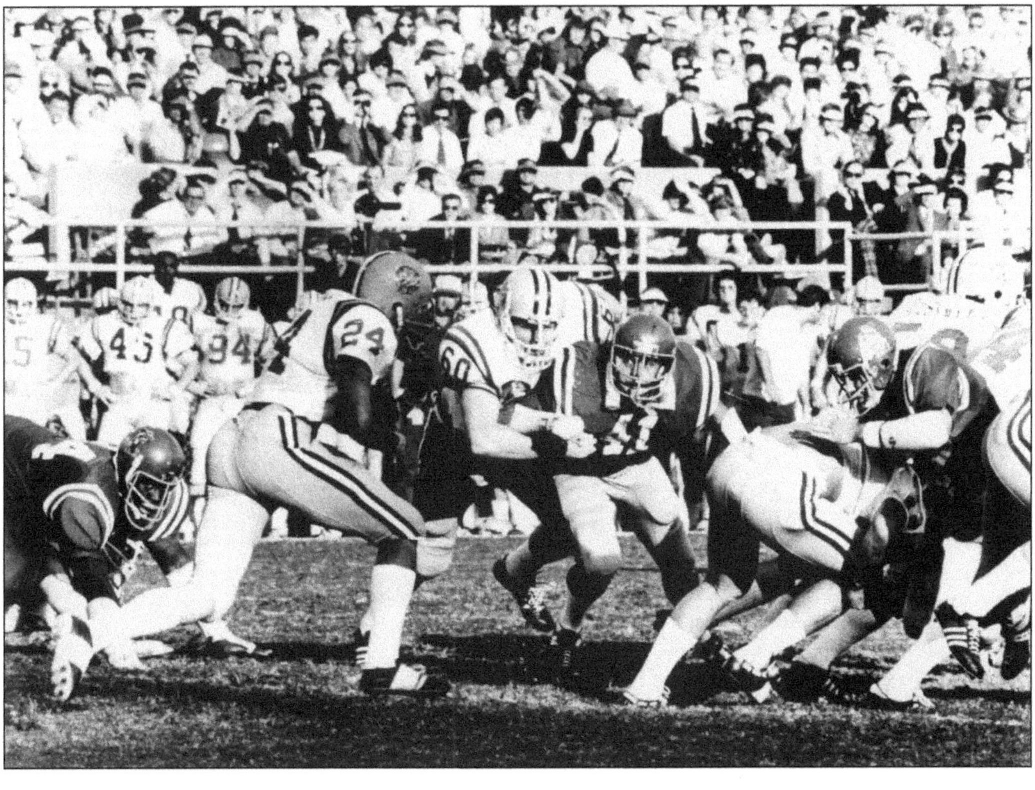

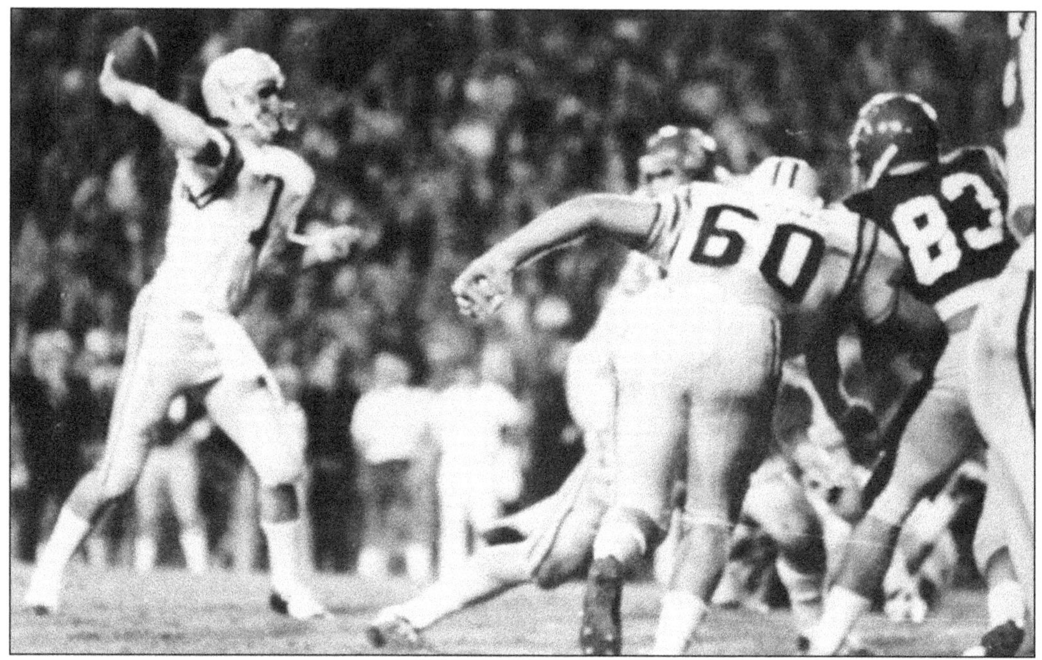

In the final second of the 1972 LSU–Ole Miss game, with the score Ole Miss 16, LSU 10, Bert Jones threw a touchdown pass to Brad Davis to tie the game. With no time left on the clock, Rusty Jackson kicked the extra point, giving the Tigers a 17–16 victory. Coach Charles McClendon said "You'd have to call this one victory one of the all-time thrills in Tiger history." (*Gumbo* 1973.)

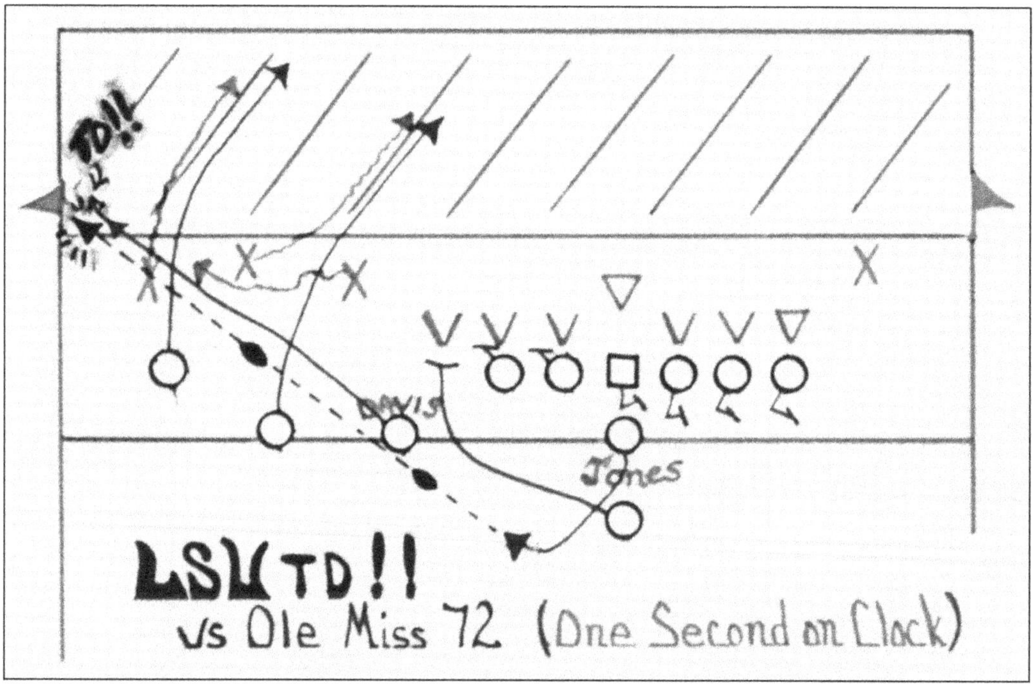

This diagram of the 1972 LSU–Ole Miss game shows how the last play unfolded: Bert Jones dropped back to pass, Davis caught the ball in the end zone. (*Gumbo* 1973.)

Cornerback Mike Williams (29), the first African American to play football at LSU, goes after the ball. Williams, a Covington, Louisiana, native, was a three-year letterman from 1972 to 1974. (LSUPC.)

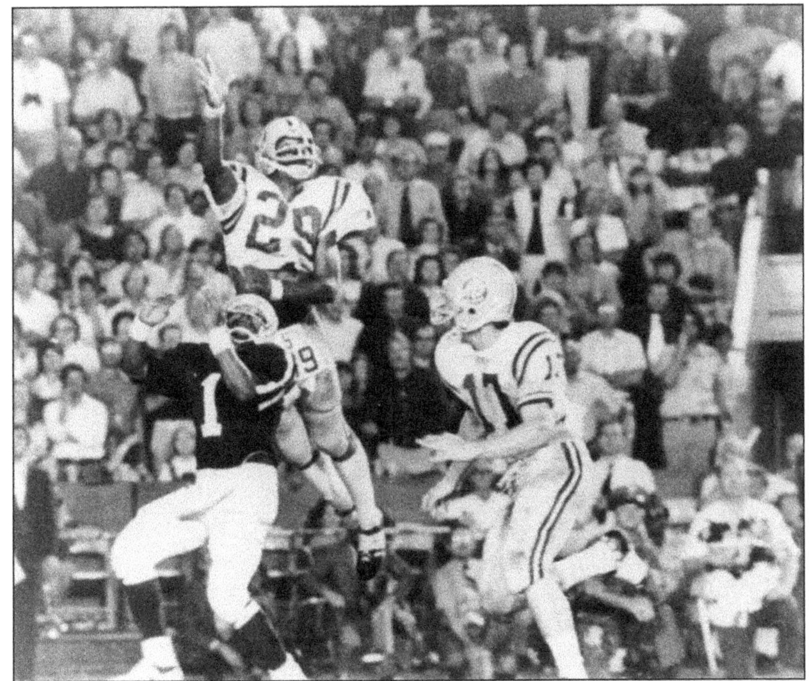

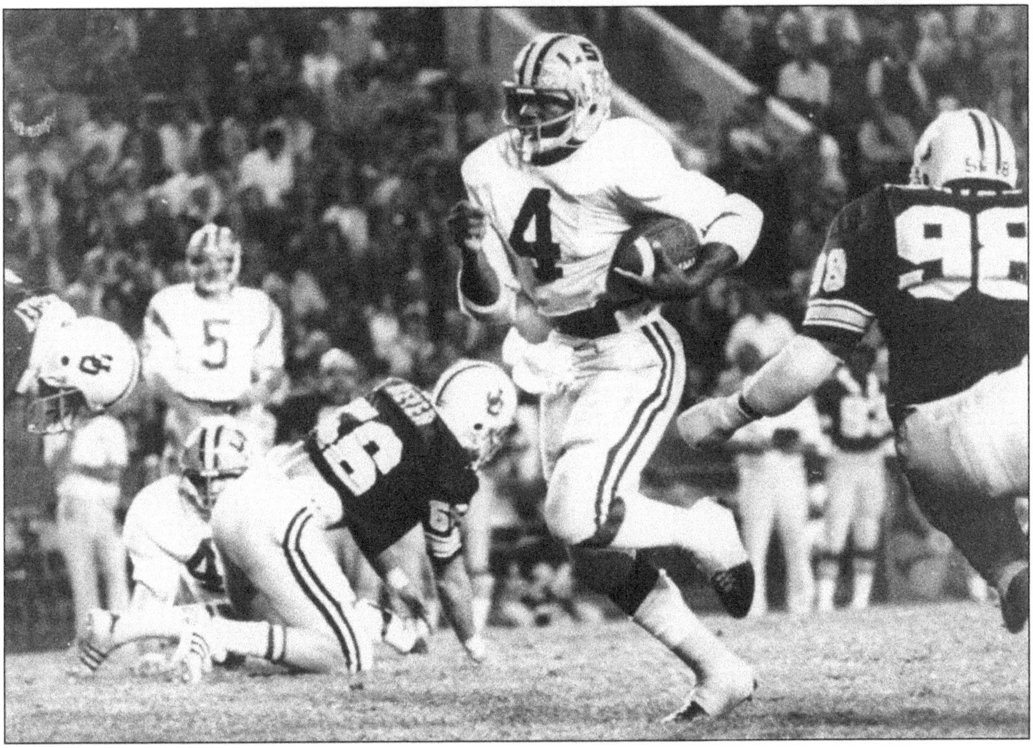

Running back Charles Alexander eludes the University of Oregon defense on October 22, 1977, on his way to helping score a 56–17 Tiger victory. Alexander was an All-American in 1977 and 1978. During the 1977 season, he set an SEC record when he rushed for 1,686 yards. (*Gumbo* 1978.)

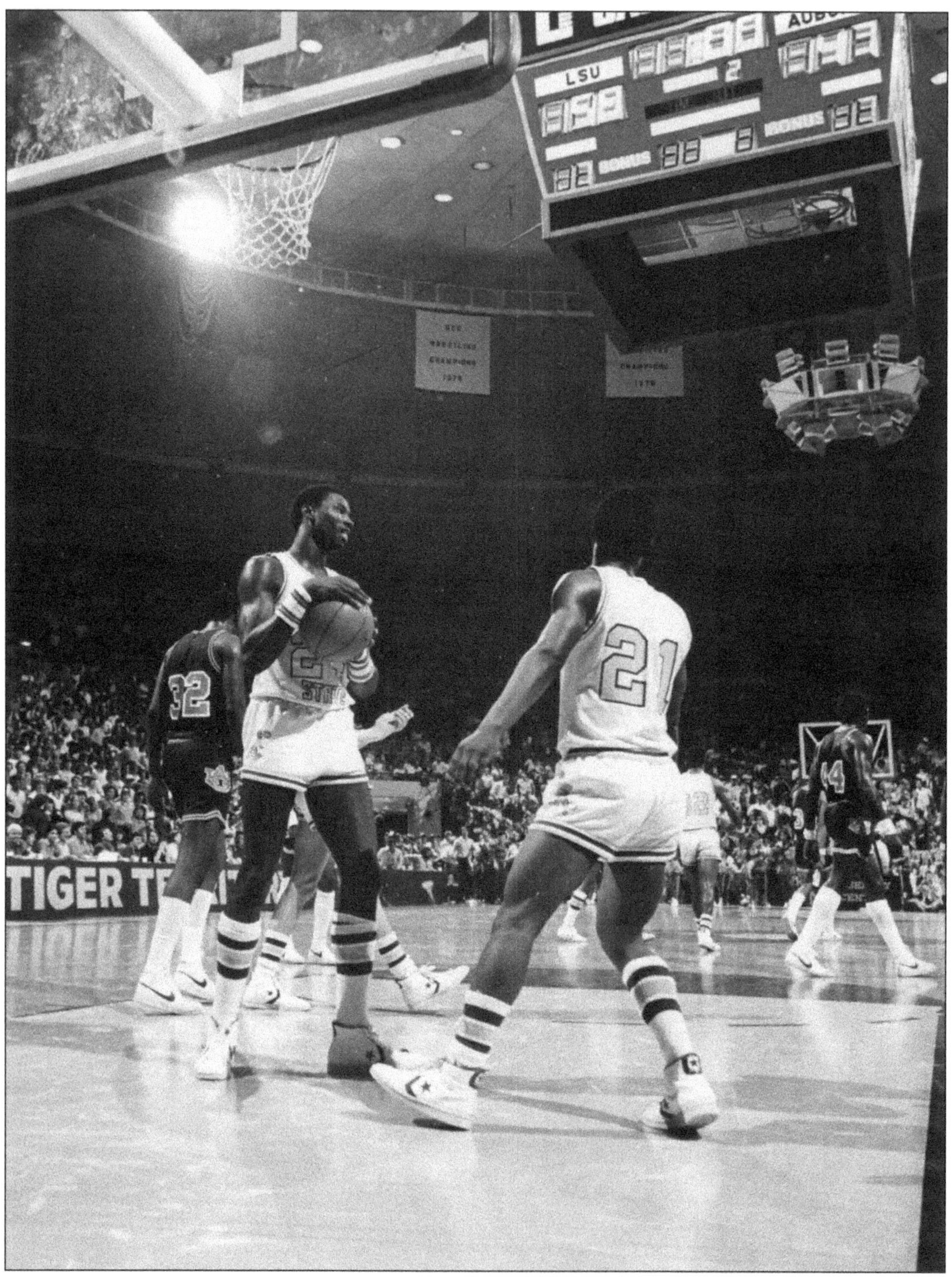

On the way to a 1981 SEC championship and their first Final Four appearance since 1953, the Tigers defeated Auburn 58–47. Seen here are guard Ethan Martin (21) and forward Leonard Mitchell (24). LSU finished the season with a 31–5 record. (*Gumbo* 1981.)

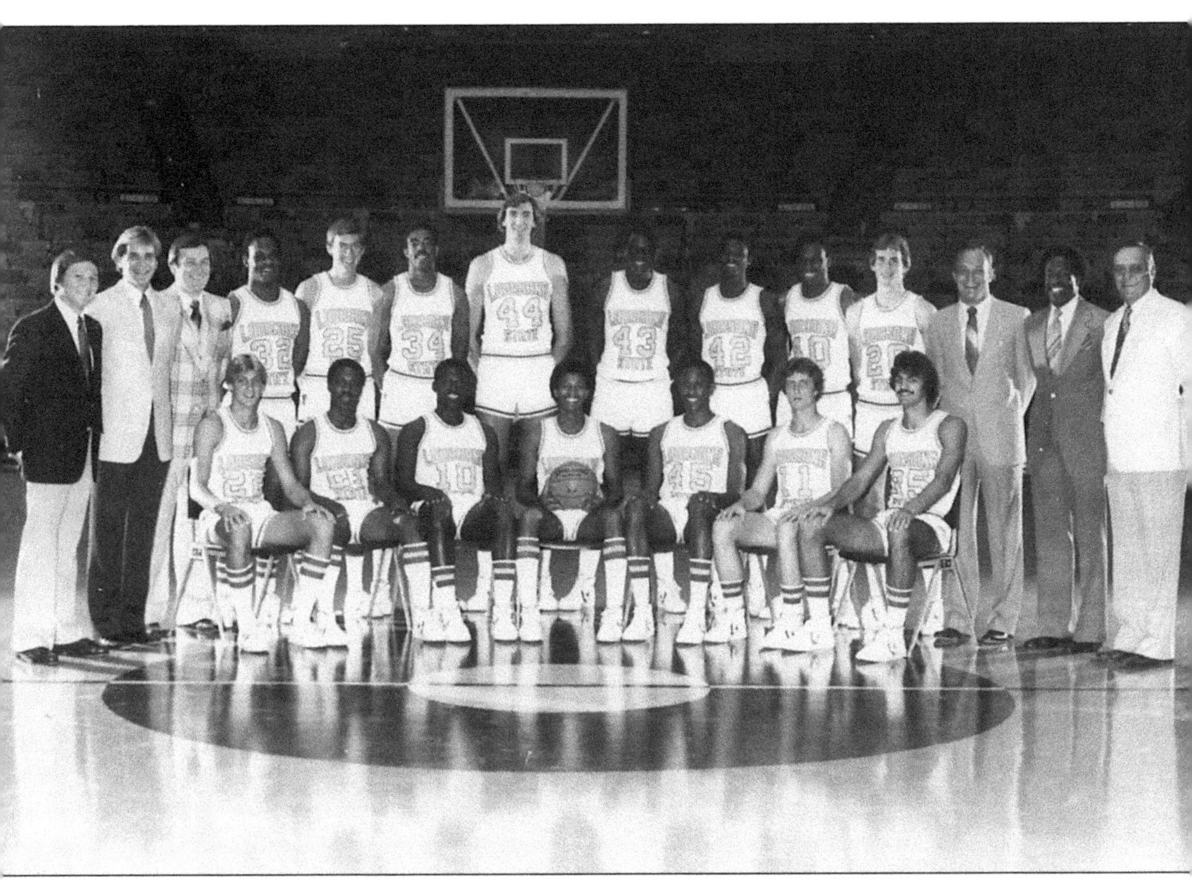

The 1981 SEC champion Tigers are, from left to right, (first row) J. Brian Bergeron, Ethan Martin, Willie Sims, Johnny Jones, Matt England, Mark Alcorn, and Brian Kistler; (second row) manager Stan Harris, assistant coach Jordy Hultberg, assistant coach Rick Huckabay, Howard Carter, Joe Costello, Tyrone Black, Andy Campbell, Greg Cook, Leonard Mitchell, Durand Macklin, John Tudor, head coach Dale Brown, assistant coach Ron Abernathy, and trainer Dr. Martin J. Broussard. (Courtesy of Steve Franz, LSU Sports Information.)

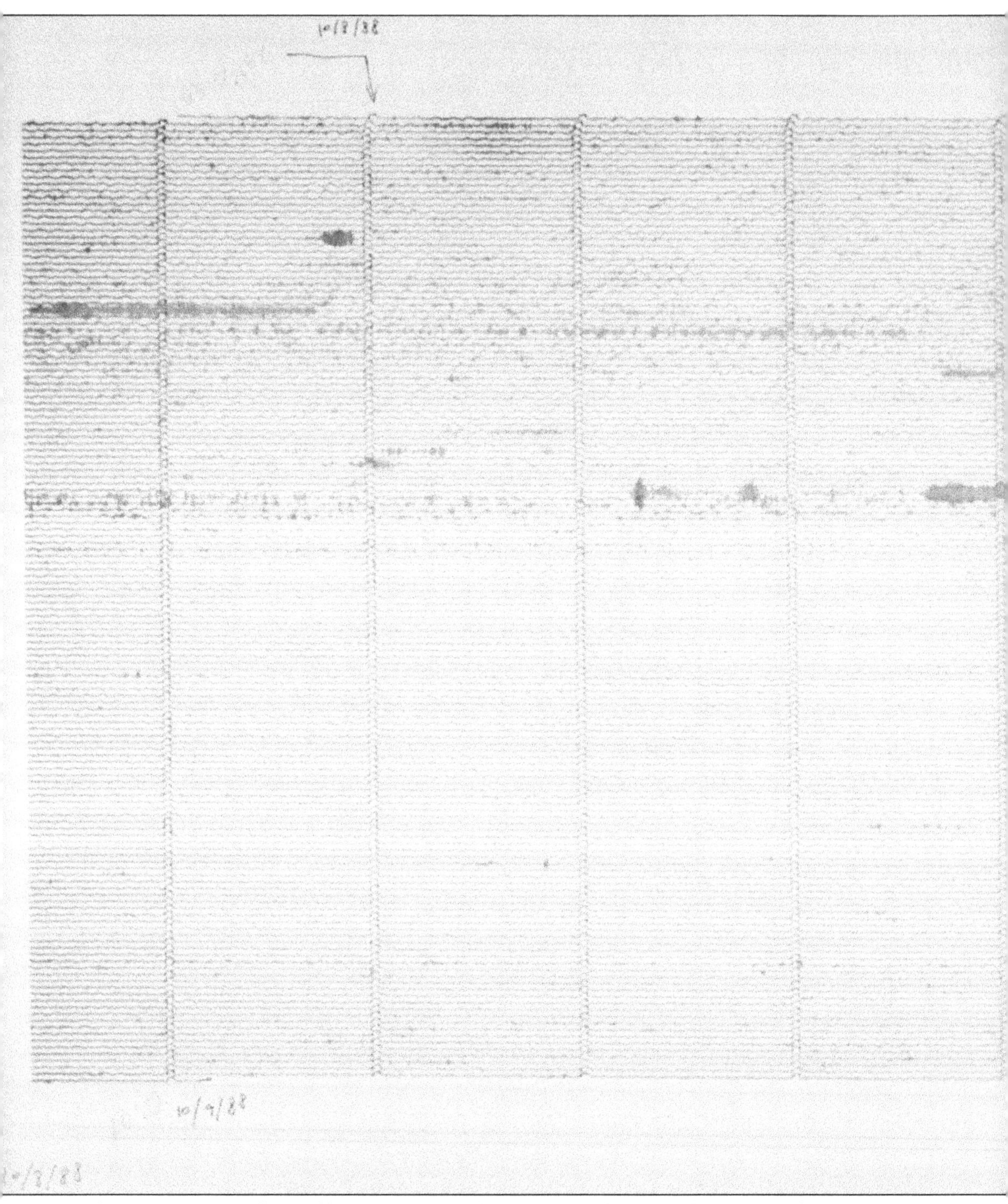

The LSU–Auburn football game on October 8, 1988, became known as the "earthquake game." With 1:47 left in the fourth quarter and Auburn leading 6–0, Tommy Hodson passed to Eddie Fuller in the end zone, tying the score. The extra point sealed a 7–6 victory for LSU. The crowd eruption in Tiger Stadium after the pass completion was so great that it registered

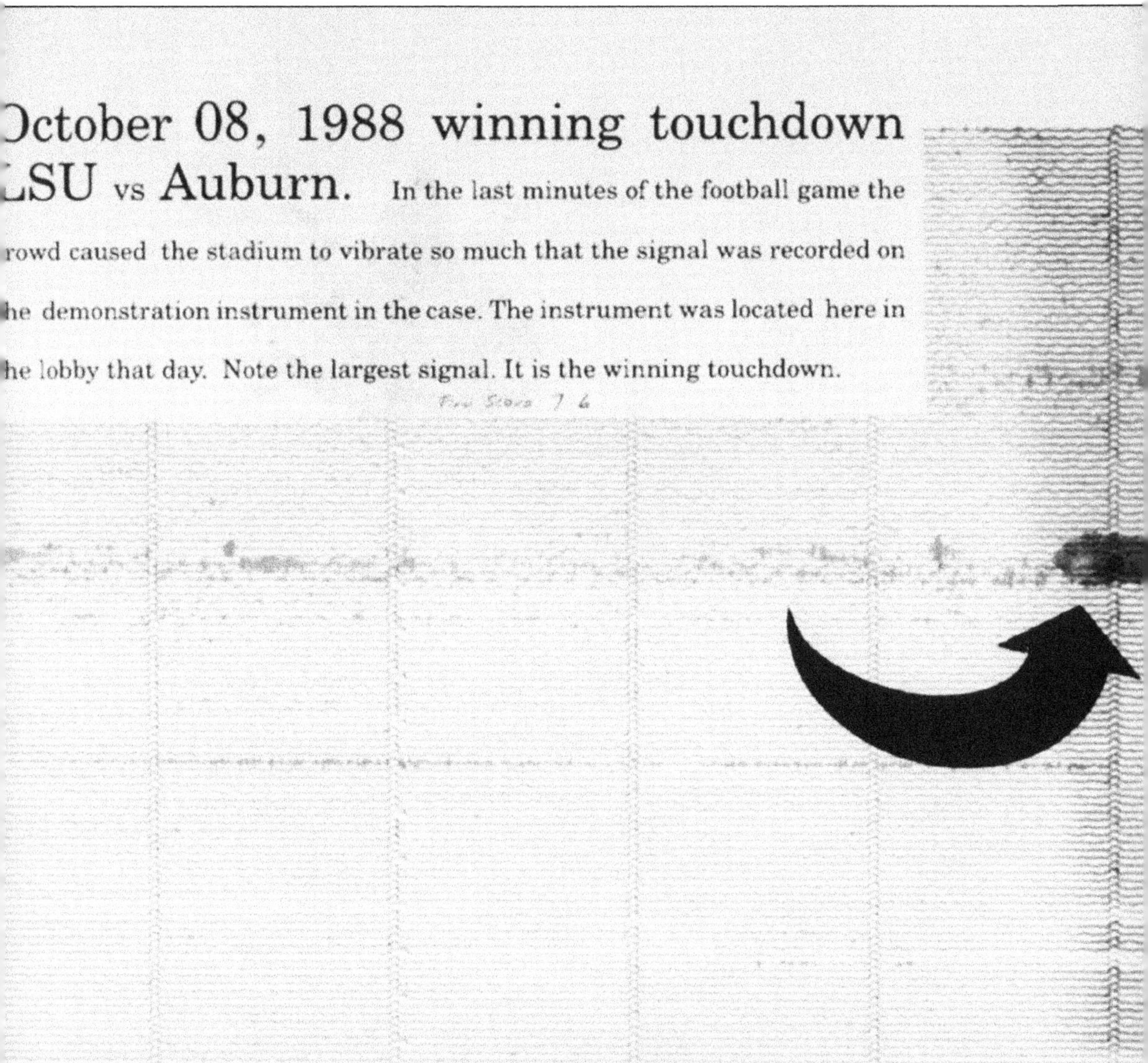

ctober 08, 1988 winning touchdown
SU vs Auburn. In the last minutes of the football game the rowd caused the stadium to vibrate so much that the signal was recorded on he demonstration instrument in the case. The instrument was located here in he lobby that day. Note the largest signal. It is the winning touchdown.

on the seismograph in the geology building. (Louisiana State University Center for Coastal, Energy, and Environmental Resources Seismogram, RG #A0402, Louisiana State University Archives, LSU Libraries, Baton Rouge, Louisiana.)

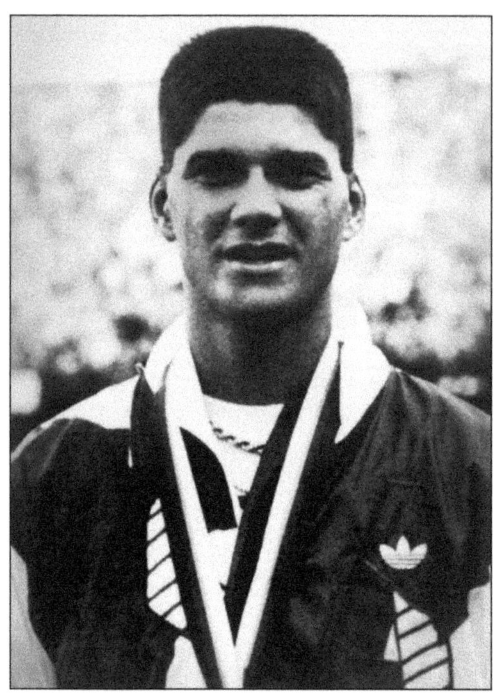

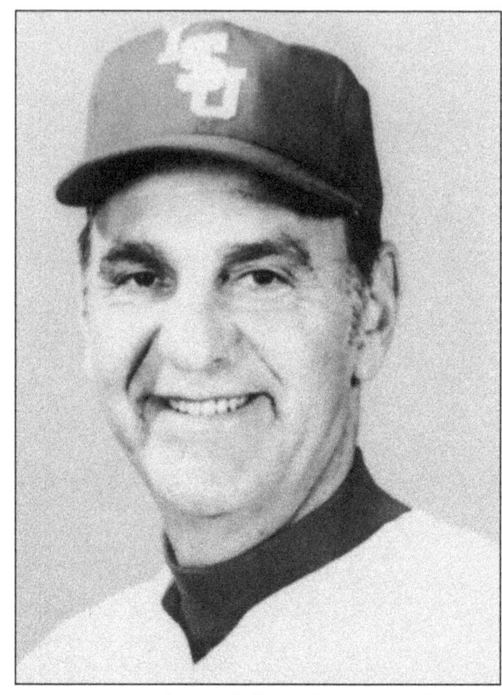

Pitcher Ben McDonald (left) and Coach Skip Bertman won gold medals in the 1988 Olympic Games in Seoul. McDonald also won the Golden Spikes award given by the United States Baseball Federation to the most outstanding amateur player. He was the number-one draft pick of the Baltimore Orioles in 1989 and played in the major leagues for 10 years. Bertman arrived at LSU in 1984 and was the pitching coach for the US Olympic team in 1988 and the head coach in the 1996 games in Atlanta. He led the Tigers to five national championships from 1991 to 2000 and seven SEC championships. (*Gumbo* 1989.)

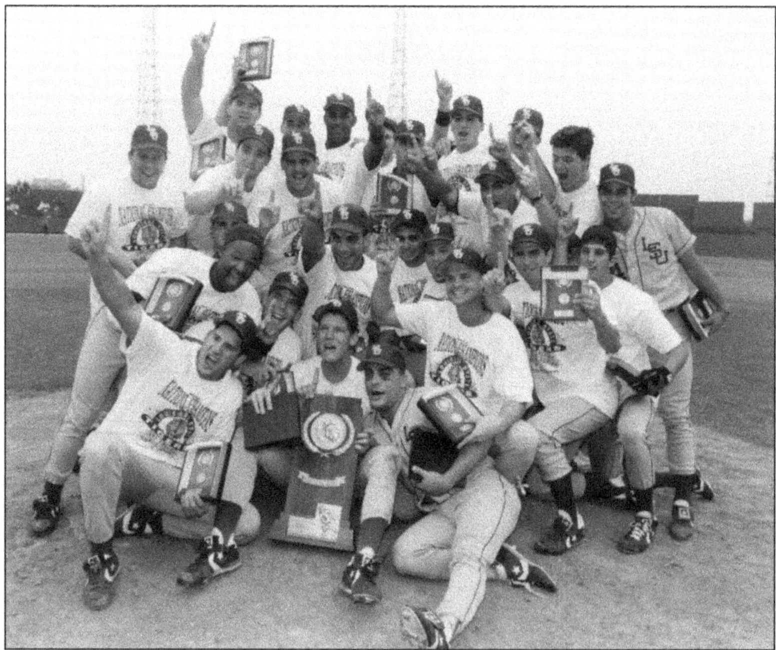

The LSU Baseball Tigers won their first College World Series in 1991. They swept their competition, defeating Florida (twice), Fresno State, and Wichita State in the final game. Catcher Gary Hymel was named Most Outstanding Player with a .500 batting average, four home runs, and 10 RBIs. (Courtesy Steve Franz, LSU Sports Information.)

Sue Gunter (1939–2005) coached the Lady Tigers basketball team from 1982 until her retirement after the 2003–2004 season. Her 500th career victory as a head coach is celebrated here against Jackson State on February 9, 1995. In 2004, she became the third women's coach in history to achieve 700 victories in a win over Arkansas. She was named SEC Coach of the Year twice, led the Lady Tigers to the Final Four in 2004, and to the Elite Eight in 1986, 2000, and 2003. (*Gumbo* 1995.)

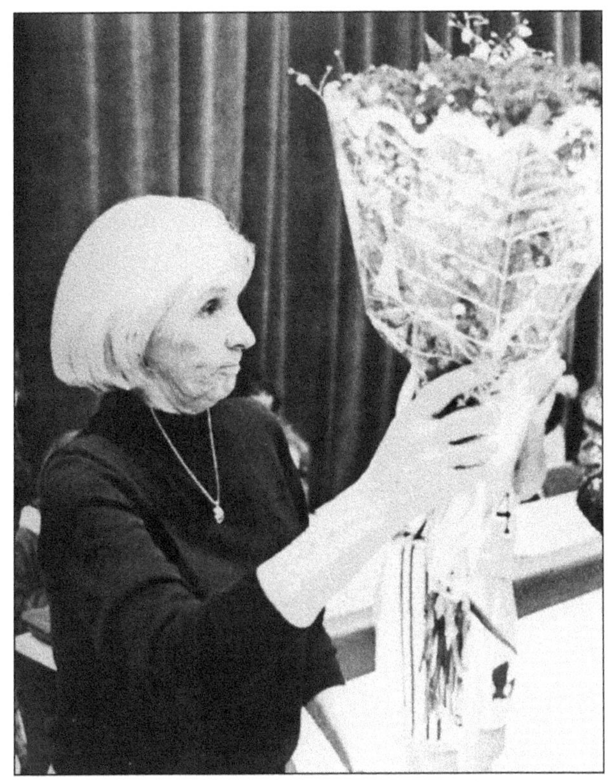

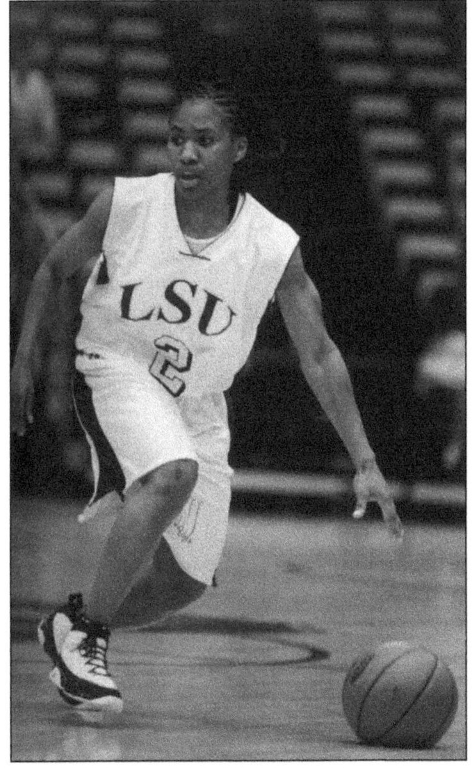

Point guard Temeka Johnson holds the team record for career assists. She played in 129 games from 2001 to 2005 and made 945 assists. Johnson's honors include first team all-SEC in 2004 and 2005, SEC Tournament MVP in 2003, and the WNBA Rookie of the Year in 2005. (*Gumbo* 2002.)

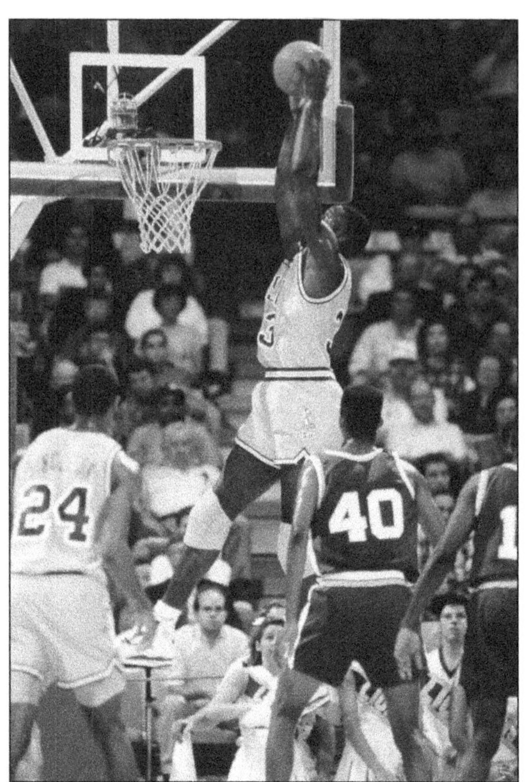

Shaquille O'Neal played for the Tigers from 1989 to 1992 and set many national and SEC records along the way. In his freshman season, Shaq blocked 115 shots and was the first player in league history to block more than 100 shots in a single season. He led the league in rebounding, averaging 12 per game. In his sophomore season, he was named Player of the Year by the Associated Press and was the first SEC player to win the Adolph Rupp Award. O'Neal's junior year was his last at LSU; he was named SEC player and athlete of the year, and was the nation's leading shot blocker, averaging 5.23 per game. These are only a few of his honors and records. O'Neal's jersey number, 33, was retired in 2000. (Courtesy of Steve Franz, LSU Sports Information.)

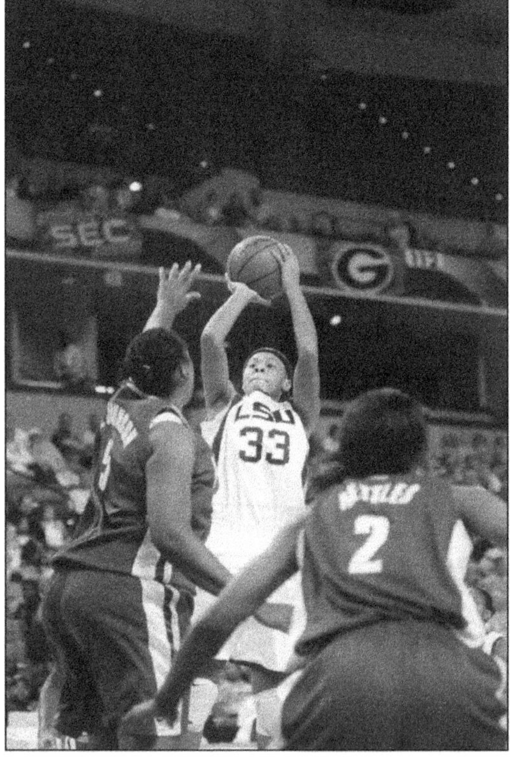

Seimone Augustus played from 2002 to 2006 and, like Shaquille O'Neal, dominated the game. She won the Naismith Award and the John R. Wooden Women's Award and started a school record of 140 games, scoring in double figures in 132 of them. Augustus was named SEC player of the year and received all-SEC honors by the league's coaches and scored in double figures in a school record 97 straight games. These are only a few of the honors and records Augustus attained while at LSU. Her jersey number, 33, was retired in 2010. (Courtesy of Steve Franz, LSU Sports Information.)

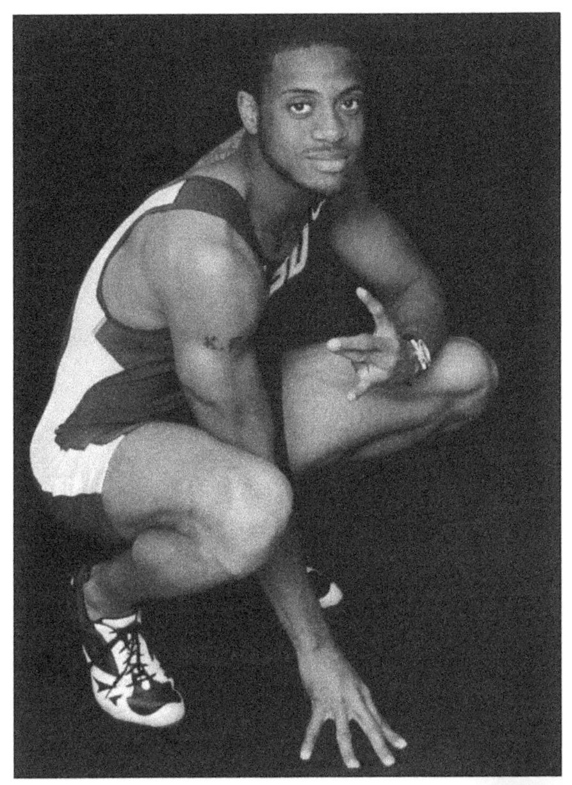

Bennie Brazell was the first LSU student athlete to win national championships in two different sports: outdoor track and field and football. Playing from 2002 to 2005, he was a member of four national championship relay teams: the 4x100 in 2002 and 2003 and the 4x400 in 2004 and 2005. The 2002 track and field team won the NCAA National Championship. In 2003, he played on the national championship football team on kickoff and punt return coverage. (*Gumbo* 2003.)

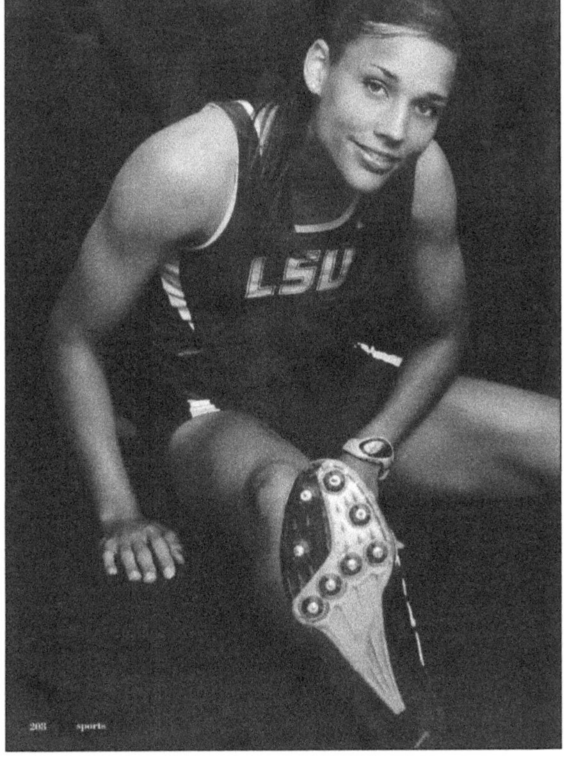

Lolo Jones was a member of the Lady Tigers track and field team from 2001 to 2004. She was an 11-time All-American and a three-time national champion. Jones was the first true freshman to win All-American honors in the indoor 60-meter hurdles. She helped LSU win titles in the 60 and 100-meter hurdles and 4x100 meter relays. (*Gumbo* 2003.)

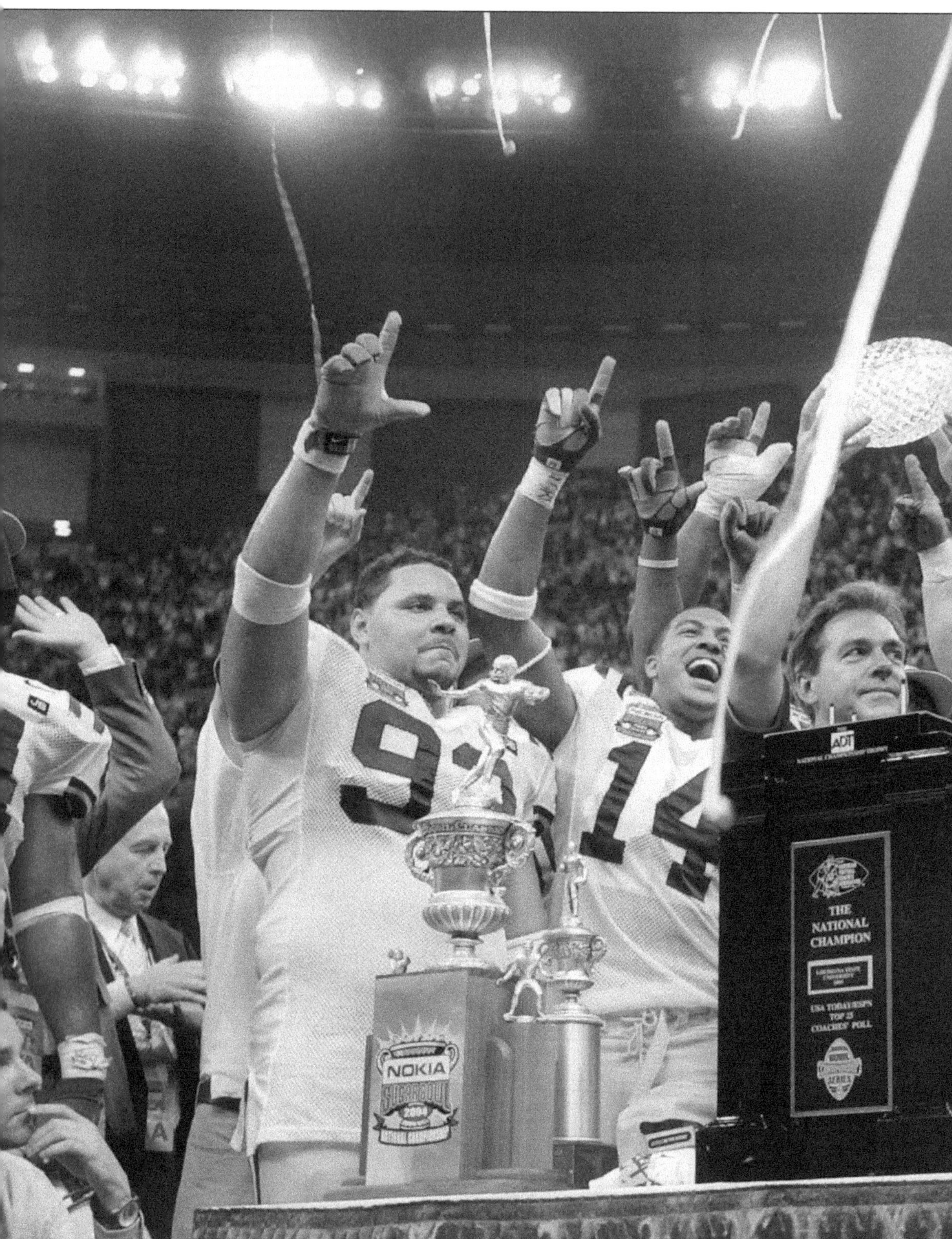
NOKIA
ADT
THE
NATIONAL
CHAMPION
USA TODAY/ESPN
TOP 25
COACHES' POLL

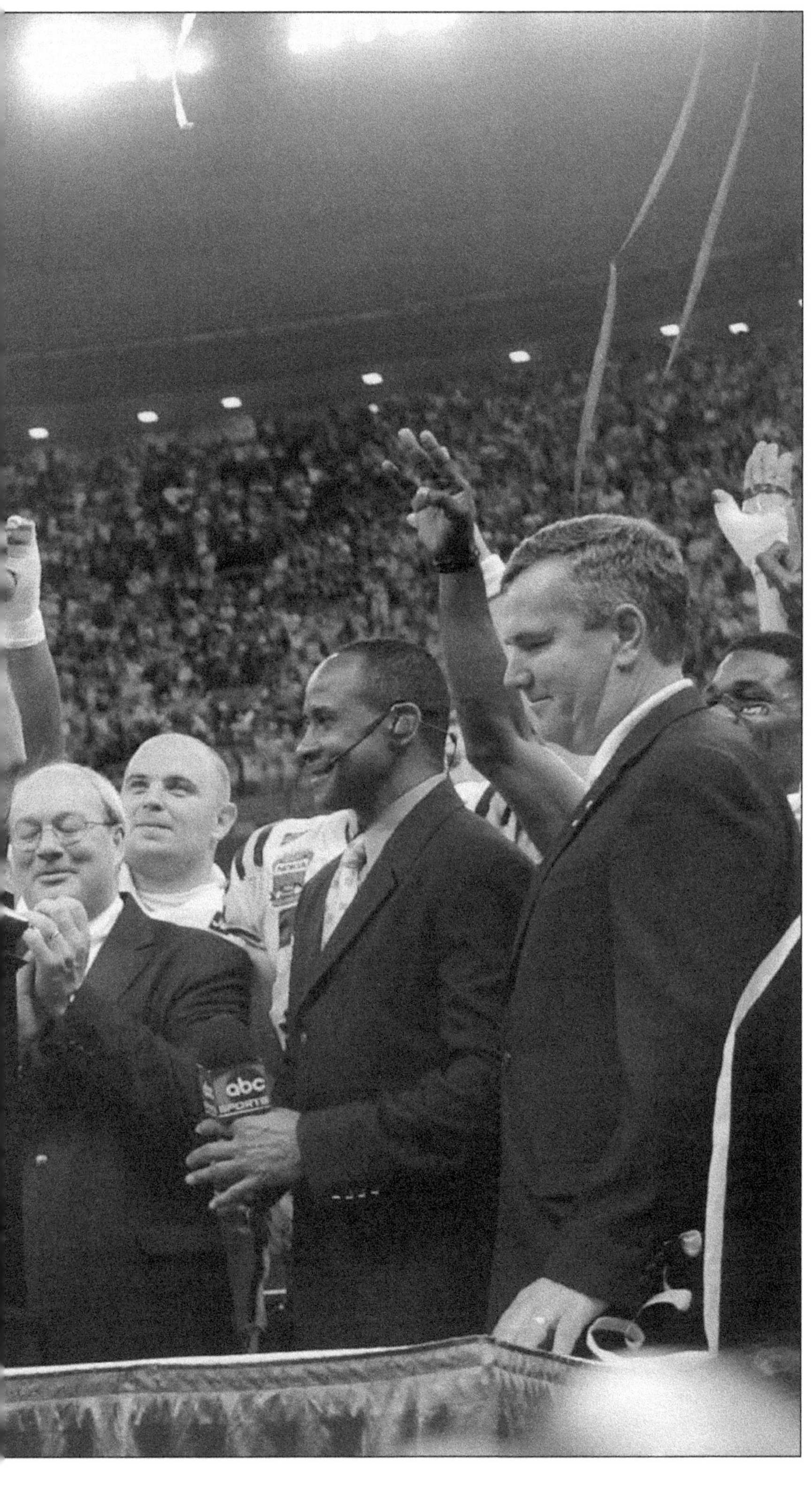

The Tigers won the Bowl Championship Series national championship in 2003. Coach Nick Saban is seen here hoisting the Waterford crystal ball in celebration after defeating Oklahoma University 21–14 in the Sugar Bowl. Others in the photograph are defensive tackle Chad Lavalais (93) and wide receiver Michael Clayton (14). This was LSU's first national championship since 1958. Going into the championship game, LSU had a 12–1 overall record and went 7–1 in SEC games. Their only defeat came from Florida. The Tigers dominated their opponents, outscoring them 475 to 154, scoring in the red zone 70 percent of the time, and sacking opposing quarterbacks 44 times for 366 lost yards. Saban was LSU's head coach from 2000 to 2004. (Courtesy of Steve Franz, LSU Sports Information.)

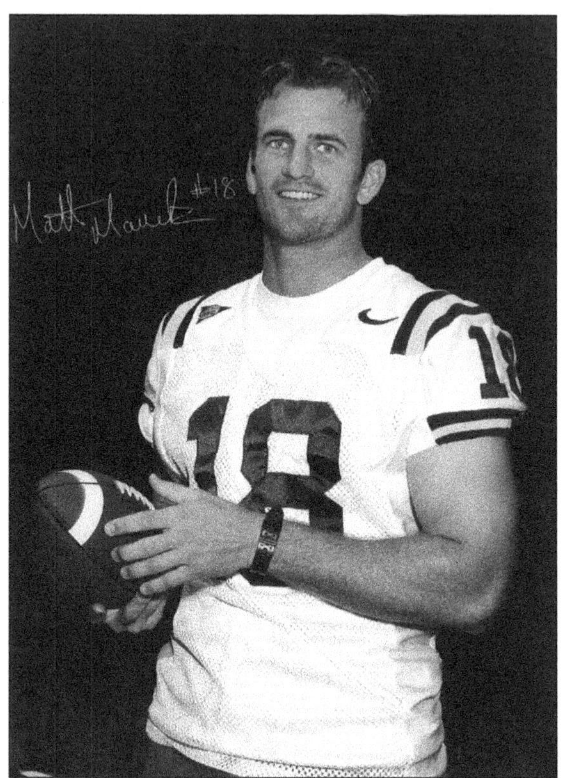

Quarterback Matt Mauck played for the Tigers from 2001 to 2003 and led them to the national championship. In his first season, Mauck came off the bench to relieve an injured Rohan Davy to win the 2001 SEC championship game against Tennessee. In the 2002 season, he received a broken foot that put him out for the year. His final season was one of the best in LSU history as he led the team to a 13–1 record and the national championship. (*Gumbo* 2003.)

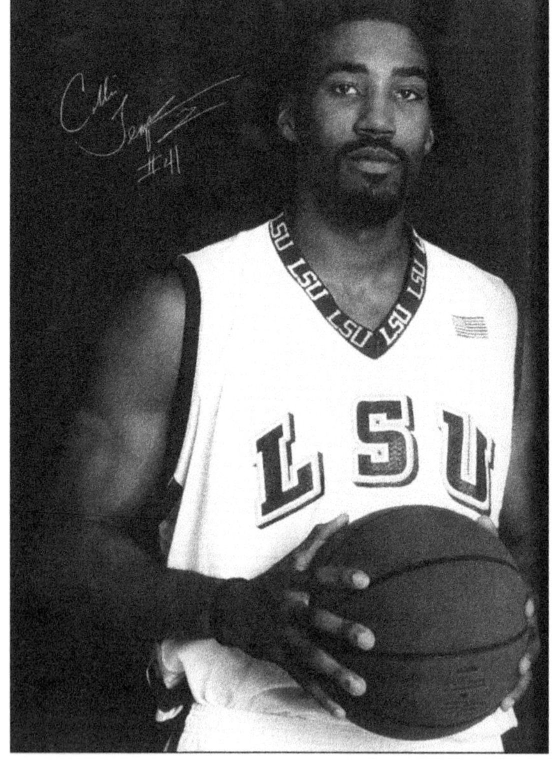

Collis Temple III played from 1998 to 2003. An injury early in his freshman year caused him to miss the 1998–1999 season, but he came back the following season as a redshirt to appear in 33 of 34 games. In Temple's sophomore year, he scored 53 three-point shots and started 28 of 29 games. Temple was expected to do well in his junior year, until a foot and ankle injuries ended his season. In his senior year in 2002–2003, Temple had already earned his master's degree in business administration, started all 32 games, and averaged 10.8 points per game. (*Gumbo* 2003.)

Bibliography

Fleming, Walter L. *Louisiana State University, 1860–1896.* Baton Rouge, LA: Louisiana State University Press, 1936.

Martin, Mark E. and Barry C. Cowan. *Historic Photos of LSU Football.* Nashville, TN: Turner Publishing, 2009.

Moore, Alison. *Sixty '60s.* Baton Rouge, LA: Ortlieb Press, 1984.

Ruffin, Thomas F. *Under Stately Oaks: A Pictorial History of LSU.* Baton Rouge, LA: Louisiana State University Press, 2003.

Soderbergh, Peter A. *Tower, Tablet, and Tree: LSU and the American Legion.* Baton Rouge, LA: Boyd-Ewing Post 58, The American Legion Department of Louisiana, 1983.

www.ingramcontent.com/pod-product-compliance
Lightning Source LLC
LaVergne TN
LVHW060625110826
845147LV00015B/940

* 9 7 8 1 4 6 7 1 1 0 9 8 3 *